N
W E
S

Napa River

Calistoga

MIKE DITKA •

Lake Hennessey

Napa Valley

29

• MOLLY CHAPPELLET

St. Helena
YAO MING •

Rutherford

FRANCIS FORD COPPOLA •

12

Oakville

Silverado Trail

• THE DISNEY FAMILY

Kenwood

Trinity Road

Yountville

JACK NICKLAUS •

Glen Ellen

Carneros Creek

BRUCE R. COHN •

MARIO ANDRETTI •

RANDY LEWIS •

Sonoma River

Napa Valley

• ROBERT KAMEN

29

Sonoma

Sonoma Valley

Napa

California Celebrity Vineyards

California Celebrity Vineyards

FROM NAPA TO LOS OLIVOS IN SEARCH OF GREAT WINE

NICK WISE & LINDA SUNSHINE

OMNIBUS PRESS

London / New York / Paris / Sydney / Copenhagen / Berlin / Madrid / Tokyo

CONTENTS

INTRODUCTION

California Dreaming

Napa Valley has come a long way since the days when it was mainly farmland and the roads were slow going because of tractors and other farm equipment. Today the roads can still be pretty clogged but now it's more likely by stretch limos full of party revelers or expensive foreign cars with passengers on their way to artisanal cheese shops or luxury spas.

In the 1980s the number of wineries in Napa doubled from 60 to 120. By the early 2000s, there were more than 230. As John Williams of Frog's Leap said, "You can't go into the steakhouse Press without tripping over a winemaker." To say that Napa has exploded is quite an understatement, the valley has been utterly transformed in the past few decades and about the only thing that hasn't changed is the soil.

Nick remembers the rustic quality of how the valley looked to him when he first visited in the 1990s. During that trip, he and his parents met Molly and Donn Chappellet, who became family friends. For this reason, we were particularly excited about returning to Pritchard Hill to interview the Chappellets for our book. Molly and Donn came to the valley in the 1960s and revolutionized both the art of growing grapes on a steep hill and the making of superb wines. Molly, an artist of rare and pitch-perfect refinement, brought aesthetics and grace to the landscape while Donn dug up the land. Together they created one of the most beautiful places in all of Northern California.

Today it would be almost impossible to accomplish what the Chappellets did: buy a piece of property and build a vineyard from scratch. An acre of land in Napa costs more than $200,000, so a huge amount of money is needed to even consider starting a winery.

But that didn't stop Peter and Rebecca Work, who bought land (not quite so pricey) in Lompoc, part of Santa Barbara County, a rather unusual place to start a winery. Yet the Works managed to build an amazing biodynamic, triple-certified organic winery, Ampelos Cellars, which produced such superb Pinots that Kurt Russell chose it when he decided to create his signature wine.

The Chappellets and the Works are clearly the exception to the rule. Today the cost factor and the risk of growing grapes in the midst of a four-year California drought have caused celebrities interested in winemaking to work with organizations such as Terlato Wine. Terlato owns several vineyards around Napa and has joined forces with golfers Luke Donald and Jack Nicklaus, as well as legendary football coach Mike Ditka, to create signature vintages. This is no slap-a-label-on-the-bottle operation. Bill Terlato insists that if you want to make a wine with his company, you must come to Napa, visit the vineyards, test the blends, and be totally involved in the process.

Another cost-saving way to venture into the winemaking game is to follow the lead of Randy

Nick Wise and Linda Sunshine celebrate the publication of their first book, *Celebrity Vineyards*, at a party at Domaine LA, in Los Angeles, California, April 2013. Overleaf: Grape clusters or works of art? On view at the B. R. Cohn vineyard in Sonoma, California.

Lewis and basketball legend Yao Ming. Both Randy and Ming source their grapes from other vineyards. Randy rents a space to make his wines while Yao Ming has joined a cooperative of superb winemakers that includes Jason Pahlmeyer, Gott, and Harrison Cellars, who share facilities and the cost of equipment. In this way, Yao Ming is working piecemeal to create his winery and saving some of the huge initial costs of starting up production.

Winemaking is, of course, more a passion than a money-making proposition, especially for celebrities who want to get into the business because they love wine and have a burning desire to use their own palate to develop their favorite tastes. Most of the celebrities we interviewed told us how much they enjoy sharing their own wines with family and friends. Plus, as Jack Nicklaus points out, it's fun to order a bottle of your own wine in a restaurant.

A Liquid Vision

Wine, like music, is infinite and there are endless things to discover. You could, in fact, spend an entire lifetime and not put a dent in either subject.

Many people consider winemaking to be one of the last real crafts in which man (or woman) can create something new from the earth and control all aspects of that creation. From field to table, the winemaker plants, sows, picks, crushes, ferments, matures, and packages his or her personal liquid vision. What a wonderful dream: to live in the countryside and make something magical from the earth.

Winemaking is both an art and a technical craft, so it involves a number of disciplines, sciences, and artistic skills. Almost every day, new advances in technology expand and regenerate this ancient art, and new wine-producing regions are popping up all over the planet.

In the early 2000s, there was an interesting development in the wine business—the advent of the celebrity vintner. Apparently, helming a winery was becoming more and more popular among the rich and famous. Why were so many celebrities getting into the trade? Many people share the fantasy of owning a vineyard and producing a signature wine, but the amount of work is overwhelming and the costs prohibitive. Could someone who had spent their life devoted to another profession actually pull it off?

Winemaking is no easy task, even under the best of circumstances, and for the most talented and dedicated of people. The accomplished winemaker must display a proficiency in a number of complex fields including horticulture, chemistry, and business, combined with a generous amount of artistry and a touch of the gambler. This is not a profession that comes quickly or easily. It requires unlimited patience. The winemaker has only one chance a year (if he or she is lucky with the grapes, that is) to get it right.

So we set out to discover whether or not these celebrities had the chops to succeed at such a complicated and rarefied business. We also wanted to know: what was it like to get into winemaking after having a successful career in another field?

Celebrities are known for making choices that can be defiant and odd—if not somewhat comical. They have created rock bands (Russell Crowe) and food products (Paul Newman and George Clooney); they've become policemen (Steven Segal); politicians (Krist Novoselic); and even exalted humanitarians (Sean Penn). Whatever their choice of second career or creative adventure, there is an underlying level of self-belief and almost overriding ambition that anything can be achieved. In our society, it is an unspoken rule that even the seemingly impossible and unattainable are available to the celebrity.

Of course, there are many reasons why someone gets interested in making wine. There can be a family tradition, love of the process, the thrill of seeing your name on a label, the challenge of combining so many skills, and so on. Wine has always been linked with a kind of sophistication that you might not associate with, say, a racecar driver or a television personality. Surely, there were some great stories out there about why and how a celebrity entered the winemaking game.

Nick Wise in the wine cellar at his family home in the English countryside. Upstairs, in this house, the final draft of this book was written during the summer of 2015, with a little help from some gems in this cellar.

Three questions were particularly intriguing to us: first, what drew these celebrities to enter such a strange, complex, elitist, and risky world as winemaking? Second, how much hands-on involvement did he or she have in creating the wine? And third, and most important, was their wine any good?

Second Career or Primary Calling?

In the course of making our first book, *Celebrity Vineyards*, we tasted some amazing wines. We traveled through Europe and Canada but discovered that the wines being made in our own backyard (California, that is) are as interesting, varied, and delicious as those we tasted in Italy, France, or Spain—sometimes even better. And most of our American celebrity winemakers were incredibly dedicated to the art of winemaking.

For some, the craft of winemaking had overtaken their first career. Robert Kamen, one of Hollywood's most successful screenwriters (*The Karate Kid* franchise and *Taken*), is also one of the most dedicated winemakers we ever met. Kamen is producing extraordinary, world-class wines and controlling every single step in the process from planting grapes to bottling. And few winemakers are more dedicated to their land and their winemaking than the Chappellets, who have devoted four decades of their life to creating some of the best wines in Napa (and the most gorgeous vineyards, tasting room, and home in all of Northern California.)

Charlie Palmer, the celebrity chef and restaurateur, had a marvelous story to share about how he got into making wine as a way of teaching his sons important life lessons and sharing the experience with them. He and his four boys do everything together, from stomping on the grapes to affixing the labels to the bottles.

Yao Ming parlayed his remarkable basketball career into what he hopes will become a family business for generations to come. Though he could have chosen to make wine anywhere in the world, he came to the Napa Valley so that he could share the wines of this region with his fellow Chinese countrymen. And speaking of China, it has become one of the premiere winemaking and wine-buying regions in the world. A good topic for a follow-up book in the future, we hope.

Our other celebrity vintners included B. R. Cohn, manager of the Doobie Brothers, racecar drivers Mario Andretti and Randy Lewis, golfers Luke Donald and Jack Nicklaus,

Signing books at a wine tasting/book party at Napa Valley's Culinary Institute at Greystone, April 2013.

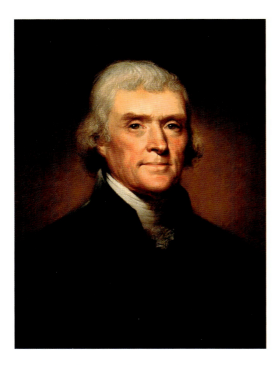

Portrait of Thomas Jefferson by Rembrandt Peale.

filmmaker Francis Ford Coppola, legendary football coaches Dick Vermeil and Mike Ditka, actor Kurt Russell, the Walt Disney family, and the estates of former TV actors Raymond Burr and Fess Parker.

The First American Vintner

Although we chose, in this book, to only focus on California celebrity vineyards, we could not write a book about celebrity winemakers without paying tribute to America's very first vintner, Thomas Jefferson, the third president of the United States. In political circles he was known as the "wine guy." Essentially, he became the middleman for the White House—picking and securing rare French wines for special occasions, a job that suited him well. Jefferson, a true wine lover and connoisseur, kept an extensive wine cellar, importing bottles from France at regular intervals.

It should be noted that winemaking in America is a fairly recent phenomenon. But in his time Jefferson was the foremost vintner in the New World, albeit not a very successful one. The grapes he brought back from Europe and cultivated at Monticello failed to produce the kind of wine he enjoyed, although today the vineyards he planted more than 200 years ago are a thriving tourist attraction in Virginia. Despite his own failure as a vintner, he was the go-to wine connoisseur for George Washington and the Continental Congress.

In 1790, Jefferson was visiting France, touring the various wine regions he loved so much. "We could, in the United States, make as great a variety of wines as made in Europe, not exactly the same kinds, but doubtless as good," he wrote home in a prescient letter. More than two centuries later, the Napa Valley would fulfill and perhaps even surpass his prediction.

Signature Wine

During the course of our research, we made an unexpected and odd observation: wine frequently tastes like the winemaker in somewhat the same way that dogs tend to resemble their owners. Perhaps it is more accurate to say that wine seems to display characteristics similar to the person who made it. We discovered that when the winemaker got his hands literally dirty in the winemaking

Nick decants wine in Napa Valley, March 2015.

process, such as Robert Kamen at Kamen Estates or Paul Smith at Vermeil, the wines tasted rugged and earthy, while elegant men and women like Randy Lewis, Luke Donald, and the divinely sophisticated Molly Chappellet create wines that are as refined in style and taste as they are. Chef Charlie Palmer conjures wines that pair with his meals—as evidenced in his signature Pigs & Pinot weekends in Healdsburg (which have raised over $600,000 for charity). Outdoorsman Kurt Russell produces wines that have originality and a discernible kinship with the land. Football coach Mike Ditka makes a red wine with the full-bodied power of a linebacker while Jack Nicklaus' wines are as trustworthy and true to form as his golf swing. Traditional winemakers like Robert Benevides at Raymond Burr, who has been making annual pilgrimages to the Mediterranean for most of his adult life, produces a port that tastes as if it was created 50 years ago in his beloved Portugal.

Regardless of their winemaking style, the celebrity vintners we've profiled are all intelligent, focused, and driven individuals with very personal reasons for attempting such a monumental task. Their dreams of breaking into the wine business reveal immensely personal stories, some filled with ambitious defiance, determination, and dedication, others with wild tales of emotional exploration packed with excitement, adventure, and even romance.

Common Denominator

The influence a celebrity can have on the public led us to first examine the lives of our chosen vintners. From the interviews, details started to emerge about how they achieved their fame and the reasons behind their initial and continual interest in wine. Some celebrities were drawn to winemaking as a means of raising money for charitable organizations. For two decades, B. R. Cohn Charity Events, the philanthropic arm of Cohn's winery, has raised over $6 million for veterans' and children's causes through 26 classic rock music festivals held at Olive Hill Estates. A portion of the profits from Jack Nicklaus' wines go to support his charitable foundations.

Aside from philanthropic considerations, we discovered that passion is what drives many of our winemakers. For both Randy Lewis and Robert Kamen, winemaking has become a per-

sonal exploration of living in harmony with the land—despite their wildly different approaches. Lewis sources his grapes from the best vineyards in Northern California while Kamen only uses grapes grown organically on his own property in Sonoma. These are very driven winemakers who have an unrelenting enthusiasm for making wine, no matter how difficult or complicated. Owning a vineyard to make wine is without a doubt a beautiful and romantic acquisition, but can nonetheless become an all-consuming ambition.

Some of these winemakers, like B. R. Cohn and the Disney family of Silverado fame, started making wine almost by accident, having bought land where grapes were already growing. After selling their grapes to other wineries, they decided to make a few bottles for themselves and the business just grew from there. Others, like Robert Kamen, started from

Nick Wise, Robert Kamen, and Linda Sunshine at the Kamen tasting room in Sonoma, California. **Opposite:** The divinely elegant Molly Chappellet with Nick Wise at Pritchard Hill, March 2015.

scratch with a plot of rocky land on a mountaintop that didn't even have electricity, plumbing, or water. Mario Andretti got into the business because it was such a treat to share wine with his friends and family.

We tried to find a common denominator among our winemakers. We explored the shared traits between them but, like wine itself, this proved too disparate, complex, and random. We had a very diverse roster of people including two football coaches, a chef, a writer, two actors, a director, two racecar drivers, two golfers, a basketball player, and a scriptwriter, so the similarities between them were few and far between, except for one important factor: these celebrities-turned-winemakers had used the benefits of fame and fortune to purposely delve into the strange and complex world of winemaking.

We learned that many of our celebrity winemakers had fond childhood memories of wine that was made or served at home with their families. Francis Ford Coppola has talked about how growing up Italian meant that his parents allowed him a little wine, mixed with water, when he was a child. These wines were called simply *rosso* and *bianco*, which became the names of the entry level wines at his vineyard. For Coppola the aura of winemaking had much to do with the love of family and family traditions.

We discovered that in the world of sports, we were most likely to meet racecar drivers or golfers. We wondered why these sports, in particular, seemed to generate so many winemakers. When we asked these guys why they had wineries, almost all of them told us that because their careers involved so much traveling, they had tasted wines from around the world, became fascinated with the process, and wanted a winery of their own. Nick has a theory about racecar drivers: their obsession with precision on the road translates into exactly the kind of precision needed to make wine—but we leave it to you to read those chapters and see if you agree.

And Their Wines Were Beautiful

Throughout our travels, we were focused on trying to gather entertaining stories and find out how and why these celebrities were making wine, but of course we always sampled all the wines. Although the focus of the book was never to rate the wines, we certainly wanted to report back on what we tasted. At the end of each visit, after trying everything the winery had to offer, we picked the two or three most successful wines from each vintner's portfolio.

The objective of each visit was to see if the wines were drinkable and it was incredible how many of these celebrities made absolutely beautiful wines. Some of them were so complex and well made that they could compete with the best wines in the world.

Though we traveled a great deal for our two books, in fact, we only covered a very small part of the world. We remain deeply interested in other parts of the planet where wine is being made. China has recently become very important in the international wine scene. Australia has always been a major producer of wine and their table wines are sold throughout the United States. Many celebrities are making wine in South Africa. And there are new wines to explore in our own backyard. We recently were thrilled when we tasted Pursued by Bear, an amazing Cabernet being made by actor Kyle MacLachlan in Washington State. (The name of the wine was inspired by perhaps the most famous of all stage directions, "exit, pursued by bear" from Act III, scene ii of Shakespeare's *The Winter's Tale*.) Nearby, football player Drew Beldsoe's Doubleback Winery is a must-see, must-taste stop on any wine tour. In fact, Walla Walla, Washington, reminded us of Napa several decades ago, and we've been thinking about writing a book on the wines of the Pacific Northwest. In short, there's a huge amount still to cover in what we hope will be future editions of this book.

Here we wanted to recount our amazing journey into the world of California's celebrity vineyards and we tried to make it fun to read. You don't have to know about technical specifics such as pH levels or sugar content. We are not interested in the highbrow, snobbish aspects of wine that seem to intimidate so many people. Wine should always be enjoyable, whether it's being drunk or read about. Instead of a textbook approach, we were aiming for more of a wine memoir, a journey into the land of both celebrity and wine.

We started out planning to stay within the boundaries of the book and write only about the wines created by our celebrity winemakers. Yet the truth is that during our many visits to Napa and surrounding areas, we tasted a lot of truly exceptional California wines being made by men and women who were not considered "celebrities" outside of Napa. Nick is an inveterate wine taster and has literally dozens of notebooks filled with his thoughts about wines he has drunk. And what a memory for wine! Nick can recall a wine he tried 20 years ago, during a tasting of 200 different vintages.

The Pritchard Hill vineyard in Napa. OVERLEAF: Aerial view of Lake Hennessey and Pritchard Hill.

Of course, he wanted to include notes on all the wines he tasted in California but since this book is not 1,000 pages long, we limited ourselves to 22 of the wines Nick considers the very best for their taste and value. Some are up and coming vineyards, some are established but only produce a limited amount and are not very well known outside of Northern California. We include Nick's Picks as an appendix at the back of this book. If you are looking for an exceptional California wine, you will find it here. And, if you're planning a wine tour of the region (an adventure we highly recommend), we suggest visiting as many of these wineries as possible. We promise you will not be disappointed in the wines you taste at these fabulous places.

Finally, we want to add that we believe wine should always be a delicious, joyous adventure and we hope this book succeeds in recreating the awesome pleasure we derived from the delectable world of winemaking.

Nick Wise and Linda Sunshine

LOS ANGELES AND IDBURY, THE COTSWOLDS, U.K

SUMMER, 2015

CHAPPELLET

Molly Chappellet

Molly Chappellet

CHAPPELLET VINEYARD, PRITCHARD HILL ®

St. Helena

A True Romance

"It is their romance with the land that makes the Chappellets' story so appealing," wrote Robyn Bullard in *Wine Spectator*. Indeed, there are few love stories so imbued with romance and wine as that of Molly and Donn Chappellet.

The couple moved to Napa Valley years before there were high-class spas, artisan cheese shops, and four-star restaurants at every turn. At one time, not too long ago, the valley looked much different than it does today, its contours weren't sculpted into pristine lines of grapevines and the streets weren't overflowing with tourists. In the 1960s, Napa Valley was the definition of rustic, it was essentially a farming community. Yes, there were a few vineyards left over from pre-Prohibition days, mostly selling their grapes for inexpensive table wine. These were jug wines, which, back then, bore names like Gallo's "Hearty Burgundy" or "Chablis." They were wines that tried to replicate a style, not develop one.

Then came people like Donn and Molly Chappellet who really defined the Napa Valley as a premiere winemaking region and the style of the wines produced within it.

Donn and Molly Chappellet today.

Molly Chappellet in her element.

Moving to Napa Valley

Donn Chappellet is a fourth-generation Californian, born in Los Angeles and educated at Pomona College. In 1952, as an ambitious young graduate, Donn co-founded Interstate United Corporation, a food service business. He and his partner invested in 64 unique coffee-making machines, buying the entire inventory from the inventor. At the time, coffee machines only dispensed instant coffee mixed with hot water. Interstate installed the machines at the Lockheed plant in California and they proved to be so successful among factory workers that soon the company was building and installing them around the country. Interstate United Corporation became the third largest company in the industry, with clients in 38 states, 7,000 employees, and a listing on the New York Stock Exchange. After running the company for four-

teen years, Donn was ready for a change of pace and a change of scenery. He sold his shares and for a short time considered getting into the cattle business but that idea evaporated after he visited Napa Valley. After much searching he discovered the Pritchard Hill vineyard on the eastern slope of the valley and knew he had found the right spot. One look at the property, and it is easy to understand why.

The family's romance with Pritchard Hill started when Donn and Molly first glimpsed this magnificent location. Steep and rocky, overlooking Lake Hennessey, the whole of the Napa Valley is on view. The land is an absolute winemakers' paradise. Following the sage advice of renowned winemaker André Tchelistcheff, who was the expert in Napa winemaking in the 1960s, the Chappellets decided to settle on Pritchard Hill's rocky slopes, becoming one of the first wineries to pioneer high-elevation hillside planting. This bold decision was also based on an ancient premise that high-elevation hillside planting was far superior to planting on the fertile valley floor.

Of course, Molly shared Donn's conviction that there was a simpler, more down-to-earth way to rear their family and produce award-winning wines at the same time. It is rare to find a couple more in sync with each other and the land as these two.

So Donn and Molly, together with their five kids (and another on the way), moved from Beverly Hills to the hills of Napa Valley. Daughter Lygia Chappellet, who was then twelve years old, remembers driving up the mountain for the first time with her family. "My father turned to us," she recalls, "and said, 'The only way this will work, is if we work it together.' I took those words very literally." So did the entire family.

Molly and artist Ed Moses with rusted vineyard wires reimagined as sculpture. OVERLEAF: The garden is adorned with many pieces of stunning pottery, brilliantly placed to feel organic to the landscape.

Meet Molly Chappellet

Born and raised in Beverly Hills, Molly studied art at UCLA and Scripps College. Her training in art was challenged by bigger canvases and three-dimensional opportunities when she moved to Pritchard Hill. With acres of land to mold and clients to entertain, she made her garden and events her artistic palette. Her work in sculpting the landscape and painting with flowers, trees, and shrubs has earned Molly's spectacular garden acclaim as one of the most unusual in the area. As an entertainer, she has been hostess to such guests as Julia Child, James Beard, Danny Kaye, Dinah Shore, Clint Eastwood, Martha Stewart, Beverly Sills, and Craig Claiborne.

Molly is the author of five books: the James Beard Award-winning *A Vineyard Garden: Ideas from the Earth for Growing, Cooking, Decorating and Entertaining; The Romance of California Vineyards*, authored with daughter Carissa; *Gardens of the Wine Country*, co-authored with Richard Tracy, which takes you on an exclusive tour of the Napa Valley's most spectacular gardens; *Into The Earth: A Wine Cave Renaissance*, brilliantly photographed by co-author Daniel D'Agostini; and *Jack Lenor*

Molly and Donn Chappellet, 1968.

Larsen's LongHouse, which celebrates Larsen's personal and artistic philosophies and his sculptural gardens.

Described as a designer, landscape gardener, author, photographer, chef, and entertainer, Molly speaks about design and gardening and hosts winemaker dinners around the country when she is not tending to her own land. She has appeared on numerous television programs including *The Regis and Kathy Lee Show, The Home Show*, and *Martha Stewart Living*. Her list of credits also includes writing articles for national magazines and daily newspapers.

With six children and eleven grandchildren, Molly takes great joy in sharing her garden with her family. In addition to regular family gatherings, her daughter Alexa's wedding was celebrated underneath one of the ancient trees overlooking Lake Hennessey.

There are, of course, beautiful vineyards today throughout the valley but few are as artistic and precise as what can be seen at Pritchard Hill where every inch of property has been designed and planted with the most exquisite eye for detail. Where others see natural rock formations or bent wires, Molly Chappellet sees sculptures and works of art.

Huge field boulders removed from the land so that vineyards could be planted were hauled up the hill to create what Molly calls her "Boulder Gardens." Somehow one enormous boulder was lowered into the family house and forms the fireplace of her living room. It is so simple and perfectly placed that it feels as though the house was built around the huge rock.

Rusting vine posts and old fence wires are recycled into huge swirling tumbleweed-like structures. Entirely man-made, they look as if they have blown in from the fields and are as natural on the land as lavender plants and sea grass. Like everything else at Pritchard Hill, the effect is effortless, elegant, simple, and in keeping with the slope and shape of the terrain. It would take days to describe in proper detail the gardens that Molly has planted and nurtured over her four decades in Napa. Taking us on a tour of the property, Molly shared the Latin name and genus of every plant, every flower and fruit tree.

The Chappellets set out to build a dream, not only producing world-renowned wines, but also to live a simpler life. As Molly explains, "A country environment has made me realize how essential it is in this age of computerized mechanization to reestablish our connection with the earth and bring back some part of that harmony and rhythm into our lives."

Certainly, there have been hundreds of individuals and couples over the last decade who've capitalized on their newly made fortunes to buy great properties and vineyards in Napa, but in comparison, there are very few who preceded the hype and actually took part in pioneering the valley as a modern-day, premiere wine-producing region. The Chappellets were (and are) unique visionaries; they were there first, they did it well, and they set the bar exceedingly high for everyone who followed.

Napa in the Sixties

The Chappellets arrived in Napa in 1967, just as a new crop of innovators was also moving in; all of them believing that Napa held enough promise to stand on the world's winemaking stage. People such as John Williams from Frogs Leap, who arrived on a Harley in full leathers, Jack Davies of Schramsberg, Bo Barrett from Chateau Montelena (whose wine won the French vs. California competition of 1976), and, of course, Robert Mondavi, the patriarch of modern Napa, all saw potential within the valley for producing serious, high-quality wines.

Donn Chappellet soon discovered that the intensity of the fruit grown on Pritchard Hill proved his intuition right. The vineyards, with their volcanic soil and warm, dry, temperate days combined with cool evenings to ensure great diurnal temperature shifts that add both power and elegance to a finished wine. Before the Chappellets purchased the vineyard it had been used to grow Cabernet Sauvignon, Chenin Blanc, Gamay, and Johannisberg Riesling. However, Donn, a true Bordeaux lover, set out, over the years, to replant the old vines and replace them with Bordeaux varieties, with the exception of a small amount of Chenin Blanc.

Molly's Chenin Blanc

Chenin Blanc is an uncommon grape to find in the Napa Valley and only about ten acres of it are grown within the whole area. Chappellet owns three of those ten acres and produces a wonderfully light but flavorsome and tangy white that's extremely drinkable. Chenin Blanc has always been grown at Chappellet. Donn and Molly first discovered the original Chenin Blanc plantings—thought to have been initially planted in 1964/65—sitting on their top terraces. Even though they loved the tiny amount of wine these old vines yielded, when the plants neared the end of their life cycle in 2004 and became much less productive, the Chappellets made the difficult decision to remove them.

Yet Molly adored the Chenin Blanc so much that Donn agreed to replant it further down the hillside and behind the unique pyramid-shaped winery that sits at the base of the property. Now fully matured, this small vineyard, which needs plenty of leaf cutting to allow for adequate sunlight, produces just as good, or better, wine than the original vineyard.

Pritchard Hill AVA?

With approximately 120 acres of planted vines, Chappellet is the biggest vineyard on Pritchard Hill. The once near-empty hillside has become home to some of Napa's most famous and prized wines. Down the road from Chappellet lies the Bryant Family Vineyard and Colgin Cellars, and adjacent to the property sits

Fog line over Lake Hennessey. Pages 36–37: View overlooking Lake Hennessey from under an ancient tree where Molly's daughter was married.

Continuum owned by Tim Mondavi.

Since it's not a legally recognized AVA (American Viticultural Area), it's difficult to pinpoint exactly where the region starts and where it ends. In 1971 Donn trademarked the name "Pritchard Hill." We asked if he would ever let the trademark become its own AVA. "I will not," answered Donn with conviction. "While discussing the idea of a Pritchard Hill appellation over the years, the challenges have become apparent. Foremost among them is the fact that it is very unclear where such an appellation would begin, and more importantly, where it would end. As a family, our concern is preserving the special essence of this place. Unfortunately, the potential reality could be quite the opposite, with an AVA that gets too big and dilutes Pritchard Hill's identity and distinctive sense of place."

The Soil

Most of the vineyards on Pritchard Hill climb higher than 800 feet above sea level, and the uppermost peaks sit above 2,000 feet. Due to the rocky terrain the soil drainage is excellent and produces grapes small in size with thick skins and powerful flavor. Yields can be modest, varying from less than a ton per acre to a few tons, depending on the vintage conditions. Rainfall is at a premium and many vineyards, including Chappellet, have "collection ponds" at the top of their properties for irrigation. Water is scarce, and its availability limits how many additional vineyards can be developed. The current total is only about 340 acres.

Pritchard Hill sits above the fog line, which is great for achieving those ever-important diurnal temperature swings that provide the grapes with great natural acidity. Terroir, of course, plays a huge role in the quality achieved within the final wines. The hill, for example, has a unique volcanic red soil (clay loam) known as Sobrante that contributes some distinctive qualities to the wines. As son Cyril Chappellet points out, the Pritchard Hill character "is tough to pin down, almost impossible." Consultant Philippe Melka, who was Bryant Family's winemaker until 2006, says it is the "the best of both worlds: Oakville sophistication with the extra intensity of a hillside."

The land is also densely mineral and various wineries have had to dynamite their way into creating soil that is viable for growing grapes. "The thing about these soils," explains Cyril, "is that we have to poke around for areas where there's enough [soil] to actually farm."

Partly Uncultivated and Totally Organic

The Chappellets are understandably devoted to their property and the land on which the grapes are grown. Only 16% of the property is under vine, the rest remains uncultivated. Rising to 1,800 feet, Chappellet's Estate Vineyards on Pritchard Hill have often been hailed as "Napa's Grand Cru." The mountainside vineyards are farmed as 34 distinctive blocks—comprising approximately 25 blocks of Cabernet Sauvignon plus plantings of Merlot, Malbec, Cabernet Franc, Petit Verdot, and Chenin Blanc. Winemaker Phillip Corallo-Titus, who has been in charge of Chappellet's winemaking program since 1990, individually ferments and ages lots from these numerous vineyard blocks, maintaining the Chappellet house style. These lots benefit from an array of different maceration and fermentation practices.

The entire Chappellet Pritchard Hill Vineyard was certified organic by CCOF in 2012. Before this, however, Chappellet was recognized as one of the first Napa Valley wineries to plant cover crops and adopt no-till farming practices. The winery is also self-sustainable. In 2008, Chappellet unveiled a 20,000-square-foot solar photovoltaic system that generates enough energy to offset 100% of the winery's electricity bill. Over 30 years, it will reduce greenhouse gases by 4,513,275 pounds. The whole of the Barrel Chai roof is covered in solar panels and the vineyard equipment runs on 50% biodiesel fuel. Chappellet also grinds grape pomace onsite that produces approximately 400,000 pounds of compost each year. In extreme draught, water pressure bombs are sometimes released to give the vines additional water. Vineyard pests are kept at bay by natural predators and the vineyard managers encourage owls and hawks to nest on the property's adjoining trees. Chappellet has no problems with sharp shooters since the estate is isolated from neighboring vineyards. While driving through the vineyards it was interesting to learn that at one stage the Chappellets were not quite happy with the orientation of the whole Pritchard Hill

This gorgeous Malbec bottle, illustrated by Carissa Chappellet, is one of the unique bottlings reserved for purchase by winery visitors and club members.

Vineyard, so they shifted all the vines towards a more north-south aspect.

Building on a belief that winemaking begins in the vineyard, winemaker Phillip Corallo-Titus works side-by-side with longtime vineyard manager Dave Pirio and associate winemakers Daniel Docher (since 2004) and Ry Richards (since 2006). From his focus on harvesting at ideal ripeness to his emphasis on maintaining the integrity of Chappellet's numerous vineyard blocks throughout the fermentation and aging process, Corallo-Titus strives to make wines that reflect both the vineyard and the vintage. In the winery, he handles the grapes very gently and uses an array of fermentation, maceration, and cellaring techniques to accentuate and preserve the distinctiveness of each varietal. "Because I've worked with our vineyards for so long and know each block so intimately, I am able to focus on the individual characteristics of each vineyard lot," says Phillip. "This diversity allows us to enjoy a great deal of freedom during the blending process, while also adding immense depth and complexity to our wines." (In addition to his role as winemaker for Chappellet, Phillip also makes wine for Titus, his family's label.)

The result is a Cabernet Sauvignon that has won incredible praise from important critics such as Robert Parker, who wrote about the 2012 vintage in *The Wine Advocate* (October 31, 2014): "Pushing perfection in Cabernet Sauvignon, this multi-dimensional skyscraper-like offering has all the intensity one expects, but it never comes across as heavy. This gives it an ethereal character that is nearly impossible to articulate, but genius is often hard to explain. It is clearly a major superstar of a great vintage."

Aerial view of the Pyramid at Chappellet.

Chardonnay also used to be grown on the property but the Chappellets were not satisfied with the results. Over the last few years they decided to source the grapes from a handful of famed vineyards in cooler parts of Napa Valley, most notably the acclaimed Sangiacomo Vineyard in Carneros.

The Chappellet Pyramid

The estate has an exquisite pyramid-shaped winery, which Molly collaborated with artist Ed Moses to design. Made out of long beams of wood, it uses a gravity-flow mechanism that's non-interventionist—meaning it minimizes abrasion to the grapes coming in and through the winery.

Recently, the Barrel Chai, a new building researched, designed, and constructed by middle son Jon-Mark, was built to house the majority of wine barrels. This allowed the pyramid to be reconfigured to accommodate guests and for the original winemaking facility to become more efficient. The open interior of the winery exposes the dramatic architecture, while providing tasting areas surrounded by stacked barrels.

The winery uses a combination of French, American, and Hungarian barrels and a variety of maturation times in the process of aging their wines. The percentage of each different barrel type varies, and the Hungarian oak is not used for the estate's top wines. The toast (the element that gives the oaky flavor to a finished wine) is medium and the barrels are "racked" quarterly during maturation, ridding the wine of excess sediment, and topped as evaporation takes a share of the barreled wine. All the wines are unfiltered and thus very flavorsome.

Simple yet elegant, as is everything at Chappellet, the winery's wooden walls are adorned with huge canvases, featuring art by Lygia

Chappellet, Ed Ruscha, and other artists. Rooms are shaped between walls of wine barrels and it is hard to imagine a more delightful setting to taste the marvelous wines on offer.

Future Generations

The Chappellets exude one of the most sophisticated personal styles of any couple that we've come across. Molly's Zen-like aura pervades the whole of Chappellet. Inside and out, the property has become a very personal reflection of Donn and Molly's impeccable taste—from the manicured vineyards and the delicately designed, deliberately unobtrusive winery, to Molly's phenomenally colored spiraling gardens and their fabulous wines.

One of the wonderful aspects of the Chappellet venture is the importance of having their original vision remain family-owned and run. Now the second and third generation have joined Donn and Molly's endeavor and proven more than capable of carrying on a unique family vision. All of the children are part owners of the winery. Cyril has become chairman of the board, Dominic is head of technical services, Carissa is director of legal affairs, Lygia is creative director, and Alexa stays actively involved on a board level. Their eleven grandchildren can often be seen playing in the vineyards where they will eventually learn the art of growing grapes and making wine. "I see achieving the full potential of our family's winery as the work of generations with generations," says Lygia Chappellet.

The barrel room at Chappellet serves double duty as the tasting room and is adorned with glorious works of art. Painting by Lygia Chappellet.

PORTFOLIO

Besides their iconic Cabernets, the portfolio also includes exceptional bottles of Chardonnay, Chenin Blanc, Merlot, Cabernet Franc, and the highly regarded Mountain Cuvée blend. Another stamp of Donn and Molly's lovely individuality are their own "Signature" wines. Donn's is a large-scaled Cabernet that shows beautiful concentration and depth, while Molly's is a unique and highly sought-after Chenin Blanc that is only sold at the winery due to its low production.

The wines are some of the most intensely flavored to come out of the Napa Valley. The reds are dark, richly concentrated, Moorish, and plush. These are deeply layered and sturdy wines with intense depth of fruit that exude an almost liqueur-like quality. The Chardonnays are creamy and lush yet always retain their rich lemon and lime flavors. The reds are capable of extended bottle age that not only "hold" but improve with time as the separate components of structure, fruit, and acidity integrate within the bottle. The whites drink beautifully on release but can also be cellared for a few years, adding extra complexity.

NICK'S TASTING NOTES

Signature Chenin Blanc, 2015

So many people adore this wine, including us, and the only problem is that so little of it is produced. Molly Chappellet has loved this tiny production of white wine since its inception in 1969. Chappellet's is one of, if not the best, example of the varietal in the entire Napa AVA. Mostly grown in France's Loire region and South Africa, the grape has the amazing ability to make not only dry but also sweet wines as the skins are prone to botrytis (the noble rot). Dry fermented versions such as Chappellet's are usually not as rich and broad in style as a Chardonnay, as the grape is typically fermented and matured in stainless steel rather than oak to preserve its varietal character. The wines reveal less body than a Chardonnay. The grape is inherently high in acidity. The color is a light youthful gold with green reflective hints and a watery broad rim. The bouquet is clean and stylish, releasing complex warm-climate aromas of poached pears, fresh hay, citrus, peach, lemon grass, liquid honey, orange blossoms, floral notes, and a hint of lanolin. The palate is medium-bodied, silky, and streamlined but mouth-filling with an almost oily texture that glides the wine over the tongue. The noticeable acidity poking through lifts the white ripe fruits to a long, fine, citrusy finish. Only available at the winery.

Signature Chardonnay, 2012

Here is the quintessential Napa Valley Chardonnay. I buy a case of this every year during the summer months and it always delivers the goods; every guest who tastes it asks about the producer. It's a big wine, succulent, juicy, and ripe but always manages to retain a French Burundian-style of restraint and elegance to keep in check its broad proportions and dense concentration of fruit. Showcasing a bright, deep, youthful gold color, it releases soaring aromas of cool-climate citrus fruits such as lemons and limes interspersed with the more tropical fruit aromas of pineapples, guavas, and bananas cloaked in fresh, creamy, new oak. The palate is full-bodied and round in the mouth with an amazing viscous texture on the tongue and deep, dense flavors of citrus, pears, baked apples, and sweet oak, leading to an extremely long, loamy finish. This cuvée is different from previous vintages, as the grapes are not estate grown but sourced from the famed Sangiacomo Vineyard on the fog-shrouded northwest corner of San Pablo Bay. The wine undergoes 100% malolactic fermentation, is matured in 40% new French oak, and is unfiltered. The clone is Wente.

Signature Cabernet Sauvignon, 2012

For more than three decades, this has been the flagship Chappellet wine. Stylistically the wine hasn't changed: as usual it's a dark opaque purple color, full-bodied with black cherry and cassis flavors, heavily oaked with a good depth of fruit, broad shouldered and plush in texture. The 2012 season offered fantastic growing conditions resulting in pristine, perfectly developed fruit with great balance and acidity. An absolutely head-turning wine with gorgeous aromas of super ripe black cherries and additional hints of plum, sage, and anise. Lush and supple with round tannins and powerful flavors.

Pritchard Hill Estate Vineyard Cabernet Sauvignon, 2012

Hands down one of the best Californian Cabernet Sauvignon wines we tasted this year. Sheer deep-veined concentration matched to a sublime sense of restraint creates a seamless elegance that drives this wine into the stratosphere. The wine reveals a deep purple hue, an opaque core, and is obviously very young. It is immensely complex on the nose with concentrated soaring black fruit aromas of liquor of cassis, black cherries, small black currants, blueberries, and a discrete but jazzy touch of red cherries. Secondary, more complex aromas of dark chocolate, damp earth, minerals, anise, a touch of red cherries and high-quality, sweet vanilla oak dance around the glass. This wine is all about precision and balance, pushing maximum levels of concentration while managing to retain a weightless feel. The depth of fruit contained is bottomless; its complexity is off the charts. Smooth and silky with tight, sweet, powerful tannins buried under numerous layers of slick black fruits, its acidity is pinpoint and carries this very concentrated Latour-like wine to an endless finish. Awarded 99+ points by Robert Parker.

GoGi

Goldie

2012

Chardonnay

Kurt Russell

GOGI WINES

Lompoc

A Disclaimer

The celebrity winemakers in this book have successful careers in many different fields—as actors, athletes, writers, chefs, racecar drivers, and coaches—and they all use their names to promote their wines, with few exceptions. The Disney family, for instance, calls their vineyard Silverado and the actor Kurt Russell names his wines after the people in his life.

Russell may not want to play on his celebrity to promote his wines but after we read about how involved he was in the winemaking process in several magazines and newspapers, we tasted his wine and were very impressed. So we contacted Kurt's younger sister, Jami, who is the business manager for the family's wine labels, and asked to interview Russell for our book. Jami was enthusiastic and introduced us to Peter and Rebecca Work, who own Ampelos Cellars where Russell's wines are created. The Works are remarkable winemakers, having created from scratch a completely sustainable and biodynamic vineyard in only the past fifteen years. We were completely infatuated with the way they honor the earth while still managing to produce remarkable wines. Nick spent many happy hours touring the Ampelos vineyards with Peter and learning about the unique farming techniques the Works have

brought to Lompoc. We wrote this chapter, leaving spaces for quotes we hoped to get from Kurt. Then, when we finally had a chance to talk to him, he asked not to be included in the book. He said he hadn't understood that our book was about "celebrities" and he did not want to promote his wines based on his fame. This was incredibly disappointing considering how much we wanted to discuss what the Works had accomplished in Lompoc.

We spoke to our lawyers, both in the U.S. and the U.K. who informed us that as long as we included a disclaimer stating that Kurt Russell declined to be included in the book, and we did not use any images of him, we could include this chapter. So please consider this our disclaimer. When we quote Kurt Russell directly in the following pages, his words are from interviews he granted to *Variety* (April 15, 2015), *Santa Barbara News* (April 9, 2015), FoxNews.com (March 20, 2015), *Huffington Post* (March 19, 2014), *Wine Enthusiast* (July, 2014), *Mercury Press* (February 21, 2011) and *Palm Springs Life* (May, 2011). Now back to the winemaking.

Keeping It Simple

"I didn't want to have a long name, Russell Estates or something," Russell told Fox News.

The expert contouring of Ampelos' vineyards maximizes the potential terroir of the region.

"I [thought] trying to slap a name on a bottle that people might recognize was not only, to me, not necessarily a good thing, I thought it was a drawback." So his wine is named GoGi (pronounced *Go-Ghee*), which was his nickname as a kid and the name his grandchildren call him. "Each year I produce a wine for a different family member," said Russell in a recent magazine article. Thus, his Chardonnay is named Goldie, after his longtime partner Goldie Hawn. He dedicated one vintage to his sister, Jody, nicknamed Baz, who was diagnosed with a brain tumor. Thankfully she recovered and Kurt labeled her wine Forbaz. A small amount, about ten cases of Viognier, is called Lulu, a pet name for his mother.

Whatever he chooses to call them, Russell's extraordinary wines stand alone for their quality, and for this he has to thank Peter and Rebecca Work who have been making wine at Ampelos Cellars since they planted their first fifteen acres in 2001. The Lompoc vineyard was well established by the time Russell met with the Works, who originally were not interested in adding a celebrity name to their label. Then they discovered the depth of Russell's commitment.

"Kurt came down to visit us and to see what we were doing," recalls Peter about their first real meeting with the actor. "From the start, he really liked our wines, so that helped, but he also admired our philosophy and asked if he could come up from Los Angeles and make some wine with us. We said to him, 'We're not really into a celebrity coming down and slapping a name on a label and being done with it. But if you're really interested, then prove it. Come down and take part in the whole process.' Funnily enough, that's what he wanted to do, so we were all happy. We soon discovered that Kurt has a really good palate and is very naturally talented at blending. He quickly learned what he wanted to get out of the grapes and express in the bottle, so it has been good fun working with him."

Peter's wife and winemaking partner, Rebecca, agrees. "Kurt has done a lot of wine tasting while making movies, so he generally knows his likes and dislikes in wine. But as he quickly discovered, there's nothing like personally carrying out the whole actual winemaking process—a complete vintage—to really develop your palate. When Kurt wants to learn something he takes the whole thing hook, line, and sinker. And now you can ask him anything about winemaking and he really understands. We have developed a great friendship and understanding together."

Russell was attracted to the wines being made at Ampelos Cellars for many reasons, including the fact that Rebecca and Peter were among the first winemakers to run a triple-certified, sustainable, organic, and bio-dynamic vineyard. Russell, who likes to be involved in all aspects of winemaking, came to depend on the Works to teach him the art of making wine. "I knew what I wanted to do, taste-wise, but I didn't have any idea how to do it," Russell told a reporter. "Peter has developed into an expert winemaker. He has this sort of fearlessness and openness. I love the way they farm."

Apparently, he was a quick learner and became a fast friend to the Works. "The reason that Rebecca, Kurt, and I get on so well is that his initial curiosity with winemaking has developed at such a pace that at this point he could easily come out here and give the exact same tour as I'm giving," says Peter. "He knows and understands the nuances between each clone, nitrogen level, vineyard yield. He's fascinated about the minutia like I am. Kurt's a tough guy and inherently loves three things all involving mechanical knowledge: flying airplanes, hunting game, and making wine. However he found out early on that only one activity out of the three might make a little return on its expenses."

And there is a lot of enjoyment in the process. "Part of the fun [for Russell]," Pat Saperstein wrote in *Variety*, "of course, is sharing his bottles with collaborators like Tarantino, who served GoGi wines at a *Hateful Eight* cast dinner recently in Telluride and likes having fine wines in his screening room. Russell returns to a favorite metaphor to describe the connection between acting and winemaking. 'It reminds me of moviemaking,' he says. 'The varietal is the genre of movie, the care in the winery is much like the casting, and the editing is the blending.'"

Russell's goal with his wine is simple: keep the winemaking small and intimate. "It's always going to be 'boutique' for me," he has said. "I want to keep it hands on. It's the thrill I get out of it. I keep mine in the barrel for a long time; I like to let the wine take its time. Because I don't have a big operation, I'm afforded the luxury of time."

And Russell's wines sell out, even without his name on the label.

The Works

Peter's family is of Danish descent, which explains his distinctive Nordic accent. His wife, Rebecca, grew up in Alaska as the daughter of a commercial sea fisherman. The couple met when they both worked for the firm Price Waterhouse. Long before they met Kurt Russell, the Works had dreamed of owning a winery.

Early in their marriage, the couple settled in Long Beach, California, working in the corporate world and indulging their love of travel. Meanwhile, they always talked about finding the perfect vineyard. They hoped to chance upon a site so tempting they could finally, without remorse, escape the city life that had dogged and bored them for many years. Even though both Peter and Rebecca had widely respected careers, behind closed doors they secretly wished for a more rural existence, closer to nature, a lifestyle far away from the stress of the rat race. They imagined gazing over hills and the ocean rather than smoggy urban skies and skyscrapers. Then, as if by a miracle, during one of their many driving trips, they came upon an east-facing, rolling cornfield with gently sloping hillsides basking in the afternoon sun.

At the time (1999), the Santa Rita Hills region was still very rural and quite unrecognized as a wine-producing region. It had no AVA designation back then (that came later, in 2001–2002) but the hillside that caught their eye looked like the perfect spot for grape growing. After a long discussion over dinner they decided to hire a geologist to evaluate the land and confirm their initial hopes. This resulted in

Peter and Rebecca Work at their superb site in the Santa Rita hills.

a positive—practically glowing—geologic analytical soil report that convinced the Works to purchase the 94 acres of contoured slopes. To this day, the farmer who sold them the property still jokes about his missed opportunity and the Works' low cost investment.

Their first long walk together through their new property and up to the big oak tree that overlooks the valley was nothing short of thrilling. "We bought the land with dreams of someday watching the nightly sunset over the hills and our dogs running through the vines," Rebecca told a reporter.

What with non-stop travel, business meetings, and conferences, the couple hardly had time to focus on their vineyard. While still working long hours in the corporate world, the Works asked their son Don to start the vineyard. Fortunately for them, Don is the head winemaker at Sea Smoke, one of the top wineries in the region.

Their first vintage was in 1999, a cuvée made by Don with bought-in grapes from the local area. In another five years, the vineyards would yield fruit that was properly matured for bottling, so the couple had plenty of time to practice on someone else's grapes. The Works edged forward in a rented custom crush facility with lots of other hopefuls, all diligently learning their new trade at a snail's pace. The wine produced was labeled Ampelos Cellars.

The vineyard's name is inspired by one of the Works' favorite places in the world: the Greek Isles. When Peter's sister married a Greek on the island of Folegandros, the Works fell in love with the region. Their affection for Greece ran so deep that they decided to christen their new property and wine *Ampelos*, which is the Greek word for "vine." What could be more perfect?

The wine club for Ampelos was named *Filos*, the Greek word for "friend." And a decidedly Greek theme runs throughout the vineyard, with each bottle carrying a Greek name and symbol relating to a special characteristic of the cuvée.

A Life-Changing Morning

After purchasing the property, the couple began the painstaking process of planning their vineyard: site-by-site, variety-by-variety, inch-by-inch. In 2001, the first fifteen acres were planted at Ampelos. Placing different varieties side by side provided a great range of red and white grapes. The Works fully understood the benefits of American viticulture law, which allows for the planting of multiple types of wine grapes on one property—an option that's unavailable to winemakers in Europe due to antiquated laws and regulations.

And then came the fateful morning of September 11, 2001. Peter and Rebecca had both just landed at Newark Airport on a routine business trip. "Peter had a meeting in the first tower of the World Trade Center, and interrupted his plan to board Path 1 of the New York Subway when his meeting was canceled," recalls Rebecca. "If he'd gotten on the train, 8:45am would've placed him under the towers as the first plane hit. Five days later, when we finally got out of the city, we went straight to our safe place—the vineyard. That is when we made the decision to quit our corporate jobs and focus all our effort on pursuing our dream of full-time viticulture. 'Someday' was no longer part of our vocabulary."

By January 2002, the Works had relocated full-time to the Santa Ynez Valley and begun

Peter and Rebecca survey their vineyard with the help of one of their two beloved chocolate labs.

tilling and nurturing the soil, preparing the vines for their first harvest in 2004. In the meantime, in 2003, while patiently waiting for their vines to fully mature, they eagerly purchased one ton of Pinot Noir and two tons of Syrah grapes from a neighbor to learn the finer details involved with winemaking. Their son Don and wine consultant Jeff Newton (of Coastal Vineyard Care Associates) proved to be excellent teachers on the bought-in fruit, and the Works literally drank in all the knowledge, tips, and techniques they had to offer.

The Vineyards

The Ampelos property sits between the Santa Rita Hills to the north and the Santa Rosa Hills to the south. Both hillsides parallel the ocean in an east-to-west direction that exposes their vines to essential cooling influences. The nighttime ocean fog and breezes roll off the ocean, blow up the valley, and blanket the day's sun-drenched vines with misty moisture that lowers their pH levels and raises their acidity (increasing the grapes' sugar concentration).

Ampelos boasts the perfect environment for the production of Chardonnay and Pinot Noir grapes; a long growing season and the diurnal temperature shifts in the region perfectly showcase their various subtle nuances. Cabernet Sauvignon and Zinfandel grapes are rarely found in these hills as the cool weather of the region doesn't promote the proper ripeness required in the grapes. The red spicy grape varieties of Syrah and Grenache, however, do grow well here due to their thick rot-resistant

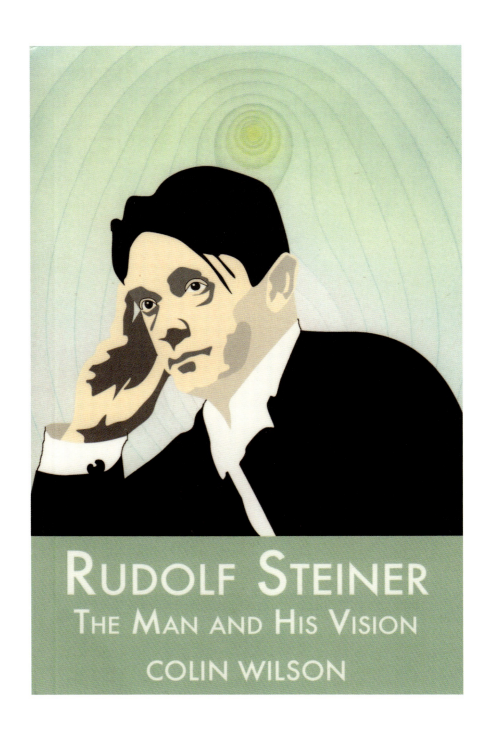

RUDOLF STEINER
THE MAN AND HIS VISION

COLIN WILSON

skins, as do a smattering of cool-climate white grapes, such as Sauvignon Blanc and Viognier.

Early on, the Works decided that the majority of their property should be planted with Pinot Noir (all estate-grown), Grenache, Viognier, and Syrah. Subsequently they've also planted plots of white Pinot Gris and Riesling grapes in small quantities as experimental varieties. The Chardonnay grapes they buy in from adjacent neighbors. The breakdown of percentage of grapes grown on the estate and bought-in from others is 80% estate and 20% (mostly Chardonnay) sourced from nearby high-quality (and continually vetted by Peter for quality control) vineyards.

Rudolf Steiner, Biodynamics, and Organic Farming

The Works have always taken a keen interest in biodynamic, organic, and sustainable farming. Everything in the house, vineyard, and winery is recycled back into the land or repurposed. Cardboard wine boxes are reused in the vineyard as protection against soil erosion; fertilizers consist of recycled horse manure, green cuttings, old stems, seeds, and spent lees from previous vintages. Alternative power sources such as solar are employed all over the property. Most importantly, no pesticides are used.

From the start, Peter—ever the trailblazer—was interested in the radical teachings of Rudolf Steiner (1861-1925). Considered the "Godfather" of biodynamic farming, Steiner was a highly respected Austrian philosopher, social reformer, architect, and proponent of

Cover of a biography of Rudolf Steiner by Colin Wilson.

esotericism. "Rudolf Steiner said we have to get back to basics and the way they used to farm before the 1900s because Germany had changed to artificial pesticides and commercial fertilizers and the farmers soon realized their yields were going down," said Peter as we walked through lush rows of sun-fed grapes. "Steiner quickly deduced it was because the chemicals were artificially manipulating their plants in the wrong way. He advised the local farmers to let their plants do what they had always done naturally, and thus 'biodynamics' was born." Biodynamic farming treats the fields, woods, plants, wetlands, animals, and people as a self-contained, self-sustaining organism, and is now practiced on more than 350,000 acres of farmland in 47 countries.

Biodynamics became popular in California during the 1970s and late '80s. Devotees believe there are "root days" and "fruit days" and a farmer should concentrate on one or the other. Farming revolves around the Earth's lunar cycles. Days are split into four divisions—leaf, root, flower, and fruit. Farming of each division is done on set days that are pre-determined by the calendar. The Works also believe in the moon's effect on a human's taste. Some days are deemed "earth days," when the flavor of wine is much less expressive than on "fruit days," when the wine seems more agreeable to the human palate.

Peter and Rebecca take the art of biodynamics very seriously, so much so that they work in symbiosis with the calendar, the moon, and vineyard water tables. They even make use of the ancient practice of burying a cow horn full of specially treated manure deep in the ground, and have planted four horns under a big oak tree that overlooks the vineyard.

The practice of biodynamics informs every aspect of their vineyard. For example, the Works only use wild yeasts (instead of commercial packets) to produce a perceived superior taste component within the fruit's flesh. "Wild yeasts provide the wine with a better structure in the mouth," Peter claims. Every decision within the Ampelos vineyard is avidly calculated and micro-managed by Peter and his consultants. Altitude, sun-exposure, soil suitability, aspect, vine spacing, and proper levels of irrigation are scrutinized day by day and hour by hour until the eventual harvest.

It must also be mentioned that the Works promote and practice this ethos in every aspect of daily life, from making wine to using solar panels. For example, instead of purchasing commercial products such as "501," Peter makes his own version using plants such as dandelion, burdock, valerian, and chamomile.

Bad Bugs

Interestingly, as the Works introduced more and more biodynamic and organic practices, the vineyards seemed to suffer less from serious pests. One of the practices of biodynamic farming is to have the crops' pests "eat each other." Thus, predatory bugs in the vineyard are eaten by mice, which in turn, are eaten by birds.

As for any threats to the health of the plants, the greatest concern is the dreaded and devastating Phylloxera bug. Fortunately, it is extremely rare in the region due to the high sand content in the soil, which hinders the Phylloxera's ability to breed. Secondly, there is the potential for grey rot when conditions become too moist due to the nightly rolling fog banks that sometimes leave behind too much moisture. A sulfur compound is sprayed every eight days to combat this form of white powdery mildew. Rain regularly makes an appearance in the winter months (on average twelve inches between November and March, usually within 20 days) and can cause both root rot and dilution of the grape juice. The Works have some unique and ingenious solutions to combat rain and its resultant damage. The first is to spray the vines with fish oil. The second method is to run their sprayer through the rows so it only blows air and thus dries off the plants. (However, it should be noted that the current four-year draught throughout California has mostly eliminated such concerns.)

The Santa Rita Hills growing season is generally considered to be dry and is prolonged with only a few drops of rain between April and September. Hail is super-rare but not unheard of. The only major pest problems are the grape-eating birds, which are deterred by laying swaths of netting on top of the vines, and the common mealy bug. Ants were introduced to keep the bugs at bay and 70 chickens work to get rid of the ants, creating a natural balance and eliminating the need for chemicals. Ladybugs are also part of the pest control at Ampelos and they are literally everywhere. Belying their beautiful appearance, these are truly savage insects that devour others without mercy; yet they have little taste for grapes, which makes them a perfect asset for any vineyard.

Network of Vines

By late 2000, Ampelos had expanded into a very serious network of vineyards. The Works had implemented irrigation and trellis systems that had the capability to selectively water separate rows and were fed by a natural well on the property.

The first fifteen acres of the estate (about 18,000 vines) were planted to run east-west and take advantage of the sun during the day. There are four feet between the vines and nine feet between the rows, allowing Peter the ideal vine and cover crop management and weed control. Each "other" row running throughout the vineyard is left fallow and seeded with various grain food crops (again providing a biodynamic environment of insect versus insect and an added benefit of stressing the vine for water as it competes against the grain, intensifying the flavor of the grapes).

There are four main levels to the slope, each is planted with suitable varietals. The Grenache sits at the very top of the curve; 230 Viognier plants are neatly rowed just below the Grenache; and placed just behind them are some Syrah. The Syrah is used solely for the production of the Estate rosé wine called "A Little Time."

Located in the middle of the main vineyard is the central Syrah block, which receives excellent sun exposure, making it well-suited for the warm-climate varietal. Below and towards the bottom of the curve and slope, the most clay-rich and water-retentive soils provide a perfect environment for the Pinot Noir. "Pinot Noir likes to get its feet wet," said Peter of the lower rows. The coolly shaded bottom row gently ends the slope and is dedicated to a newly planted Riesling experiment.

In 2004 the property yielded fifteen tons of Pinot Noir and six tons of Syrah, which remain the estate's primary varietals. Flowering starts with the Viognier and Pinot Noir grapes followed by the Syrah and then finally the thick-skinned Grenache. This flowering period between April and May is tricky due to "shatter," where grapes don't fully flower due to frost and literally burst on the vine. Harvesting of the fully ripened grapes follows the same progression as flowering, beginning with 250 vines of the white-grape Viognier in October and concluding with the harvest of the Grenache grape at Thanksgiving, which gives one a good idea of the extended "hang-time" the grapes enjoy due to the region's uniquely long season.

In 2005 another ten acres were planted at Ampelos just to the right of the original fifteen acres, totaling 25 acres of the two varieties. However, the estate grows numerous other small plots of varietals, some just experimentally, in an effort to see how or if they will mature. As Peter explains, "We continually persist in experimenting with different grapes and winemaking styles, as we are major believers in the journey being the destination."

Harvesting

Weird looking "refractors" (they resemble a single-eye metal binocular) used to gauge the present sugar-levels within grapes are usually employed by winemakers to determine the ideal time to harvest. At Ampelos, refractors are rarely used past the initial grapes' maturation stage. The Works think the instruments' findings are too formulaic and do not allow for the unique natural variations of every terroir. The eyes, hands, noses, and tongues of the couple and their consultants decide when to ultimately harvest the ripe grapes. As Rebecca explained, "A happy vine's major job is to propagate. It actually yearns to propagate. It desperately wants to produce the best fruit

in the vineyard that will entice a certain bird to take its fruit and not its neighbors' fruit. So the vine is going to tell you visually *'I'm at my optimal level, I can't get any better than this or I'm going to shut down and I'm done.'* You watch those signs carefully and that's how you decide to pick."

Harvesting times can alter vintage to vintage due to individual climatic differences between years. "Winemaking is not a recipe like beer production," explains Peter. "If I want to make an IPA beer, I follow the recipe. In winemaking there's no half cup of this and a half cup of that." Picking is carefully done by hand, often aided by the family and even Kurt, during this frantic time.

Clones

The Works and Kurt Russell are particularly fascinated by the use and blending of clones and the character each clone expresses, especially when making a particular blend from separate barrels. By combining increments of each desired barrel (a wine changes flavors with maturation in barrel) flavors build and can form a direction and vision. The Works and Russell create "blended" cuvées, utilizing different clones of the same variety. Some clones add structure such as tannin, while others add color (pigmentation), mouth-feel, richness, or flavor of fruit.

"Kurt is easy to work with, which is a plus, and has a very good palate," says Rebecca. "It's funny because after his first vintage, which he really enjoyed so much, he came back

It's been a long but satisfying journey from Wall Street finance to California winemaking, but there's nothing Peter Work would rather be doing.

after the second harvest and said, 'OK let's do it the same!' and we said, 'Look we are not making Coca-Cola wines here, every vintage is different, every year will have differences.' He looked at us after a glass of the second vintage of his pre-set favorite blend and said, 'This is not exactly the taste that I first fell in love with a year ago.' We explained that as a winemaker one has to work with the nuances that each vintage offers and those attributes won't be exactly the same from year to year. So it took him a few vintages to really work out the inner mechanics of how winemaking works, but he's an extremely fast learner. And at this point, let me tell you, he's not at all afraid to express exactly what he wants to achieve."

Blending wines is perhaps the most challenging and interesting part of winemaking. "I've been able to formulate my own taste," Russell told blogger Gabe Saglie, "and it's blending that is the most challenging, yet the most rewarding."

Staying Small and Sustainable

Peter is now firmly in charge of the various vineyards, while Rebecca is happy to be involved with the finances and the blending of the cuvées inside the couple's tin-shed winery. Their winery is simply an artificially cooled garage within the city limits of Lompoc. Resembling a vast complex of huge grey warehouses bordered by the Vandenburg Airforce Base and an unforgiving-looking federal penitentiary, it is situated in a sheet metal hanger.

Air-conditioned and humidity-controlled, the winery is stacked with barrels neatly racked and packed towards the rear of the house; piles of cardboard and equipment cover every area of the room. Cleanliness is paramount in all wineries and Ampelos is no exception. Generally, a winery is very damp. Gallons of water are used daily in an attempt to keep nasty bacteria such a Brettomices from contaminating the equipment and thus the wine. Brett is a common problem in the wine world and is tremendously difficult to fully eliminate. Many a winemaker has lost a vintage under the belief that their Brett problem was eradicated, only for it to make a bewildering reappearance once under cork.

Peter says their commitment is "to stay small and be sustainable." Ampelos Cellars produces a meager 5000 cases of wine every year, while Kurt Russell's production is limited to 1000 cases.

Melding the New and Old

The team practices a mixture of both old and new winemaking processes but insists on being as eco-friendly as possible. After harvesting late in the year, the grapes are transported (as gently as possible) to the winery and sorted in accordance to their designated vineyard blocks or lots and then placed in a near-freezing cold room that avoids the use of environmentally damaging dry ice. The process of de-stemming takes place with particular attention paid to the Pinot Noir. No crushing, only gentle pressing is employed, so as not to produce overly extracted, aggressively tannic wines from this finicky grape. "We just let the grapes do what they want to do," explains Rebecca. For the whites, a cold fermentation in stainless steel tanks is used to retain volatile fruit esters and prevent secondary fermentations. Wild (indigenous) yeast fermentation and wild

ML fermentation is induced (the bought-in Chardonnay grapes being the only exception, as they receive a processed mixture).

Once fermented, the wine is then transferred to oak to mature, with the Grenache and Syrah spending up to three years in cask. Tough-skinned grapes such as Grenache and Syrah require extended barrel maturation to soften and tame their thick tannic skins. Some grapes can handle and benefit taste-wise from a dollop of new oak.

Ampelos utilizes a combination of oak barrels, though the winery is very conscious about oak; the types, the toast levels, and the maturation times. They have a preference towards a less oaked, more inert style of wine that expresses pure clarity of fruit. Russell prefers more oak maturation in his wines but never veers towards a "creamy," over-the-top California style. "Kurt does like a touch more oak in his wines, that's his personal preference. But he never likes too much of a 'toast' [a bigger toast results in an oaky flavor]. Most are lightly toasted and in fact some experiments have even involved blending un-oaked wines," says Rebecca. "Generally at Ampelos we don't like too much toast on our wines; they are aged for a maximum of two years in barrel and one in bottle before release for the public. We use barrels more for the softening of tannins and the wines' mouth-feel than for the overt creamy oak flavor influence transferred by the wood."

There are other methods for achieving added complexity and Ampelos employs one of these to the full: the ancient technique of *bâtonnage*, a French term for manually stirring the "lees," or sediment, within a white wine—usually a Chardonnay. The fruit for the Chardonnay purchased from the Santa Rita Hills is bright, lush, and ripe; a perfect vinous base for *bâtonnage*. "Kurt really likes his Chardonnays made on the lees and personally stirs his barrels," explains Rebecca.

Boot's Barrels

In the middle of the Ampelos warehouse sits a stack of wine barrels in a square block shape. Stacked three barrels high and ten barrels long, the barrels appear cradled like rotund babies held captive in a heavy metal frame. Each row contains barrels of grape varieties and clones from the different vineyard blocks and plots. Identification is a difficult process with personal codes scrawled in fading chalk in the damp darkness. The once bright two-by four-foot caramel barrels are stained and streaked with vertical bright blood-colored drips from the numerous "Bung" tastings.

The Ampelos barrels are usually matured for an average of sixteen months before being filled and situated on the rack. There is, however, a secreted two-barrel stash of super juice that's reserved just for the Ampelos wine members—the Filos. Recognized as the two best barrels of the harvest, they are marked with the word "Row" and are matured in special Boot's barrels. As Rebecca explains, "The Boot's barrels that we use are all cut on a descending moon. We know for a fact that the 'moon takes in' [as it descends], whilst on an ascending moon the 'Earth takes in.' We irrigate the vineyard on a descending moon because the Earth takes up less water and thus drives the vine towards deeper geologic penetration than on an ascending moon. So the intent with these barrels is to cut the wood down so all the flavors or sap flows gently into the wood itself, creating a better-balanced and flavorsome barrel."

Eco-friendly Wines

By the late-2000s, Ampelos Cellars gained notoriety in the U.S. as not only the first sustainable, but also organic and biodynamic vineyard and winery. The aim was to produce eco-friendly, natural wines with no added yeasts, tannins, artificial bacteria, or coloring. Considered to be the new leaders of environmental winemaking in the region, the Works, in conjunction with the Wine Institute and California Association of Winegrowers, implemented the new Sustainability Grape-Growing Principles in 2003. Avidly conscious about being environmentally non-toxic, the Works have solar powered their property and even have gone as far as to have Rebecca make their own safe bio-washing detergents and hand soaps. One can immediately sense in Peter and Rebecca the connection and personal pride they feel towards their vineyard, along with the respect they have developed for the planet through the practice of growing grapes and making wine with their own hands, from their own land.

When the Works first purchased Ampelos, there were very few established vineyards in the Santa Rita Hills area except for the now widely respected early pioneers of the region, such as Sanford, Alban, Clos Pepe, and Au Bon Climat, among a handful of others. Now the area is bursting with a new generation of well-hyped international vinous stars in addition to Ampelos, including Sea Smoke, Domaine de la Côte, Sandhi, Babcock, Foley, and Melville, among others.

PORTFOLIO

Kurt Russell's wines are a perfect reflection of the quintessential wines made in the Santa Rita Hills. There's a wonderful lushness about them that is apparent in all the wines of the region. Without a doubt, they are purposely fashioned in a very Burgundian style, highlighting elements of delicacy, elegance, and purity of fruit rather than extracted power. Throughout all Kurt's wines, there's a noticeable trait—a wonderful pure streak of ultra-ripe fruit that flashes across one's mid-palate and sinks deep into the middle of the tongue. When Nick told Rebecca that this seemed to be a trademark of the wines produced at Ampelos, she smiled with recognition.

The wines at Ampelos are never heavy or thick; they seem to float across the palate with the previously mentioned elegance and a silky quality. These wines are endowed with ripe concentration; European in style but with a definite dash of California sunshine. They also age superbly in the cellar as witnessed from an older cuvée, kindly opened by the Works during our visit, that had developed into a solid wine with nuances of a forest floor, deep aromas such as moss, damp earth, and interesting hints of fungus.

"Goldie" Chardonnay, 2012

This is a very bright, light-gold-colored wine; reflective, silky, and round in the glass. An expressive creamy nose bursts with a mélange of smooth, pure lemons and limes bolstered by excellently judged, unobtrusive oak that supports rather than masks the sun-ripened but not baked fruit. Good acidity with a very long, lush, mineral-infused finish indicates that this wine originated from a prolonged growing season. Fine but unfiltered, 25% new French oak. Twice-a-day *bâttonage* in barrel to promote extra complexity. Less matured in new oak (a third less) than the regular Ampelos cuvées, as is Kurt's preference. I thought this was a really lovely, very high-class Chardonnay made from carefully selected, well-sourced fruit in the AVAs.

"Jillybean" Pinot Noir, 2010

"A great Pinot chases its own tail," Russell told Fox News. "My dream was to make a world-class Pinot." He succeeded. His Pinot Noir grapes are sourced, picked, sorted, and blended by Kurt with help from the Works at Ampelos. The color is gorgeous, a bright ruby crimson—vibrant, alive, and youthful. The nose explodes with a cornucopia of red and black fruits that jump from the glass. Aromas of red and black cherries, raspberries, chocolate notes, and spices are subtle and restrained but with obvious high-quality accents of new French oak and forest floor scents, creating extra complexity. In the mouth the wine is gorgeous, silky, supple, and sweetly ripe, coating the tongue but with restraint written all over it. The balance of fruit and acidity is pinpoint, the tannins are tight yet sweet and lengthen out to a long, sensual, juicy finish. Note: Kurt's wines are slightly less oaked than the usual cuvées made at Ampelos—21 months versus the typical 26 and 30 months. Kurt also keeps his juice on the skins for only about month.

Hudson Bellamy "A Little Time" Sauvignon Blanc, 2013

Hudson Bellamy is a pet project of Kate Hudson, the daughter of Goldie Hawn and Russell's stepdaughter, and Matt Bellamy, the singer from the rock band Muse, who were once engaged and have a son but are no longer together. Kate was inspired to make the wine because of Kurt. Her wine is clean and bright, with a very shiny, pale lemon color and reflective, youthful watery hints. Grassy on the nose but not herbaceous; it has more lightly tropical aromas of lush pink grapefruit, sherbet, and cut lemons and limes, but with California sunshine/ripeness. Not super dry. Subtle tropical notes, minerals, and citrus fruits on the light-bodied, flavorful palate. Expertly constructed with precisely balanced levels of acidity to fruit, so as not to become sour. Ripe, with reoccurring starburst flavors, this is a well-made and fun, yet nonetheless serious, wine.

2009

Yao Ming

❖

Cabernet Sauvignon

NAPA VALLEY

Yao Ming

YAO FAMILY WINES

Napa Valley

The New Winemaking Cooperative

The business of winemaking has changed dramatically in the past 50 years. It used to be that if you wanted to start making wine, you would buy a chateau and then purchase the surrounding vineyards. Grapes were turned into wine at the property's winery and then matured at the chateau before bottling. Everything was done "in house." Over the last five decades, however, everything has changed. Why buy a chateau? Why have a winery? In fact, why have a vineyard? The cost to start a winery from scratch is almost completely prohibitive, except for huge companies who can afford such an extravagance.

The trend in winemaking now is towards lower start-up costs: grapes can be sourced from different vineyards; equipment can be rented, shared, or borrowed. Even so, in recent years, only a handful of individuals have actually created their own wine from scratch, which is one reason we were so eager to see how Yao Ming had planned his start-up from the ground up.

Our interest took us to the Napa Valley and an initial meeting with Tom Hinde, president and director of winemaking for Yao Family Wines. We had an appointment to meet Tom in what turned out to be an unobtrusive, secluded lot in Napa. A sentry at the gate, who checked our identifications, gave the place a military feeling, though, as we later learned, having a guard seems appropriate where tens of millions of dollars of wine are being stored. In the center of this compound stood a half dozen tall modern buildings throbbing with activity. We were impressed to see that some of our favorite wines were being made in this place, including Jason Pahlmeyer.

We entered one of the offices and met the gregarious, good-looking Tom Hinde, who had a wide smile and a powerful handshake, one that suggested he has ripped up a few vines in his time. Hinde is considered to be one of the top wine experts in California, with experience ranging from vineyard cultivation to winery management and hands-on artisan winemaking. His impressive resume spans three decades of directing, working, and managing some of the best wineries in California, including the innovative Flowers Vineyard and Winery, a specialty Pinot Noir and Chardonnay producer at Stonestreet Winery, Vérité Estate, La Crema, and the Hartford Family Winery. Recently he worked at Kendall-Jackson Wine Estates,

OVERLEAF: Yao Ming and Tom Hinde, president and director of winemaking for Yao Family Wines.

developing two high-quality Cabernets—Lakoya and Cardinale. Another extremely important, if not vital, attribute is that Hinde has managed to leverage his longstanding grower relationships, enabling Yao Family Wines to source some of the best fruit in the Napa Valley. Tom has a Bachelor of Science degree in Business Administration from the University of Toledo and a winemaking certificate from the highly regarded University of California, Davis. This is a man who knows his wines and the business of winemaking.

Hinde talked with us about the development of this unique winemaking operation, a huge business that spans the globe. In the beginning, Yao Ming explored the idea of branding wines with an established winemaker and soon discovered that his famous name was much in demand. "But then he looked around Napa Valley and saw a whole bunch of different people like Jason Pahlmeyer who didn't have wineries. Those guys came here from different places and Yao realized he didn't have to co-market," explains Hinde. "I was contacted by Yao's team and told they wanted to start a winery. They asked if that was possible and I said of course, it is what people in Napa Valley do. I said he could start Yao Family Wines on his own. And he did. We went ahead and filed our federal permits, leased out vineyards, leased space at the ranch, bought barrels, and hired our vineyard manager, Larry Bradley. We started as an authentic Napa Valley winery."

Hinde then outlined the way the business had been grown through sharing the facilities with Jason Pahlmeyer, Gott, and Harrison Cellars, among others. They all use the same equipment, sharing the rent and the problems that every winemaker faces. "It's actually a great place to make wine," says Hinde. "There is a wonderful sense of collaboration here."

In this way, "Yao Family Wines could 'piecemeal' the winery in stages, thus spreading the cost over several years," explains Hinde. With his connections to grape growers, there was no need to purchase vineyards. As for a winery, yes, they needed one, but their communal winery was serving that function very well. One thing they had to purchase though was the barrels. "You definitely have to invest in barrels," Hinde says. "And the need for some of our cuvées is 100% new French oak barrels. They are expensive." The Family Reserve requires two years in barrels.

As for the future, they do have plans to eventually buy a vineyard or two and then an estate. We wanted to know if they were also planning to enter the newly transforming vinous China. "Most probably," replied Tom with a smile.

Hoops and Grapes

Yao Ming is arguably the most famous basketball player to be making wine in California. Certainly, as a 7-foot 6-inch Chinese athlete, he is unique to the Napa Valley. After an astonishing career in professional sports, the charismatic Yao Ming chose Northern California as home base for his winemaking venture.

In October of 2013 he explained why to Katie Bell of Forbes.com. "When I realized I might not be able to play basketball much longer, I began to think of things I might enjoy when I was done playing. At the same time, China was just discovering fine wine, mostly French wine like Bordeaux. I knew about Napa Valley wine because of my time in the United States, so I felt I could help introduce people to something new.

When I was presented with the opportunity to have my own wine, it was very exciting. I was introduced to a lot of great people, including my current team and our winemaker, Tom Hinde, and I felt it would be a good opportunity."

Hinde explains that Yao Ming, "has a passion for wine. His father drank Bordeaux with him and helped him develop a palate. Ming spent a lot of time in California and fell in love with California wines. He owns a restaurant in Houston called Yao and, being in the food and wine business, developed even more of a passion for wine."

His passion for red meat also played a role. On November 28, 2011, Yao Ming explained to Jason Chow of *The Wall Street Journal* that his interest in wine was sparked by his love of Texas steaks. "In Texas, they are famous for their steaks, which are usually paired with great wine. I tried some excellent Napa Valley wines at dinners with teammates and friends, charity events, and other get-togethers. This is when my passion for wine first started."

Part of Yao's incentive to start a winery in Napa, as opposed to buying an established vineyard in Pauilliac or Saint-Émilion, was to bring the flavor and ambiance of Northern California to his native China. "I saw a great opportunity to introduce fine wines from Napa Valley to China," says Yao. "Napa Valley wines are the wines that I enjoy the most, and I wanted to bring a taste of that back home to China. I want to make wines I am proud of, and to share them with Chinese people, but also share the culture of Napa Valley; the traditions of enjoying wine with food, and bringing family and friends together. Napa Valley is one of the most beautiful places I've ever been, and that is also why I wanted my wine to be from there."

The venture has been a great success. Within 39 months, Yao Family Wines sold more than $8 million of wine while receiving stellar reviews from critics. The June 2013 issue of *Wine Enthusiast Magazine* gave the 2009 Napa Valley Cabernet Sauvignon 95 points and rated the Family Reserve a 97. Wine critic Steve Heimoff, wrote that "Yao's Family Reserve bursts with upfront, delicious blackberry, crème de cassis, and dark chocolate flavors that are wildly sweet on the mid palate, but then finish thoroughly dry. It immediately establishes itself among the elite Cabernets of Napa Valley."

Even the ultimate judge of wine tasting, Robert Parker, praised Yao Ming's wines. In *The Wine Advocate*, October, 2013, Parker wrote, "I am aware of all the arguments that major celebrities lending their names to wines is generally a formula for mediocrity, but that is not the case with Yao Ming. These are high-class wines. The two Cabernets are actually brilliant, and the Reserve bottling ranks alongside just about anything made in Napa."

And the wines have won enthusiastic fans from around the world. When the Yao Family Wines made their first appearance at a charity auction for the Special Olympics East Asia last November in Shanghai, the inaugural bottle sold for 150,000 yuan (or $23,499).

The Year of the Yao

Born in Shanghai on September 12, 1980, Yao is the son of two Chinese professional basketball players, Yao Zhiyuan and Fang Fengdi. At birth he weighed eleven pounds, more than twice the average Chinese newborn. At nine years old, obsessed with basketball, he was on the court ten hours a day and honed his skills by attending a junior sports school. The following year, Yao measured 5 feet 5 inches and was examined by sports doctors, who predicted he would grow to 7 feet 3 inches. The prediction fell short by three inches.

At thirteen, Yao was signed to the Shanghai Sharks and after playing with the junior team for four years, he joined the senior team, where he averaged ten points and eight rebounds a game in his rookie season. His next season was cut short when he broke his foot, which he claimed decreased his jumping ability by four to six inches. Still, Yao played on their senior team for five years in the Chinese Basketball Association (CBA), winning a championship in his final year.

It was at this time that Yao first played for China in the 2000 Summer Olympics and, together with 7-foot-tall teammates Wang Zhizhi and Mengke Bateer, was dubbed part of the "The Walking Great Wall." By the end of his career Yao had led the Chinese national team to three consecutive FIBA Asian Championship gold medals (in 2001, 2003, and 2005). He was also named the MVP of all three tournaments.

Basketball, however, was not the only thing on the young player's mind during the Summer Olympics. The pins he collected during the event would play a big role in his personal life. In 1998, when he was seventeen, Yao met a 6-foot 3-inch beauty named Ye Li. Also a basketball player, she played for China in the 2004 Summer Olympics. She has admitted that when they met, she "did not like him at first." But Ming was persistent and presented her with the pins he had collected and won at the Olympics. The gesture did the trick and they were married in 2007. They now have a daughter, Yoa Qiniei (Amy) who was born in 2010 in Houston, Texas.

Team Yao

When Yao decided to enter the 2002 NBA draft, he was helped by a group of advisers that came to be known as "Team Yao." The team consisted of Yao's negotiator, Erik Zhang; his NBA agent, Bill Duffy; his Chinese agent, Lu Hao; University of Chicago economics professor John Huizinga; and the vice president for marketing at BDA Sports Management, Bill Sanders. Though it was widely predicted that Yao would be the number one pick, some teams were concerned about whether the CBA would let Yao play in the United States.

Previously, Chinese NBA basketball star Wang Zhizhi had refused to return to China to play for the national team. China was not going to let that happen again. This time the CBA stipulated that Yao would have to come back to China to play for their national team. They also said they would refuse to let him go to the United States unless, amazingly enough, the Houston Rockets took him as a first draft pick. After assurances from Team Yao, the CBA gave permission on the morning of the draft. When the Rockets picked Yao, he became the first international player to be selected first without ever having played U.S. college basketball.

Yao did not participate in the Rockets' preseason training camp, instead he had to play for China in the 2002 FIBA World Championships. For Yao's first U.S. game, in Miami on December 16, 2002, the Heat passed out 8,000 fortune cookies, an Asian cultural stereotype. In an earlier interview in 2000, Yao said he had never seen a fortune cookie in China and guessed it must have been an American invention.

Yao's rookie year in the NBA would later be the subject of a documentary film entitled *The*

Yao Ming is probably the only 7'6" Chinese basketball superstar making wine in Napa Valley.

Year of the Yao. He also co-wrote, along with NBA analyst Ric Bucher, an autobiography entitled *Yao: A Life in Two Worlds*.

His Rookie Season

Before Yao's rookie season, many commentators, including Bill Simmons and Dick Vitale, predicted he would fail terribly within the NBA. The retired pugnacious Charles Barkley said he would "kiss the ass of Kenny Smith" (a famous commentator) if Yao managed to score more than nineteen points in one of his rookie-season games. Yao played his first NBA game against the Indiana Pacers, scoring no points and grabbing two rebounds. He scored his first NBA basket against the Denver Nuggets. In his first seven games, he averaged only fourteen minutes of court time and four points, but on November 17 he scored twenty points on a perfect 9-of-9 from the field and 2-of-2 from the free-throw line against the Lakers. Barkley made good on his bet by kissing a donkey's buttocks on national television.

Yao finished his rookie season averaging 13.5 points and 8.2 rebounds per game. He was second in the NBA Rookie of the Year Award to Amar'e Stoudemire, and a unanimous pick for the NBA All-Rookie First Team selection. He was also the recipient of the *Sporting News* Rookie of the Year Award and the Laureus Newcomer of the Year Award.

Long Dream Come True

In the 2004 Athens Olympics, Yao carried the Chinese flag during the opening ceremony, which he said was a "long dream come true." He then vowed to abstain from shaving his beard for half a year unless the Chinese national basketball team made it into the quarterfinals of the 2004 Olympics Basketball Tournament.

Ultimately, China lost to Lithuania in the quarterfinals by 26 points, eliminating them from the tournament. Yao's nineteen points a game were the second-highest in the Olympics, and his averages of 8.2 rebounds and 1.5 blocks per game were third overall.

Back home in Houston, the Rockets' head coach Rudy Tomjanovich resigned because of health issues, just before the start of Yao's sophomore season. Subsequently, longtime New York Knicks head coach Jeff Van Gundy was hired and began focusing the offense on Yao.

It was just the right adjustment for Yao, Van Gundy, and the Rockets. Yao soon averaged career highs in points and rebounds for the season, topping out at 41 points and seven assists in a triple-overtime win against the Atlanta Hawks in February 2004. The Rockets made the playoffs for the first time in Yao's career, claiming the seventh seed in the Western Conference. In the first round, however, the Los Angeles Lakers eliminated Houston in five games. Yao averaged 15 points and 7.4 rebounds in his first playoff series. He was voted starting center for the Western Conference in the 2004 NBA All-Star Game for the second straight year and finished the season averaging 17.5 points and 9 rebounds a game.

One of the controversies that swirled around Yao's career was his relationship with the brilliant Shaquille O'Neal. On January 17, 2003, just before a game between the Lakers and the Rockets, O'Neal said, "Tell Yao Ming, Ching chong-yang-wah-ah-soh," which prompted accusations of racism. O'Neal denied that his comments were racist, and claimed he was only joking. Though Yao conceded that O'Neal was probably joking, he also acknowledged that most Asians would not see the humor. In that 2003 game, Yao scored six points, blocked O'Neal twice in the opening minutes, and made a game-stealing dunk with ten seconds left in overtime. Yao finished with 10 points, 10 rebounds, and 6 blocks; O'Neal recorded 31 points, 13 rebounds, and 0 blocks. O'Neal later publically admitted that he was ashamed he had insulted Yao.

In 2003, the NBA began offering ballots in three languages—English, Spanish, and Chinese—for fans voting on the starters for the NBA All-Star Game. Yao was voted to start for the West over O'Neal, who was coming off three consecutive NBA Finals MVP Awards. Yao received nearly a quarter million more votes than O'Neal, and became the first rookie to start in the All-Star Game since Grant Hill in 1995. In 2005, with 2,558,278 votes, Yao broke the record previously held by Michael Jordan for most All-Star votes.

In total for 2005, the Rockets won 51 games and finished fifth in the West making the playoffs for the second consecutive year, where they faced the Dallas Mavericks. The Rockets won the first two games in Dallas, and Yao made thirteen of fourteen shots in the second game, the best shooting performance in the playoffs in Rockets history. However the Rockets lost four of their last five games and lost Game 7 by 40 points, the greatest Game 7 defeat in NBA history. Yao's final averages for the series were 21.4 points and 7.7 rebounds with a 65% shooting average. During his fifth season, Yao averaged a career-high of 25 points per game.

Height Has Its Disadvantages

Being 7½ feet tall definitely has its advantages on the court, where you can dunk at head level or receive high-placed passes around the hoop. But such enormous height has its disadvantages in the form of injuries. Feet, spine, and knees are especially vulnerable and Yao was no exception to the rule.

After missing only two games out of 246 in his first three years of NBA play, in 2005 Yao endured an extended period of inactivity for his fourth season. He was diagnosed with osteomyelitis in the big toe on his left foot, and surgery was performed in December 2005. He suffered a broken bone in his left foot in a game against the Utah Jazz on April 10, 2006. The injury required a full six months of recuperation, threatening his participation in the 2006 FIBA World Championship. However, he recovered before the start of the tournament and in the last game of the preliminary round, scored 36 points and 10 rebounds in a win against Slovenia to lead China into Round 16. In the first knockout round, however, China was defeated by eventual finalist Greece. Into his fifth season, Yao was injured again, breaking his right knee while attempting to block a shot on December 23, 2006. This time, he was out for 32 games and missed what would have been his fifth All-Star game.

On November 9, 2007, Yao played against fellow Chinese NBA and Milwaukee Bucks player Yi Jianlian for the first time. The game, which the Rockets won, was broadcast on nineteen networks in China, and was viewed by over 200 million people in China alone, making it one of the most-watched NBA games

in history. In the 2008 NBA All-Star game, Yao was once again voted to start as center for the Western Conference. On February 26, 2008, however, it was reported that Yao would miss the rest of the season with a stress fracture in his left foot.

The next season, Yao played 77 games, his first full season since the 2004–05 season, and averaged 19.7 points and 9.9 rebounds, while shooting 54.8% from the field, and a career-high 86.6% from the free throw line. The Rockets finished the regular season with 53 wins and were fifth seed in the Western Conference. Facing the Portland Trail Blazers in the first round, Yao finished with 24 points on 9 of 9 shooting in the first game, and the Rockets won 108–81, in Portland. The Rockets swept all their games in Houston, and advanced to the second round of the playoffs for the first time since 1997, and the first time in Yao's career.

The Rockets faced the Lakers in the second round, and Yao scored 28 points, with 8 points in the final four minutes, to lead the Rockets to a 100–92 win in Los Angeles. However, the Rockets lost their next two games. Yao was diagnosed with a sprained ankle after Game 3. A follow-up test revealed a hairline fracture in his left foot, and he was out for the remainder of the playoffs. Yao underwent a successful operation to insert screws in his foot to strengthen the bone.

After his surgery, Yao stated if he could not play in the 2008 Summer Olympics in Beijing, "it would be the biggest loss in my career to right now." On August 6, as part of the Olympic torch relay, Yao Ming carried the flame into Tiananmen Square. In the Opening Ceremony, he carried the Chinese flag and led his country's delegation. Yao scored the first basket, a three-pointer, in China's opening game against the United States. "I was just really happy to make that shot," Yao said after the Americans' 101–70 victory and eventual gold medal. "It was the first score in our Olympic campaign here at home and I'll always remember it. It represents that we can keep our heads up in the face of really tough odds."

On December 16, 2010, it was announced that Yao had developed a stress fracture in his left ankle, related to an older injury, and would miss the rest of the season. In January 2011, though he couldn't participate, he was voted the Western Conference starting center for the All-Star Game for the eighth time in nine years. Yao's contract with the Rockets expired at the end of the 2010–2011 season, and he became a free agent.

On July 20, 2011, Yao announced his retirement from basketball in a press conference in Shanghai, citing injuries which forced him to miss 250 games in his last six seasons. In eight seasons with the Rockets, Yao ranked sixth among franchise leaders in total points and total rebounds, and second in total blocks. His retirement sparked over 1.2 million comments on the Chinese social-networking site Sina Weibo. Reacting to Yao's retirement, NBA commissioner David Stern said Yao was a "bridge between Chinese and American fans," and that he had "a wonderful mixture of talent, dedication, humanitarian aspirations, and a sense of humor." Even his old nemesis Shaquille O'Neal said Yao "...was very agile. He could play inside, he could play outside, and if he didn't have those injuries he could've been up there in the top five centers to ever play the game."

In 2009 Yao returned to China and purchased the Shanghai Sharks, the team that had launched his career when he was just a teenager.

A Wealth of Gratitude

By any standard of professional sports, Yao Ming has earned a huge amount of money in his career. In addition to his substantial salary from the Rockets, he participated in many promotional campaigns, becoming the spokesperson for such companies as Nike, Reebok, Pepsi, Visa, Apple, and McDonalds, to name a few. (He sued Coke for image infringement over a TV commercial and won. However, it should be noted that because he was more concerned with protecting the rights of all the players Coke featured, not just himself, he only sued for $1.) The commercial ads pushed his annual average personal earnings to $51 million a year. He led the Chinese "Rich List" for six consecutive years.

Yao's humanitarian career began in 2008, when he created the YAO MING Foundation in response to the devastating earthquake in Sichuan Province, China. The foundation's long-term mission is to provide educational opportunities for children in the United States and China, and has committed to rebuilding five schools in the earthquake region. The new earthquake resistant schools will provide top-level education to more than 1,400 students. The foundation has also made grants to help rebuild four playgrounds in Houston that were destroyed by Hurricane Ike. Yao has pledged $2 million to the foundation, and has committed to personally covering all the administrative costs.

Yao serves as a global ambassador for the Special Olympics. He is also involved with environmental causes. In an effort to save sharks from extinction, he and Sir Richard Branson recently joined forces with WildAid, and Yao has made a global appeal to ban shark fin soup.

The Yao family is passionately involved with many charities but most notably SAARS, which supports underprivileged children, countries hit with emergency situations, and animal conservation, especially elephants and white rhinos. (Yao helped fund and produce a documentary highlighting their plight.)

Yao Ming is currently earning an economics degree in China's Shanghai Jiao Tong University, a skill he felt would help him run his many enterprises. "I am involved in several businesses," explains Yao. "In addition to Yao Family Wines, I am also the proud owner of the Shanghai Sharks, the team that I once played on, and several other interesting ventures. I find business fascinating. I am attending school and taking classes to learn more. I believe my studies will help in the success of my businesses and my foundation, which is very important to me. The more knowledge I have, the more I can contribute."

From Courtside to Tasting Room

In November 2011, Yao Ming announced the establishment of his Napa Valley wine company, Yao Family Wines. Ming formed a formidable winemaking team, led by Tom Hinde and consulting viticulturist Larry Bradley. He's lucky to have these two consummate professionals who've both worked for some of the best estates and companies in the California. "He likes balance in the wine," says Yao of Hinde, "everything has to work together."

Speaking of Yao, Hinde responds in kind. "He notices when something is too far in one direction, and he always asks to pull it back."

Larry Bradley has a long and extensive background in both developing and managing vineyards around the globe. His particular expertise lies in soils and his extensive resume includes vineyard management and viticulture consulting with Clos du Val Winery, Clover Hill (Australia), Domaine de Nizas (Languedoc, France), Elyse Winery, Falcor Winery, Flowers Winery, Morisoli Vineyards, Taltarni Winery (Australia), and V. Sattui Winery, among others. Larry has advanced degrees in plant science from the University of California.

Yao Family Wines sources its grapes for the YAO MING Napa Valley Cabernet Sauvignon from high-quality vineyards that have gained a reputation for producing excellent fruit. The vineyards are located from north to south along the Napa Valley where the variation in climate and soils provide grapes with distinct characteristics that can add to the final complexity of the blend. The vineyards include: Sugarloaf Mountain Vineyard, Tourmaline Vineyard located in Coombsville and Tulocay, Circle S Vineyard on Atlas Peak, Broken Rock Vineyard in Soda Canyon, and Wollack Vineyard in St. Helena.

At harvest time, Tom, Larry, and Yao select the individual blocks they aim to blend. The grapevines are pruned in winter to achieve balanced green shoots in the spring. The vines are thinned at six different phases during their development, until they have the ideal fruit-cluster-to-vine-canopy ratio. This balance is essential to achieving a low grape yield, rich flavors, and optimum ripeness.

Once at the winery, grapes are hand-sorted and de-stemmed, then lightly crushed and placed in stainless steel tanks. Tom tracks each lot of grapes from individual vineyard blocks and ferments them separately under cold temperature-controlled conditions. He uses artisan winemaking techniques throughout the entire process to allow the character of the vineyards to speak in the wines.

The basic character of the wines forms early in the fermentation process. Fermentation is conducted using native yeasts from the vineyard, which create subtle nuances in the wines from each individual site. The wines undergo an extended maceration and stay in contact with the grape skins and seeds to extract more color, tannin, and flavors. Following fermentation, the wines are gently pressed in a traditional wooden basket press. They are then aged exclusively in 100% French oak barrels for at least eighteen months. Individual barrels from each lot are then hand selected by taste for the final blend.

The company released its inaugural wine under the brand name YAO MING®. Yao Family Wines appointed Pernod Ricard (China) as its sole and exclusive importer and distributor in mainland China. Yao Family Wines has become the biggest seller of high-end Californian wine in China. Today, 15% of the winery's revenues come from the U.S., compared to almost zero in late 2011.

The Yao Family Wines inaugural launch was in 2009 when they released a limited supply of the YAO MING 2009 Napa Valley Cabernet Sauvignon and YAO MING 2009 Family Reserve Cabernet Sauvignon to select wine shops and restaurants across the U.S.

The wines are all of extremely high quality including the entry-level Napa Crest label. Stylistically they are reflective of wines produced in the French region of Bordeaux, especially those from the "Left Bank" commune of Paulliac, created around a base of Cabernet Sauvignon, as opposed to the wines of the "Right Bank" (right of the River Gironde) that are generally softer and richer, due to the higher percentage of Merlot used in the overall blend.

Napa Crest is an approachable, full-bodied, concentrated blend of Napa Valley Cabernet Sauvignon, Merlot, and Petit Verdot grapes. It's probably one of the more serious entry-level wines that I've come across in the valley. Next level up the ladder sits the Napa Valley Cabernet Sauvignon; the 100% Cabernet Sauvignon Estate wine is more structured, with a deeper-veined concentration at its core than the Napa Crest, and reveals overall a more refined mineral sensibility. Last is the amazingly expensive ($625) yet very impressive 100% Cabernet Family Reserve, which combines grace and power; the elegance of Paulliac paired with the concentration of Napa Valley fruit. It's expertly crafted and structured to ensure a long cellar life. The last two cuvées are only available by joining the Yao Family Wines mailing list.

NICK'S TASTING NOTES

Napa Crest, 2010

Presents a dark crimson color with a slightly aged bricking rim. Produced from all five Bordeaux varieties—Cabernet Sauvignon, Merlot, Petit Verdot, Malbec, and Cabernet Franc—this wine comes from the cool 2010 vintage and reflects a very Bordeaux-like profile. Even though this is an entry-level wine, it is nonetheless a high-quality and expensive wine in its own right. Classic Bordeaux-like nose with small-berried cassis fruit, black and red cherries, pencil-lead, graphite, vanilla oak, and some complex earthy aromas. A touch of savory age follows through on the back end. On the palate the wine has good flesh and ripeness for a 2010. It sits on a medium-concentrated firm frame, with an initial attack of cassis fruit from the Cabernet leading on to black cherries that carry into a fleshy mid-palate from the Merlot in the blend; structure is gained from the Malbec and then finally the Petit Verdot adds a touch of red fruit spice to the long finish. Reflective of the cool climate vintage, the wine is restrained, a touch austere, but reveals nice symmetry. High acidity and grainy tannins ensure some further bottle age and make it superb with light meat dishes. Very Left-Bank St. Julian Bordeaux-like in style.

YAO MING Cabernet Sauvignon, 2010

A step up from the Napa Crest bottling, this wine presents better depth of fruit, more complexity, and deeper veined concentration. Still Left-Bank Bordeaux in style, it's obvious that besides the cool vintage, there is a determined aim towards achieving elegance and grace within the wine. The wine has a dark ruby-crimson color with purple highlights. It shows a touch less age than the Napa Crest on both the rim and the very Bordeaux-like bouquet. Aromas of cigar box, pencil lead, earth, smoke, leather, vanilla, and spice intermingle with the scents of cassis, black and red cherries, and blueberries. Less obviously fleshy than the Napa Crest bottling, the wine is similarly medium-bodied but more deeply seated, exhibiting a rich mineral core of dark smoky fruits and complexity. High acidity and firm tannins ensure a sweeping uplift on a long finish, making this a very high-quality wine that pairs exceptionally well with food. Similar to a ripe, concentrated, yet elegant St. Estephe from Bordeaux. Allocation through the wine club only.

YAO MING Family Reserve, Cabernet Sauvignon, 2011

Produced from an extremely cold vintage, this wine has all the elegance the year had to offer plus it's extremely concentrated, utilizing microscopic yields and berried fruits from the famous Howell Mountain. It presents a very dark bloody crimson color with a wide watery rim that indicates youth. Extraordinarily complex nose, exhibiting secondary aromas of pencil lead, licorice, wild herbs, cola, and chocolate with mineral and floral notes. It's medium-bodied but deeply concentrated with a silky-smooth mouth-feel. This powerful wine leaves an almost delicate impression and refined flavor on the palate. Contains excellent structure with tight, dense tannins and high acidity from the vintage conditions. With lovely delineation, this wine is streamlined, has good length, and will improve over the short term. Allocation through the wine club only.

2012 CHARDONNAY
CARNEROS

LUKE DONALD
COLLECTION

Luke Donald

LUKE DONALD COLLECTION

Rutherford Hill, Sanford, and Terlato, Napa & Lompoc

Chicago's West Side

The Terlato Wine Group (TWG), one of the world's premier, family-run, global wine empires, can trace its origins back to when Anthony Paterno opened a small retail store on Grand and Western Avenues on Chicago's West Side in 1938. Back then, customers would fill their own pitchers with wine tapped directly from an oak barrel. This small operation eventually bloomed into a full-service wine, liquor, and grocery operation.

In 1956, Anthony Paterno's daughter, Josephine, married the enterprising Anthony Terlato, who, at the urging of his friend Robert Mondavi, joined his father-in-law's company. In 1959, the Terlatos welcomed son Bill into the family and in 1960, another son, John.

Throughout the 1960s and '70s, the company assembled a portfolio of best-in-class wine suppliers, which included selections of Alexis Lichine and Frank Schoonmaker, and encompassed most (if not all) of the French classified Bordeaux growths and Estate Burgundies. The portfolio also showcased the wines of Champagne Roederer, Beaulieu Vineyards, Robert Mondavi's first vintage in 1967, Joseph Drouhin, and Louis Latour.

In terms of distributing these wines, the company innovatively targeted fine restaurants. This approach was contrary to industry convention, but leveraging the link between fine wine and fine dining became one of the core philosophies of the family business. As Bill Terlato recalls, "The company ended up controlling 60% of the restaurant wine-list

Bill, Anthony, and John Terlato have built one of the most progressive and forward-thinking wine groups in the world.

business in Illinois simply by concentrating on efficiently supplying restaurants with quality product. It was an historic move for us as a company." Within a few years they expanded far beyond Illinois, becoming the premier wine distributor in the United States.

In the late 1960s, the company began importing prestigious brands on a national basis, adding a smattering of them into their portfolio. They also expanded their Illinois distribution business by buying, or starting, highly respected wine companies. Direct Import, RG Distribution, the Cream Wine Company, and the Vintage Wine Company were among those added to the organization.

The Father of Pinot Grigio

Anthony Terlato is universally credited with introducing Italian wines to the American public. By 1966 he was importing the brand Sicilian Gold, an Italian wine that would soon become the standard for modestly priced table wine in America. Then came Gancia, a sparkling wine imported from Northern Italy, which was also extremely popular.

In 1972, with the introduction of Corvo, the company established a category that did not previously exist in the U.S. market: Sicilian wines. Within four years, Corvo became one of the best-selling Italian wines in America. The company would eventually import over 400,000 cases a year. Following such a success, Anthony Terlato realized that the new American wine consumer was looking for ever-higher quality wines.

Anthony's reputation was further enhanced when he introduced Santa Margherita Pinot Grigio to America in 1979, which grew into a

The debonair Bill Terlato in his Chicago office.

major brand, thereby establishing an entirely new wine category in the U.S. Today, Pinot Grigio is the second best-selling white wine (after Chardonnay) and the most popular and fastest growing varietal in the United States.

In 1984, the *Wine & Spirits* restaurant poll revealed that Santa Margherita Pinot Grigio was, "the most requested Italian wine in U.S. restaurants." By 1988 it was named "the most requested imported wine in U.S. restaurants," an honor it continued to hold for many years. In 1984 Anthony Terlato was conferred the decoration of Cavaliere Ufficiale, Motu Proprio, becoming the first American in the wine industry to receive this honor. It's no wonder then that he garnered the nickname, "Father of Pinot Grigio."

While Terlato Wines has moved on and Santa Margherita is no longer part of their portfolio, the company has launched a new Pinot Grigio under Terlato's own name, from the Friuli Colli Orientali region—one of the most respected regions in all of Italy for white wines of exceptional quality. (At press time, the new Terlato Friuli Pinot Grigio was in high demand from restaurants coast to coast.) The new wine is handcrafted, estate bottled, and produced in partnership with renowned viticulture experts Marco Simonit and Pierpaolo Sirch. It has quickly become recognized as the best-in-class Pinot Grigio.

The Third Generation

After attending Loyola University in Chicago, Bill Terlato returned to the family business. Under the tutelage of his father and grandfather, he literally started his career on the bottom-most rung. "It was in the early '80s when I started with the company in sales and did a stint in every role within the organization," remembers Bill. "My father believed we needed to understand that the business had many different facets and each had to be mastered. I got every rigorous, labor-intensive job. I was given the longest hours working in the warehouse and the most challenging delivery and sales routes. I was totally stuck in these roles, which were obviously meant to demonstrate that there was no favoritism, and test my commitment. My father wanted to show that he wasn't favoring family over staff. Many of my colleagues felt bad for me as they thought he was being unnecessarily hard on me."

Once he passed that rigorous initiation, Bill started working in the office—selling, buying, and managing the Chicago accounts. During his early tenure, after tasting thousands of wines from around the world, Bill gained a reputation as an adept and proficient sales representative and evaluator. "There's no substitute for experience," says Bill. "If you want to be knowledgeable about wine you have to taste a lot of it, and if you don't, you'll never develop the expertise. My father was always intrigued with all the world's wines. He encouraged us to try as many different wines as possible from as many different regions around the globe. We were constantly exposed to different wines."

In terms of the business, Bill Terlato realized that California, Bordeaux, and Italy were just the tip of a very big and quickly expanding vinous iceberg and that there were vast amounts of serious opportunities in the "new world." He was eager to move forward with Terlato's expansion. "We had a great opportunity to become not only distributers but also vintners," explains Bill. With the company's stellar history in the wine business, Bill felt they'd earned a formidable reputation as an ambitious, trustworthy, profitable, and well-connected company. He was correct. Soon producers were vying to join Terlato's network.

California Dreaming

While both his grandfather and his father made remarkable and innovative strides in the business of importing wine, Bill Terlato's vision was to bring global expansion to the family business. He initiated a strategic move into winery ownership in the U.S. In 1987 the family added established California brands to their portfolio including Rochioli, Markham, and Rutherford Hill. The purchase of Rutherford Hill signaled the start of several very significant winemaking ventures for the company that continued with further investments in California properties and vineyards such as the classic Stag's Leap

District winery, Chimney Rock, the well-sited Terlato Family Vineyards (with vineyards located throughout Napa Valley and Sonoma), and majority interest in the groundbreaking Pinot Noir and Chardonnay producer, Sanford Winery, in Santa Barbara County. These investments have made TWG one of the most acclaimed suppliers of premium California wines in the country.

Star properties around the globe were vetted when they came on the market and, if deemed suitable, became part of the portfolio and not solely as financial investments, but rather for their long-term potential. Unlike companies such as Constellation or Diageo, Terlato wasn't interested in making or importing cheap, voluminous quantities of Yellowtail or Two-Buck Chuck-style wines. Terlato wanted to assemble the very best of the world's wine producers. Some are well-known icons such as Gaja, Il Poggione, Nino Franco, and Anselmi in Italy, or Michel Chapoutier and Ramonet in France. It was quite obvious by the late 1980s that Terlato was one serious company with a solid vision of quality at the heart of each venture.

In 1994, Bill Terlato was appointed president and Anthony Terlato became chairman. Since then, TWG has become one of the largest wine marketers, importers, and winery owners in the U.S., accounting for one out of every five bottles of wine (over $20) sold in America. Since 2012, Terlato wines have earned more than 2,200 ratings of over 90 points, more than any other wine company in the world. "As a company and family we were and are continually on the lookout and actively striving to acquire top quality, expressive properties," explains Bill. "We also want to portray a continually innovative vision with a concerted emphasis on always offering or introducing

Chimney Rock's wines epitomize the distinctive Cabernet qualities of the Stag's Leap district.

something new to our buying public." In 2007, for example, Terlato excelled once again by adding five outstanding South African brands: Cirrus, Engelbrecht Els, Ernie Els, Guardian Peak, and Rust en Vrede.

How does TWG decide what they want to acquire? Is there a game plan? "People always ask how we pick our wines," muses Bill. "I always simply say: We will never sell anything that we would not be proud to drink ourselves and share with friends and guests. We are excited when we feel we've identified something unique that our wine consumers are going to appreciate, hopefully even before they know it exists. There are different roles in the industry and we feel ours is to pioneer, innovate, and introduce people to new things."

From Golf to Celebrity Vineyards

Bill Terlato has become known in his hometown of Chicago. When he's not in a vineyard or working around the globe, he is most likely on a golf course. He happens to be an avid amateur golfer. He carries a handicap that varies from 1 to 4 and, besides some success over the years in club championships and invitational tournaments, he has also played for nine years in the Pro Am (professional and amateur competitions) at Alfred Dunhill Links in Britain. Some of the people we interviewed said that he could have competed with the best pros, though Terlato disagrees. "I've played with virtually every top touring pro," he told Chicago's *Daily Herald*. "I am smart enough to understand I'm good but not nearly good enough to compete professionally."

Still, his love of the sport had one other advantage; it was on the golf course that

Terlato Estate Vineyards includes a vast and unique group of properties; like a jigsaw puzzle, each piece completes the overall picture.

Terlato formed lasting friendships with the three sportsmen who would eventually partner with him to make signature California wines: golfers Luke Donald and Jack Nicklaus, and Chicago's legendary football coach, Mike Ditka. "All these friendships came through an interest in golf and wine," says Bill. "Then one thing led to another."

Bill Terlato has said that the idea of creating a line of celebrity wines was not something the company was particularly interested in pursuing. "We didn't really have a desire to do something like that," he admits. "We only work at the highest end of the market." Still, when he realized that all three of these sports figures were genuinely interested in wine and creating a quality brand, he began to change his mind.

Ultimately, these Terlato wines would debunk the myth that only small boutique wineries could make handcrafted wines, and prove that a global company could create a worthy specialty wine.

Women in Wine

One of the unique aspects of Terlato is that it has two women winemakers in Napa Valley (and two assistant winemakers who are also women!). At Rutherford Hill it was especially interesting for us to meet the amazingly talented Marisa Taylor, as impassioned and knowledgeable as any winemaker we encountered in

Marisa Taylor (Top), head winemaker for Rutherford Hill, and Elizabeth Vianna (Bottom), winemaker at Chimney Rock, exemplify how women are impacting a trade previously dominated by men.

all of California. Taylor also manages the entire winery and oversees management of the surrounding vineyards, ensuring the continuity of quality grapes grown and sourced. She has developed her own unique style while remaining true to the "house style" of Rutherford Hill.

As an aside, we just want to mention that the advent of women winemakers in positions of authority throughout California is both encouraging and long overdue. Why this didn't happen sooner is a mystery. It's long been acknowledged that females possess a superior sense of smell and taste to their male counterparts. When we asked Marisa how she felt about this, she replied, "I think women were there all along, it's just now about us getting the proper recognition."

Women like Marisa, her colleague Elizabeth Vianna at Terlato's Chimney Rock Winery, as well as legendary winemakers Cathy Corison (Corison Winery in St. Helena), Heidi Barrett (Amuse Bouche, Paradigm, Lamborn, Kenzo, Au Sommet, and Vin Perdu, among others), Kris Curran (Sea Smoke and others), and Helen Turley (Marcassin Vineyard) are making that happen in their own quiet way.

Marisa is a deft winemaker, which became most obvious when we tasted the celebrity wines she handcrafted; each reflecting the personality and style of the celebrity in question. Luke Donald's portfolio is very European—styled after his own vinous heritage. Jack Nicklaus' wines are as precise as his work on the putting green and Mike Ditka's are as exuberant as his personality.

Putting Skin in the Game

"All three of our celebrity wines were born from a very close relationship with Bill Terlato,"

Bill Terlato and Luke Donald are good friends on and off the golf course.

explains Marisa. "Luke Donald has for many years been a close friend of Bill's; Nicklaus is also a long-term family friend; and Ditka is a large-than-life figurehead in Chicago due to his association with the Bears. Bill met him years ago at their golf club and they formed a close friendship."

Friendships aside, Bill explained that they all participate in the winemaking process. "Bill has a very strict rule that if you are going to make a wine in conjunction with us you have to 'put some skin in the game' as Ditka would say," adds Marissa. "You have to be involved and come out to Napa, tour the relevant vineyards, explore, find and develop your own style, and be part of the barrel tasting and blending to finalize the vision."

Terlato himself is involved with the whole process. "There's no doubt that Tony and his sons won't release a wine they are not happy with," explains Marisa. "They watch and vet every step of these 'celebrity wines.' They express what style would suit and if it does indeed pair and reflect the personal style of each individual. They really involve themselves in what they want to achieve and that primarily presents

The family business: Bill Terlato, Anthony Terlato, Jo Terlato (Bill's daughter), and John Terlato.

itself in the blending process, which can take many hours. So it's a good format, especially for me as winemaker, as I want as much involvement as possible to achieve my goal."

My Name on the Label

The process proved to be very successful. "I think all three of our celebrity partners enjoyed making their wines," says Bill. "I was pleased that we identified what would work for each of them. They all said to me the most important factor was that their wine be a high-quality product because 'my name is on the bottle!'

And I remember saying, of course, you forget my name is on the label too!"

Of the three celebrity wines, we wanted to know, which does Bill prefer? He diplomatically declined to pick one, saying that each was an exceptional example in its own right. "Luke's wines are much more European in style than Jack's or Mike's and they are designed to pair with food," explains Bill. "Luke's wines are more Merlot-based while Jack's are more Cabernet-centric, bigger and bolder. Mike Ditka's wines are huge, meaty, rich, and reflect his character but are also crafted around the food served in his restaurants, which are steakhouses."

Terlato launched its first "celebrity wine" with Luke Donald in 2008, with the 2006 vintage wines. Subsequently, many other people have approached Terlato, seeking to have their names attached to a quality wine. But joining the Terlato portfolio is not so easy. As the lovely Liz Barrett, vice president of corporate communications and public relations, told us, "There have been quite a number of celebrities who've approached us and it has just not worked out. We are extremely selective. Just the other day a big Italian TV food star called and was very eager to make a good wine with us. So we said, 'Okay, come meet us and we'll see if we share the same vision.' She said, 'No, no, I need you to come to New York City, I don't have time to travel to Chicago or Napa Valley.' Immediately, we scuttled the project. It's just how we do business. Our partners need to be engaged and invested in the process from the very start."

Luke Donald and the Game of Golf

We began writing this chapter while watching the British Open at St. Andrews in July 2015, where Luke Donald was comfortably sitting in 9th place within the top pack of pros. It was a return to form for the dashing Englishman whose youthful good looks and short game are considered by many to be the finest on the green. His recently revamped swing once again propelled him not only back into the top tier of golf professionals, but also into the hopes and

Tangley Oaks, the headquarters of Terlato Wines, is in Lake Bluff, Illinois, a suburb about 30 miles north of Chicago.
PAGES 88–89: Aerial view of Rutherford Hill.

Luke Donald in his element.

prayers of English sport fans. No matter what the sport might be: tennis and Andy Murray, Formula One and Louis Hamilton, football and Wayne Rooney or, indeed, golf and Luke Donald, England is absolutely fanatical about supporting their sporting heroes. (Unfortunately, he didn't make the final cut of the British Open, which was eventually won by the American, Zach Johnson.)

For millions of fans, golf is far and away the most civilized and sophisticated of all the professional sports to play and watch. Golf is ancient, precise, slow, rule-heavy, pointedly gentrified, and inherently steeped in age-old traditions. It is one of the more personally reflective of modern sports, as there are no cars or teammates to hide behind, so the style of the player—from his swing to his trousers—is continually on display. Luke Donald personifies the sophisticated, stylish gentleman on the green and he has built a trademark brand that incorporates his own personal style, unique character, and European upbringing. His wines were created to celebrate and showcase that very image.

The Luke Donald Brand

Luke's "lifestyle" brand includes many high profile sponsors. In 2003 he signed with the sports management company IMG and developed a multi-year contract to play exclusively with Mizuno fairway woods, irons, and wedges. It is a primary sponsor for Donald; he still carries a Mizuno bag and sports their trademark visor as part of his deal. (It has been rumored that Donald receives $1 million just for wearing the visor, and this could quadruple if he wins a major event such as the Masters.)

Luke also enjoys sponsorship deals with Footjoy, who supplies his personal shoes, Rolex, and the Royal Bank of Canada, as well as Zurich Insurance. In February 2007, Polo Ralph Lauren reported that Donald had signed a multi-year contract with the luxury apparel company. Luke also continues to serve as a brand ambassador for the RLX Golf range. These sponsors were carefully chosen to craft the image of a sophisticated gentleman.

Donald's manager was keen on having Donald put his name to a line of wine and suggested some winery contacts. Donald, however, was not very receptive because, being very particular about wine, he didn't like the overall quality of his manager's suggestions. Then, coincidentally, they both landed on the same page. As Bill recalls, "Luke told his manager, 'I have a friend in the wine business who could do this really well.' His manager said, 'This time I've found a great wine company that could produce a very high-quality, serious portfolio of wines for you. It's called Terlato.' So we all ended up having a meeting and things just took off."

Coincidentally, Bill Terlato and Luke Donald had been friends and golfing partners for

many years before either of them broached the subject of creating a Luke Donald wine. Golf coach Pat Goss, who worked with Luke and was also a friend of Terlato, introduced them in 1999. "He was a very respectful young man," remembers Bill. "I also met his wife, who was his girlfriend at the time, and we became good family friends."

Between tee-offs over the next few years, conversations about wine started to take place between the two men. As Donald recalls, "We formed a good, friendly relationship soon after meeting. Bill would bring me wines to try as I was starting to develop a cellar and I became interested in his work. I really began to learn a lot about wine from Bill. Plus, when I was young I had a head start, growing up in England where we drank wine with our meals. I expressed an interest in having my own brand of wine; Bill had a good think about it and finally decided that yes, I was serious about making a personalized, but also serious wine. We had never talked about the idea or even the possibility of producing a wine together when we first met."

Working in Napa

Even before Luke Donald started working with Marisa Taylor at Rutherford Hill, he had a well-formed palate. "When I was young, my parents drank predominately French wines: Bordeaux, Burgundies, Rhônes but specifically Bordeaux so they were my first learning templates," explains Donald. "I fell in love with that Bordeaux style, absolutely adored its unique deep aroma and taste, which is much earthier than most American wines, but they're hard to replicate, especially in the extremely warm climate of Napa Valley."

The first decision about how to achieve Donald's vision involved choosing grapes from different cool-climate vineyards that had good altitude and excellent diurnal temperature shifts from day to night, thus ensuring levels of acidity much more similar to a European wine than one from California.

In the winery a gentle rather than extracted style of winemaking was practiced and maturation and levels of oak were measured rather than slathered. This resulted in a lovely balanced wine and, as the label states, a "Claret" style of Californian wine.

"The first wine Marisa and I worked on was the red Claret," says Donald, "and I specifically wanted a drier Bordeaux style. I was looking for a very precise blend of different grapes." Both parties were serious about making a personally expressive wine for Luke that could compete with the best. They took their time to develop exactly what he was looking to achieve.

"Luke's wines are a great reflection of his love for the 'old world style' of winemaking," says Marisa. "He's quite a complex guy; he's a professional golfer, yes, but he's also definitely an artist. Creating blends is a skill that absolutely requires an artistic flair. An advantage for us in the U.S. is that we have more relaxed rules than in Europe, which I think enhances the winemaking process; it gives you a wider palate to work with. I like to think of this with Luke's wines. I want him to exercise his flair for expression. With his blends we went back and forth. Bill Terlato was there. I remember coming back into the room with another blend and he put his glass down and told me to take it away. Luke wanted to try something with more spice and red fruits. He knows exactly what he wants to achieve in creating a very personalized

Bill Terlato and Luke Donald tasting Luke's latest blend.

wine. And hey, by the way, in the end the next blend I came out with was the one we finally used."

Luke remembers their vinous experiments with fondness. "I like the blended style and we ended up going through eight or nine different blends," he recalls, "and we finally came up with two blends that we brought to lunch. Both were exceptional with food and that's what the wines of Bordeaux are all about, so I was very happy. My claret is 44% Cabernet, 43% Merlot, 12% Cabernet Franc, and 1% Petit Verdot."

As for Donald's Chardonnay, the grapes at Rutherford Hill were chosen with re-spect to the individual profile he and Marisa wanted to achieve. The general style of Ruth-erford Hill has always leaned towards plush, fruit-forward wine; yet, of course, one that consistently expresses its origins or "sense of place" proudly. In this case, Marisa and Don-ald were able to craft a noticeably more delicate and subtle wine, more restrained than what is usually made at Rutherford Hill, while still re-taining impressive depths of fruit and flavor.

"My wine is marketed a little towards the younger generation. It has my initials on the label, not a picture of a vineyard," says Donald. "I think younger successful people are into wine."

But what, we wondered, did Donald really want to achieve with his wine venture? "He doesn't need to do this from a financial perspective," explains Bill. "He never did it because he thought this was going to be lucrative. The idea was that he could share his wines with family, friends, and business associates." Bill, however, does concede that Donald is very ambitiously brand-centric and a good wine portfolio easily adds sophistication to that brand. "He wanted something with his name on it, something that positively reflected his taste and that he could be proud of. The wines are made in a boutique style, and he felt the portfolio, if done very expertly, could also add gravitas to his 'Luke Donald' brand."

The Game of Golf

Born on the 7th of December, 1977, in Hemel Hempstead in Hertfordshire, England, Luke Donald has described himself as "half Scottish." His late father was from Stranraer in southwest Scotland. However, despite his Scottish ancestry, Donald plays golf as an Englishman and proudly represents England.

As a schoolboy Donald attended the Rudolf Steiner School in Kings Langley and later the Royal Grammar School in High Wycombe, a

LEFT TO RIGHT: Bill Terlato, Luke and Diane Donald, Tony Terlato, and John Terlato.

suburb not far from London. He played junior golf at the Hazlemere and Beaconsfield Golf Clubs just outside London and twice became the club champion of Beaconsfield, first at the unbelievably young age of fifteen. Donald's brother Christian also played junior golf and caddied for Luke.

Donald subsequently accepted a golf scholarship at Northwestern University in 1997 where his coach was Pat Goss. In 1999, he won the individual NCAA Division I Men's Golf Championships title, beating the scoring record formerly held by Tiger Woods. Donald shares the Northwestern University school record of 202, for a 54-hole tournament score. He also became the first amateur to win the Chicago Open in 2000.

In 2001 Donald made his debut as a professional at the Reno-Tahoe Open. Immediately he was recognized for his deft precision and for possessing one of the best short games in the world.

Donald has played mainly on the U.S. PGA Tour but is also a member of the European Tour. In 2011, he ascended to the top spot in the world rankings, which he held for 40 weeks. He made history by becoming the first player ever to finish number one on both the PGA and European Tour money lists in the same season, and won Player of the Year honors on both tours. He was appointed Member of the Order of the British Empire (MBE) in the 2012 Birthday Honors for services to golf.

In May 2012, Donald regained the world number one ranking. He held it for a further ten weeks. Donald had spent a cumulative total of 56 weeks as the World Number One and over 200 weeks in the top ten. He retained his title at the BMW PGA Championship at Wentworth on May 27, 2012, with a four-

Luke Donald holding the BMW PGA Championship trophy at Wentworth, England, 2012.

stroke victory over Justin Rose and Paul Lawrie. He shot all four rounds in the 60s, including a final round 68 with five birdies and only one bogey to claim victory. He became only the third player to successfully defend the European Tour's flagship event, alongside Nick Faldo and Colin Montgomerie. The victory was Donald's seventh title on the European Tour and resulted in a return to World Number One for the fourth time. In November, Donald won his third tournament of 2012, the Dunlop Phoenix Tournament in Japan. In doing so, he overtook Tiger Woods and returned to second place in the world rankings.

In the first event of the 2015 European Tour season at the Nedbank Golf Challenge, Donald led the tournament after 54 holes. However, he was unable to hold onto that lead after 72 holes and took third place. Donald had to face sectional qualifying for the U.S. Open for the first time in eleven years due to his fall to 66th place in the world ranking. He managed to finish at the top of his qualifier at the Bears Club to seal a spot. At the time of this writing, Donald has played in sixteen events, has made the top ten twice and the top 25 four times.

A Career in Winemaking?

Despite his hectic global schedule, Luke Donald is happiest at home with his family. He met his future wife, Diane Antonopoulos, a Chicago native, while attending Northwestern University in Evanston, Illinois. He proposed in June 2006, and the couple married on June 24, 2007, on the Greek island of Santorini. They have three daughters and own homes in Northfield, Illinois, and Palm Beach Gardens, Florida. Donald studied art theory and practice in college, and to this day enjoys painting and drawing when not on tour. In 2002, one of his oil paintings was auctioned off by the PGA Tour for charity. Donald and his wife are avid collectors of contemporary art.

He and Bill Terlato remain great friends. "Our families are very close," says Terlato. "We both have houses in Florida, we brought up our kids together and he doesn't live far from us in Chicago. We travel together often and generally spend quite a lot of time in each other's company. I have to admit a lot of our friendship revolves around gastronomy. Luke is a genuine, passionate 'foodie' and so am I. He knows every top restaurant, he's very knowledgeable about the up and coming chefs, and he definitely enjoys his meals. My wife Debbie also adores his wife and as friends we very often go out to dinner together. I'm familiar with his palate, his likes and dislikes. I don't think there's a restaurant we haven't hit; his capacity to absorb and understand flavors is impressive."

As for Donald's future, it may contain more winemaking. "I play a sport where I'm free to compete as long as I want," says Donald. "Wine is a hobby now and I have a lot to learn. In my later life, I would love to shift gears more towards making wine."

PORTFOLIO

Donald's red blend, produced from the main Bordeaux varieties grown in the Napa Valley, is a true reflection of his European heritage. Stylistically this could easily pass for an excellent Cru Bourgeois. The wine is bright and fruity, exhibiting restraint and delicacy. In overall style the wine is without a doubt typically Californian but with a sense of European restraint and, thus, never comes across "fat" or heavy.

As for his whites, as an Englishman, Donald is particularly fond of a steely European style of juice. It's more purposely crafted with a slightly higher tone than the usual California Chardonnays, displaying notes of green apples, cashew nuts, and minerals. The wine is excellently balanced with good acidity. Still, being made in California definitely adds an extra layer of richness to the fruit and the overall feel. This makes them extremely approachable and drinkable, even without food, though with food, they really shine. The style they achieved adds richness to white meat dishes yet never overpowers them.

NICK'S TASTING NOTES

Viognier, 2012

The grapes for this white wine were sourced from the famous Sanford & Benedict vineyard in the Santa Rita Hills just north of Santa Barbara. This fragrant wine expresses a wonderful sense of individuality, juiciness, and floral characteristics. The relatively cool climate and diurnal temperatures allow good acidity to form within the grapes. It's a water-white-colored wine, and expresses the typical varietal scents of orange blossoms, green apples, apricots, honeysuckle flowers, peaches, and clean minerals. A good expression of the grapes, it binds the varietal flavors of orange blossoms to an uplifting acidity and a silky-textured mouth-feel. Matured in stainless steel, making the grapes' natural varietal character become the wine's main focal point. Un-oaked in style, yet assuredly ripe, with a long, tangy, floral finish.

Chardonnay, 2012

Made from grapes that were sourced from Carneros' cool Pope Valley, this is more of a steely, Burgundian-style Chardonnay rather than an overtly creamy, tropical, Californian-style. Thus it's a bright and clean wine with an appetizing light gold color and aromas of pale, cool-climate fruits that are also expressed on the palate. Flavors of pears, limes, and lemons mingle with macadamia nuts, minerals, and a touch of new oak that braces rather than smothers the fruit. A lovely grip of zesty acidity holds the fruit in check and leads to the wine's fine cut-citrus finish.

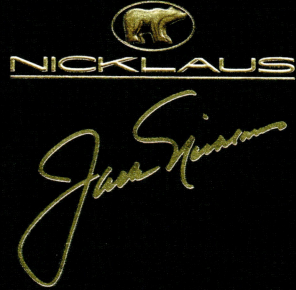

PRIVATE RESERVE

NAPA VALLEY

Jack Nicklaus

JACK NICKLAUS WINES

Chimney Rock, Rutherford Hill, and Terlato, Napa Valley

A Career for the Record Books

Jack Nicklaus, nicknamed the Golden Bear, is considered by many to be the greatest professional golfer of all time. His career has been nothing short of phenomenal; his accomplishments almost beyond description. He has 117 worldwide professional victories. He holds the record for winning the most major championships (eighteen). With 73 PGA Tour victories to his credit, he is third, behind only Tiger Woods with 79 and Sam Snead with 82. Nicklaus holds the outright record for the most wins at the Masters (six) and the Players Championship (three). He played on six Ryder Cup teams (twice as captain) and the Presidents Cup team four times. For 24 straight seasons, from 1960 to 1983, he made at least one top-ten finish in a major championship, and that's yet another record.

After his first year on the PGA Tour in 1962, Nicklaus received the PGA Tour Rookie of the Year award. In 1966, he became the first golfer to ever win the Masters Tournament for the second year in a row and also won the Open Championship, completing his career slam of major championships. Between 1971 and 1980, Nicklaus would become the first player to complete double and triple career slams for four professional major championships.

In addition to being named the PGA Tour Player of the Year five times and topping the PGA Tour money list eight times, Nicklaus has also received the Bob Jones Award and the Payne Stewart Award, among others. He played in 146 consecutive major championships between 1962 and 1998 and has made 20 holes-in-one during his professional career. Nicklaus was inducted into the World Golf Hall of Fame in 1974 and into the Canadian Golf Hall of Fame in 1995.

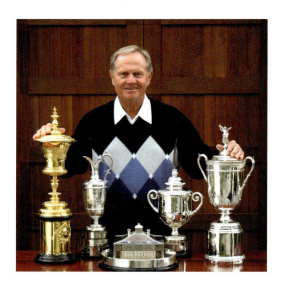

The Golden Bear with just a few of his many trophies.

Jack Nicklaus, fourteen years old, with his father, Charlie, on the golf course, 1954.

Nicklaus maintains a legendary status among golfers for driving the longest and straightest balls on the PGA Tour. In his youth, he won the official long-drive contest at the 1963 PGA Championship with a belt of 341 yards and 17 inches (312 meters). This amazing record lasted for over 20 years. As his career matured, so did his playing style, adapting to fit every new era in the game. As fellow golfer Gary Player stated, Nicklaus had, "the greatest mind the game has ever known."

A Mid-Life Triumph

Before the start of the 1986 Masters Tournament, Tom McCollister of *The Atlanta Journal-Constitution* wrote that Nicklaus was "... done, washed up, through." Nicklaus responded by telling a reporter, "I kept thinking all week, 'through, washed up, huh?' I sizzled for a while. But then I said to myself, 'I'm not going to quit playing the way I'm playing. I've played too well, too long to let a shorter period of bad golf be my last.'"At age 46, Nicklaus won the 1986 Masters, becoming the oldest golfer in history to do so, a record that still stands today.

That mid-life triumph generated an ocean of accolades and commentary. Noted golf historian Herbert Warren Wind wrote that the achievement was, "nothing less than the most important accomplishment in golf since Bobby Jones' Grand Slam in 1930." Author Ken Bowden commented, "There have been prettier swingers of the club than Jack Nicklaus. There may have been better ball-strikers than Jack Nicklaus. Other golfers have putted as well as Jack Nicklaus. There may have been golfers as dedicated and fiercely competitive as Jack Nicklaus. But no individual has been able to develop, combine, and sustain all of the complex physical skills and the immense mental and emotional resources the game demands at its highest level as well as Jack Nicklaus has for as long as he has."

And sports columnist Thomas Boswell noted that, "Some things cannot possibly happen, because they are both too improbable and too perfect. The U.S. hockey team cannot beat the Russians in the 1980 Olympics. Jack Nicklaus cannot shoot 65 to win the Masters at age 46. Nothing else comes immediately to mind." This victory was his eighteenth and final major title as a professional.

Nicklaus joined the Senior PGA Tour in January 1990, when he became eligible, and by April 1996 had won ten of the tour's tournaments, including eight major championships, despite playing a very limited schedule. At the age of 58, Nicklaus made another valiant run at the 1998 Masters, where he tied for sixth despite being hampered by a painful left hip. His last competitive round in the U.S. took

TOP: Nicklaus with his driver, circa 1960.
BOTTOM: Nicklaus displays one of the most amazing swings in the history of golf; he was known for his abilities to drive the ball almost beyond belief.

Jack Nicklaus receives the Medal of Freedom from President George Bush, November 2005.

place on June 13, 2005, at a Champion Tour's Bayer Advantage Classic in Kansas. On July 15, 2005, he made his final appearance at the Open Championship at St. Andrews. There he told reporters, "I'm very sentimental and the place gets to me every time I go there. In May I walked around and welled up with hardly anyone watching me. St. Andrews was always where I wanted to finish my major career."

In November 2005, President Bush honored the Golden Bear at the White House with the Presidential Medal of Freedom; the highest honor the Office of the President can award an American civilian. At 75 years old, Jack Nicklaus was named either, "Golfer of the Century," or "Golfer of the Millennium," by almost every major golf publication in the world. *Sports Illustrated* called him the best "Individual Male Athlete of the 20th Century"; ESPN named him one of the ten greatest athletes of the century. On March 24, 2015, Nicklaus received the Congressional Gold Medal, an honor that's only been bestowed upon seven athletes.

Setting His Own Course

"Jack Nicklaus has found a remarkable second career in doing everything," wrote Alan Shipnuck in September 2014. Indeed, Nicklaus' life off the golf course might be considered as record-setting as his athletic career.

Along with his four sons and son-in-law, Nicklaus founded Nicklaus Design, a company that designs and builds golf courses. Since then, he has been involved in the design of 290 courses in 39 states and in 36 countries, which is nearly 1% of all the courses in the world. His courses have staged more than 900 tournaments and championship events. Currently, the company has more than 45 golf courses under development in nineteen countries.

In 1992, he founded Nicklaus Golf Equipment, which sells a huge range of equipment for different stages of aptitude and ability on the green. Nicklaus is in partnership with Rolex, Shaw Floors, Sub-Zero, and Wolf kitchen equipment. He endorses pens, calendars, custom greens and turf, headgear, shoes, bottled water, flavored Arizona lemonade, and real-estate ventures. He sells videos of golf tips and instructions and is also an accomplished author having published his autobiography as well as books on course design and golf techniques. His *Golf My Way* is one of the best-selling instructional golf books of all time. On his website, he offers sports memorabilia and limited-edition, signed handprints—some in 14-carat gold.

Nicklaus is currently working on a line of ice cream. "I just love to stay busy and find new challenges," he says—a profound understatement.

Of all Nicklaus' accomplishments, perhaps his most important is his family. He and his wife, the former Barbara Bash, have been married since 1960; they have five children and 22 grandchildren. They've lived in the same house in North Palm Beach since 1965. And it was in the basement of that house that Nicklaus learned an important, if not costly, lesson about wine. After his 1972 Masters win, Augusta National GC chairman Clifford Roberts gifted Nicklaus several cases of 1947 and 1952 Chateau Lafite Rothschild, two celebrated vintages of what some consider the best wines in the world. "I used to get all sorts of great wines given to me, but I wasn't really a drinker and Barbara didn't drink much either. It used to give me headaches," reports Nicklaus. So he stashed the Lafite in coolers in the basement of his Florida house, but the tropical climate was not kind to the delicate wine. "I wound up with the most expensive vinegar in the world," says Nicklaus. "This was back in the day when those wines cost about $1000 a bottle." Today, if you could find such a bottle, it would cost at least twice that amount.

The Wine Business

As with Luke Donald, Jack Nicklaus's wine venture with the Terlato Wine Group was born out of his friendship with Bill Terlato and the sport of golf (to learn more about the Terlato Wine Group see p.79). Terlato and Nicklaus met during a golf tournament in Jupiter, Florida, after Bill won a country club championship

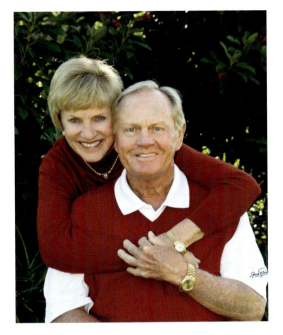

Jack Nicklaus and his wife, Barbara, have been married since 1960.

and Nicklaus handed him a trophy during the awards ceremony.

Nicklaus had been thinking about going into the wine business for a long time. "My objective was to find a way to create a brand that was going to last beyond my lifetime," he says. "It made sense to have a wine in my business. I'm not an expert, but I know what I like. We researched it for many years. Bill was a member of the Bear's Club in Chicago. I called and asked to pick his brain. One thing he said was that if I did it, I had to do it right. I liked the sound of that."

"Of course, Jack had been approached by other winemakers but he eventually came to me," Bill Terlato recalls. "He said, 'I know you are in the wine business and I'd like to sit down

Jack and Barbara Nicklaus unveil the logo for one of the their charitable foundations, the Nicklaus Children's Hospital.

and talk wine with you.' So we sat down and I told him that it wouldn't be a case of just finding a commercial wine to slap his label on because we aren't the sort of people for that. I said you need to be involved, need to know about the wine, participate in the tasting and blending, understand the vintage, where it came from, the vineyards and the lots. So he says thank you and leaves.

"A few days later, he returns and says, 'I've thought about it and, yes, I want to make a wine with you. The reason is because out of all the companies we approached, you honestly didn't sugar coat the problems or the potential. Plus everyone is telling me you're the best company to take on such a personally serious project.' And I was sitting there with Jack Nicklaus, thinking: he has a real connection with the land, he's designed and created the best golf courses all over the world, he already understands the importance of location, terroir,

and development. He's even developed different strains of grass that thrive better in certain locations. He understands that vines conform to environmental factors, so he's serious about the land and what it can provide."

Nicklaus and Bill Terlato share a love of playing the course and a life-long appreciation of the land—be it through nurturing the best grapes or transforming tracts of sand into contoured structures of golf artwork. "We immediately felt a mutual respect and connection sparked by a shared passion for quality and vision to create something that embodies the high standards of both our families," explains Nicklaus.

In fact, since our interview, Terlato and Nicklaus have launched another project named Jack's House Wines. The two partnered to create a Chardonnay and Cabernet Sauvignon inspired by a mission to give back. Ten percent of the proceeds from the sale of each bottle of Jack's House Wine benefit the new Jack's House Foundation, a non-profit organization inspired by Jack Nicklaus' own philanthropic spirit.

Hard at Work

Nicklaus had a vision for his line of wines: he wanted to create various tiers, like he does with his golf clubs, for example, so that people could choose the product that would best suit their taste and budget. As Bill says, "Jack came to Napa and spent a lot of time with us visiting the vineyards. The thing with his wines is that he wants everyone to enjoy them, even his charities. This is one reason he makes wine and other products, to generate income for his charitable organizations. He and his wife Barbara are very involved with building hospitals and houses for

An intensive tasting and blending session is a crucial part of how the Terlatos strive to produce the highest quality handcrafted wine. Here we see a tasting with both the Terlato and Nicklaus families.

the impoverished in Florida. Jack personally felt that this journey into wine could bring in more funds to help those ventures."

Like Luke Donald, Nicklaus was enthusiastic about making his own wines and happy to travel to Napa to create his portfolio, though it wasn't an easy process. "We had literally hundreds of wine samples on the desk and he was insisting we go through different samples from different vineyards, different areas of Napa, different varying altitudes and many different lots of grapes as he really wanted a crafted 'unique customized blend' for each wine. We certainly gave him some direction in terms of 'pedigree' of grapes. We ended up with six to seven blends, potential options, for each of the wines," explains Terlato. "And then we tasted through all of them—white to red—scoring them. Jack did the final taste through and picked the blend for each where he felt he had identified something particularly unique that he liked."

Nicklaus remembers that *Golf Digest* took a picture of him sitting at a table with about 200 glasses of wine lined up in front of him. Nicklaus laughs when he remembers the photo, explaining, "The caption underneath read, 'Jack Nicklaus hard at work.'"

The Chimney Rock Connection

As a counterpart to his red wine, Nicklaus wanted to produce a signature white for his wife, Barbara, whose favorite wine is Sauvignon Blanc. Jack and Bill went through various cuvées at Rutherford Hill (one of the wineries owned by Terlato), but Jack couldn't exactly nail down Barbara's specific taste preference. They toured different vineyards, looking at specific blocks—vineyards at higher altitudes, and warmer or cooler sites, yet nothing was working. Soon they realized they had to get Barbara involved with the process of making her own wine. "Jack really wanted to make a Sauvignon Blanc that Barbara would love so he asked her to come down and taste through the samples, to become really involved with the creation," recalls Terlato.

Barbara almost immediately picked a sample from Chimney Rock, Rutherford Hill's sister winery down the road. Designed to look like a white Spanish-style villa, Chimney Rock is located in the prestigious Stags Leap District of Napa. Chimney Rock grapes have always been sourced from their impressive surrounding estate vineyards and they have developed a serious reputation for the classic, powerful Stags Leap reds. However, they also have a fantastic Sauvignon Blanc vineyard on the property.

Terlato introduced Jack and Barbara Nicklaus to Chimney Rock's winemaker Elizabeth Vianna, who showed them around the vineyards. They tasted further samples of her Sauvignon Blanc. Barbara was smitten with the results and knew that the grapes from Chimney Rock would make her white wine the perfect companion to Jack's red.

Under Vianna's direction, the winery hand-harvests whole-cluster pressed grapes, a method that helps preserve the aromatics of citrus, stone fruit, and green apple. Using an innovative method, the wine is barrel fermented with a portion of the wine matured in French oak and the balance in stainless steel barriques.

The result is a wine that releases lush fruit at the front palate followed by a rich and textured mid-palate and a long finish. It retains finesse and complexity and is very drinkable. There were now two signature Jack Nicklaus wines, a his and a hers, which perfectly complimented each other.

Aerial view of the Chimney Rock winery.

Wine for a Sportsman

As with all of our celebrity winemakers, we wanted to know what Jack Nicklaus hoped to convey with his wines and we discovered that his portfolio proved to be a true reflection of his persona as a sportsman. Nicklaus was one of the first televised figures in sport; for TV viewers he transcended the green as Roger Federer today does the tennis court. On the small screen in our living rooms, Nicklaus became one of the first athletes to really embody the "modern day" sportsman brimming with confidence, strength, and commitment. Viewers became enraptured by his otherworldly display of talent. Nicklaus managed to sculpt seemingly impossible shots out of nowhere, always determined to stay in the game and never surrendering until the last shot.

Similarly, his wines are crafted in a style that's direct, precise, restrained, elegant, and not in the least ostentatious; much like the way Nicklaus operates on the golf course. Overall, the wines display an impeccable sense of balance. It's as if Jack himself is guiding us down par 12 at St. Andrews. And the wines are serious examples of premium red Napa winemaking. They are supremely well made, delicious, and reasonably priced.

Even the look of the bottles is in keeping with Jack's brand. The beautiful, elegant labels are designed to feel clean, confident, and sophisticated, much like the wine itself.

A Hole-in-One Wine

Jack Nicklaus signature wines were an immediate hit with the public. The 15,000 cases of the 2008 vintage, released in 2011, were 70% sold out before they even hit the market (more than half the pre-orders were from China). As of 2010, Terlato has been selling about 10,000 cases annually. The success of the portfolio was very rewarding, but there is another reason Nicklaus enjoys being in the wine business. "It's fun to walk into a restaurant and order your own wine," he says with glee.

Jack Nicklaus continues to create more vintages of signature wine. His most recent, the Golden Bear Commemorative Series, was launched in June of 2015 at the Memorial Tournament presented by Nationwide. In an on-air interview, standing next to Bill Terlato, Jack Nicklaus said, "A couple of years ago we launched a Cabernet and a Private Reserve Es-

Making wine is a family affair for the Terlato and Nicklaus clans.

tate wine. On this occasion we're introducing a Private Reserve blend. It's a 1.5-liter bottle of white wine, a Bordeaux blend of grapes. We're only producing one thousand bottles and we're going to do that for the next eighteen years. Each year commemorates one of the eighteen major championships I won. So hopefully I will be around for those eighteen years. And then, fifty years from now, Bill Terlato and I will drink the first bottle, because Bill says that in fifty years the wine will be just perfect!"

PORTFOLIO

Nicklaus's wines purposely try to express his vision of a great Napa California wine. They are neither swathed in, nor buried beneath, a wave of stodgy maple syrup or oak flavors. Nicklaus is a craftsman at the highest level and his wines are a combination of elegance and power. They are as true to aim as the man himself—linear, precise, and refined but requisitely very tasty. These wines have pinpoint balance and express wonderful purity of fresh ripe fruits within the entry level red and white wines. The Reserve Red is more structured, darker in profile, and a good candidate for a few years additional cellar age to come together.

There also happens to be a current trend sweeping Napa where the style of red wine has shifted towards a fresher, less new-oaked, more restrained and terroir-driven profile. Nicklaus's wines certainly qualify in this manner; stylistically they are very forward-thinking.

NICK'S TASTING NOTES

Private Reserve White, 2012

This Napa Valley Sauvignon Blanc reveals a beautiful, very bright, shimmering lemon color. The nose explodes with floral aromas, grapefruits, lemons and limes, pears, minerals, and other ripe white stone fruits with a tiny lick of oak. In the mouth the wine has a lovely silky texture that positively glides over the palate. The introduction of 5% wild yeast to the fermentation process provides some unique complex notes of starburst candies and sherbet as well as slightly grassy notes to the palate. Neither particularly tropical nor herbaceous, this is a lush, juicy, drinkable wine. The wine is barrel fermented in a blend of 18% new French oak, 54% used French oak, and 28% stainless steel.

Cabernet Sauvignon, 2009

Created from a splendidly dry, warm vintage, this Napa Valley wine has a deep crimson color with an opaque purple core and some creeping age on the rim. The wine has a briary black-fruit profile, revealing clean aromas of ripe red cherries, raspberries, plums, and black currants. Matured for 21 months in French oak, the wine has excellent balance in the mouth, not too big or extracted, with an obvious accent on fine elegance from beginning to finish. Nicklaus prefers to achieve a more European style with precise, bright flavors and a very "seamed," "linear" structure. This is Nicklaus's entry-level portfolio Cabernet and it does have less dimension than its bigger counterpart yet it still reveals good concentration, power, and ripeness. This is not a weak-willed wine. Like the rest of his portfolio, it shows restraint and good medium complexity, especially for an "entry level" wine. The easiest drinking red cuvée in the portfolio, this wine is created from a combination of primarily Cabernet Sauvignon and a touch of Petit Verdot grapes. Thirty-nine hundred cases produced.

Private Reserve Red, 2009

This Napa Valley Cabernet Sauvignon-based blend is a noticeable step up in seriousness from the regular 2009 Cabernet cuvée. Concentration and complexity has definitely been ratcheted up a level and makes this a very serious wine in its own right. Only 1400 cases are produced and it sees 50% new French oak in maturation. Again, this was produced from the fantastic warm and dry 2009 vintage. It has a deep garnet color with a touch of browning age on the rim. The expressive nose soars with aromas of black-spectrum fruits such as black plums, black cherries, cracked black pepper, and blueberries as well as sweet vanilla oak. Much bigger, bolder, and more concentrated on the palate than its little sibling, yet still with a similar sense of elegance. Fine but bold sweet tannins plus nice uplifting acidity shuttles the wine towards a long, lush, assured finish. This Bordeaux-style wine was awarded 90 points by *Wine Spectator* and is made up of 81% Cabernet Sauvignon, 10% Syrah, 5% Merlot, 2% Petit Verdot, and 2% Malbec grapes. This is a serious Bordeaux blend from the New World.

mike
DITKA

THE CHAMPION

COACH'S BLEND

NAPA VALLEY

Mike Ditka

MIKE DITKA WINES

Rutherford Hill and Terlato, Napa Valley

A Sports Icon

Mike Ditka is a legendary and beloved sports figure, especially in his hometown of Chicago. He is known for his lifelong achievements and personal passion, primarily in the field of professional football.

As a player, he was a driving force on the 1963 NFL Champion Chicago Bears, and as a coach he won the Super Bowl with the 1985–86 Bears. In 1988, his fearsome blocking and 427 career receptions for 5,812 yards and 43 touchdowns earned him the honor of being the first tight end ever inducted into the Pro Football Hall of Fame. In 1999, he was ranked number 90 on *The Sporting News'* list of the 100 Greatest Football Players. By any measure, Coach Ditka's mark of excellence in sports is indelible.

Ditka was named to both the NFL's 50th and 75th Anniversary All-Time Teams. As a coach for the Bears for eleven years, he was twice both the AP and UPI NFL Coach of Year (in 1985 and 1988). Over a total of fourteen seasons as a head coach, Ditka amassed a regular-season record of 121–95 and a post-season record of 6–6. And he is a media icon, currently headlining for ESPN.

When he was inducted into the Pro Football Hall of Fame, Ditka told the crowd in Canton, Ohio: "In life, many men have talent, but talent in itself is no accomplishment. Excellence in football and excellence in life is bred when men recognize their opportunities and then pursue them with passion."

Early Years

He was born Michael Dyczko on October 18, 1939, in the Pittsburgh-area town of Carnegie, in western Pennsylvania, a place known primarily for coal mining. His father was a welder of Polish and Ukrainian descent; his mother, Charlotte, was Irish and German. As the surname "Dyczko" was difficult to pronounce, the family changed it to "Ditka." Along with his younger siblings—Ashton, David, and Mary Ann—the Ditkas settled in Aliquippa, just outside Pittsburgh.

At Aliquippa High School Ditka excelled at football under the tutelage of head coach Press Maravich, who recognized his potential. Ditka attended the University of Pittsburgh where he was a three-sport athlete, excelling at baseball and basketball, as well as football. But it was through football that he really showed exceptional talent, starting in all three seasons, leading the team in receiving, and, surprisingly, also serving as the team's punter. A first team selection on the College Football All-America Team in his senior year, he was considered one of the best tight ends in college football history.

The Chicago Bears drafted Ditka fifth overall in the 1961 NFL Draft. In his first season, Ditka managed 58 receptions and introduced a deft style of play to the tight end position that had previously been dedicated to simply blocking. He also scored twelve receiving touchdowns, which earned him Rookie of the Year honors, making him the youngest player to achieve such a feat. It was the beginning of a long and distinguished career as both player and coach in the NFL, where he was All-NFL four times and a perennial Pro Bowl selection.

Mike Ditka and Tom Flores are the only two people to win an NFL title as a player, an assistant coach, and a head coach. Ditka is the only person to participate in both of the last two Chicago Bears' championships, as a player in 1963 and as head coach in 1985.

He has said that his guiding philosophy of life is: "Everything that happens in life starts right now. Your thoughts become your words and your words become your actions. Your actions become your habits and your habits become your character. Your character defines your destiny."

The Restaurant Business

After his many successes on the football field, "Da' Coach," as he is known, took on what some consider an even more brutal profession: the restaurant business. His landmark restaurant, Ditka's, located in the heart of Chicago's gold coast, is known for steaks and chops—including the signature "Da Pork Chop" and what some consider the best burger in Chicago. Ditka often shows up at the restaurant to greet customers and pose for photos. In fact, hospitality is what makes his restaurants so special and he has said that his goal was always to create "a Ditka experience." The original restaurant was, and is, so successful that four other locations were soon added to his growing empire in Arlington Heights, Oakbrook, Pittsburgh, and most recently at the Veequiva Hotel and Casino in Phoenix, which features "Da Coach's Meatloaf."

It was only a short leap from opening restaurants to making wine. Why not serve a signature top-quality wine to enjoy along with his top-quality meats? And wine was also a passion of the Da' Coach. "I've been interested in wine my whole life," says Ditka. "French, German, Chilean, Argentinean, Australian, New Zealand, South African—I've had 'em all. I've had every kind of wine there is. I now lean more to the Cabs, but I drank Merlot for a long time. I've had a lot of Silver Oak and Jordan in my life. If I had a penny for every glass of wine I've had in my life, I'd be a millionaire. If being a wine expert means you have to drink it over a long period of time, then I'm an expert!"

Another Golfing Connection

Mike Ditka met Bill Terlato of the Terlato Wine Group (to learn more about Terlato see p.79) about 20 years ago when they were paired up on the links. Their shared interests, aside from golf and wine, include sports, food, and good cigars. Together they recognized the opportunity to create an approachable collection of superior quality wines at attractive price points that would delight the patrons at Ditka's restaurants as well as his numerous fans.

Val Warner, Mike Ditka, Bill Terlato, and Ryan Chiaverini tasting wine on "Windy City Live," Chicago, October 2012. OVERLEAF: Entrance to the magnificent Rutherford Hill Winery, which is well worth a visit if you are in Napa.

At the time that the two began discussing going into business together, Ditka had a wine portfolio that he asked Bill to pick up. Terlato suggested several modifications including ditching the cartoon likeness of the Coach on the label and replacing it with images that highlighted the Coach's football career. They created different blendings and new branding, such as the tagline, "Raise Your Game!"; and released the new Ditka portfolio in 2012. The changes proved successful and more retailers were willing to stock the wine on their shelves. Before the re-launch, most of Ditka's wines were sold in his restaurants; today they can be purchased from more than 400 retailers nationwide.

A Problem for Forever

In his restaurants, the new wines were a big hit with fans. At the time of their release, Ditka told an interviewer, "We just got it into the restaurant, and we're already sold out. I hope it's a problem we have forever! Everyone will buy it once, maybe because of the name, maybe not. But I think they'll buy it again. It's one of these

Coach Mike Ditka.

Bill Terlato and Mike Ditka are not just friends but also ambitious partners in the wine business.

deals where, when you order it, you don't expect the worst and you don't expect the best, but it turns out to be a hell of a lot better than you expected."

The overhaul far surpassed the expectations of even Bill Terlato. "Of the 10,000 cases of the newly labeled Ditka wines that were made for the first year on the market (beginning in October 2012), about 8,000 sold out in the first six months," explains Bill. "That was up from about 5,000 cases that sold over the previous 12 months. We didn't anticipate that early success and we were left with only 2,000 cases in the market for a six-month period." [It should be explained that red wine needs a three-year lead-time for production, so Terlato has to project how much inventory they will need in the future.] "To anticipate today's demand, we

Bill Terlato and Coach Mike Ditka promote their wines at a Walgreens event.

would have had to make the decision three and a half years ago," says Bill. "There's much more support for the brand today than there was in the past and we are having double-digit growth year after year."

As a result, Terlato ramped up production of Ditka's wines, making 16,000 cases for 2016. As expected, Terlato took some grief from Da' Coach for not anticipating the demand. "I went to Coach and he looked at me and said, 'Did you make enough wine?' I said, 'No,' and he replied, 'I knew that. I just wanted to hear you say it.'"

Award Winners

The wines were not only a financial success but became award winners at the prestigious San Francisco Chronicle Wine Competition, the world's largest American wine competition, which includes a field of 5,500 wines from all over the United States. The judging panel is made up of 60 accomplished and influential wine journalists, professors and educators of enology, winemakers, and sommeliers from all over the country. Ditka's "The Icon" Cabernet Sauvignon 2010 won the gold and "The Champion" Red Blend 2010 took home the silver.

In a lifetime filled with awards, though, winemaking is only part of a blessed life for the Coach, whose popularity in his hometown continues to thrive. "I'm just having fun with it," explains Ditka. "Probably the best thing is when you stop taking yourself so darn serious. And I quit. I don't take myself so seriously anymore."

PORTFOLIO

If any of the Terlato celebrity vintners proudly celebrate their own persona it has to be Mike Ditka. Stylistically, his wines are unabashedly Californian. The Cabernets, in particular, are solid, full-bodied, full-oaked, inky, super-rich examples of big Napa winemaking.

The Mike Ditka collection consists of "The Player" Pinot Grigio, "The Player" Merlot, "The Coach" Sauvignon Blanc, "The Coach" Cabernet Sauvignon, "The Hall of Famer" Chardonnay, "The Hall of Famer" Pinot Noir, "The Icon" Cabernet Sauvignon, and "The Champion" Coach's Blend. The last two are admirable wines due to their sheer density and weight of fruit.

NICK'S TASTING NOTES

"The Champion" Coach's Blend, Napa Valley, 2010

This is a "meritage" blend, which traditionally indicates a wine made from various red Bordeaux grape varieties, usually Cabernet Sauvignon, Merlot, and Cabernet Franc. Reflective of Ditka's stature, this a huge, burly wine, stacked and packed with masses of ultra-concentrated black cherry fruits, dark chocolate, and swaths of lavish new vanilla oak. A real crowd pleaser, it's decadent with a luxurious mouth-feel that is lush and dense on the palate and supported by medium tannins and some well-needed acidity to hold up the ballast of muscular fruit.

"The Icon" Cabernet Sauvignon, Napa Valley, 2010

This is the second of Ditka's Meritage wines, with grapes sourced from different altitude vineyards in the Napa region. It is slightly less "overtly" fruity in comparison to the Coach's Blend, and a touch more structured, perhaps because of some extended cellar age. However, it displays the same purple opaque color and crème de cassis nose and it's hard to tell the subtle difference between the two cuvées. Meaty, exotic spices and licorice accents overlaid with almost over-ripe black cherries and vanilla pod aromas on the nose. Not a subtle wine, yet neither is Ditka. It's very broad shouldered, solid, and muscular. Most of Ditka's bottles sell out in his steakhouses, so keep in mind that these wines were especially designed to be enjoyed with red meat. This version, despite its purposely brawny weight, seems better constructed. The Coach's Blend feels a bit more disjointed, being a touch more jammy with a slightly less acidic and tannic structure. Overall, the wines feel akin to falling into a deep comfy couch. Powerful and super-concentrated, this is a proud American Cabernet.

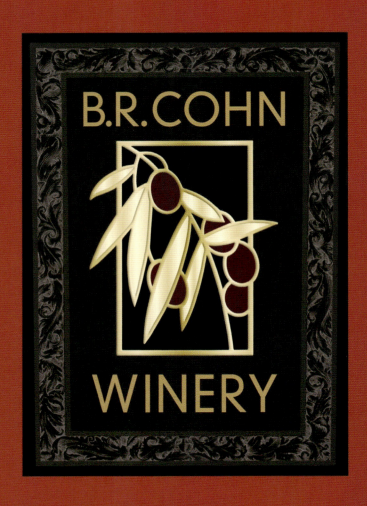

Bruce R. Cohn

B. R. COHN WINERY

Glen Ellen

Days of Wine and Music

One of the most beautiful places we visited in Northern California was the B. R. Cohn Winery on the site of the picturesque Olive Hill Estate Vineyards. Located in the center of the Sonoma Valley (also known as the Valley of the Moon) and surrounded by 140-year-old, majestic, rare French Picholine olive trees, its main building is an elegant, whitewashed Craftsman-style farmhouse. The grounds are immaculate and laid out with an artist's eye for nature's inherent grace and sensuality. We first came to Olive Hill in March 2010 to interview and taste wine with the larger-than-life character of Bruce Cohn himself, an avid vintner and manager of a famous rock band, the Doobie Brothers.

Upon entering the house that serves as tasting room and office (and was once Cohn's family home), we noticed a black-and-white photo on the wall of a rail-thin man with a massive 1960s Afro and beard. Was this the man we were going to meet? Did this guy look capable of producing world-class wines? In this photo at least, Bruce looked better suited to growing something more suggestive of the band's moniker.

However, the man who greeted us in his office seemed a few generations away from that stereotype. The Afro was gone; he was more meat, less hair, but one could still sense that underneath was the same man who had won the hearts of the long-haired Doobies.

Throughout our interview, we found him to be easygoing, affable, humorous, friendly, and knowledgeable. He couldn't have been more accommodating and congenial, generously spending hours discussing his childhood, the early years managing the band, and sharing various opinions on how and where to grow the best grapes and make the finest wines possible in Sonoma.

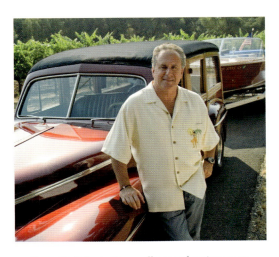

Bruce R. Cohn is also a collector of antique cars.
OVERLEAF: The B. R. Cohn vineyards in Sonoma.

B. R. Cohn Winery

Everything about Cohn's operation was thoughtful and well executed, including the olive branch logo on all the B. R. Cohn products. [Coincidentally, one of Nick's first vinous memories—admittedly 20-odd years ago—was of a bottle of B. R. Cohn Cabernet and, as he was too young to drink, this memory is solely due to the elegant logo.] This lovely design still appears on every product the estate sells and is a wonderful example of simple but effective branding.

Bruce Cohn—like the winery and wines that bear his name—reflects a sense of perpetual motion. His energy boggles the minds of those of us who are decades younger. On his desk were a pair of telephones: one for his vineyard business and the other reserved for music dealings. His two executive assistants were similarly divided into two separate enterprises, and it seemed to us that everyone there had to work overtime just to keep up with the boss.

The winery itself sells over a 100 different products, ranging from dog collars and silver teaspoons to gourmet food, handcrafted vinegars, and extra virgin olive oils, which have garnered a huge reputation for excellence and quality.

Born Into Music

Cohn's interest in music may well have been genetic. Born in Chicago in the late 1940s, he hails from a musical and artistic family. "I came up through music," explains Cohn. "My aunt and uncle played with the Chicago Symphony. My mom was a professional backup singer who sometimes sang with Sinatra when he was in Chicago, and Dad was a classically trained tenor who sang Italian arias. But in that era you could not make a living in classical music unless you were [like a] Pavarotti."

Cohn's father was also a partner in a family-owned shoe business and, though it was quite successful (and is still going strong after 90 years), it held little interest for the tenor who sang under the distinctly non-Jewish name Robert Conati. When Bruce's younger brother, Marty, was diagnosed with asthma in the mid-1950s, the senior Cohn sold his share in the shoe business and moved the family to San Francisco. In 1956, on a weekend family jaunt to the Russian River, Cohn's father impulsively bought a ranch as a second home for his family (without consulting Cohn's mom). "He didn't know anything about ranching," laughs Bruce. "He couldn't tell a screwdriver from a wheelbarrow." Though the ranch was only supposed to be used for weekends and vacations, four months later the family packed up and moved there full-time. "The ranch had no central heat, no insulation," remembers Cohn. "There were only wood-burning pot belly stoves, and my brother and I had to chop wood for them."

A couple of goats were purchased to eat the weeds and, within six months, the herd grew from 8 to 32. More goats were acquired and before long Bruce and his brother were milking 115 of them by hand, twice a day, seven days a week. After a contractor absconded with their money, the family had to complete the dairy barn themselves. Bruce put in the concrete and his mom did all the electrical work. "We had to wear boots when it rained so we wouldn't be electrocuted," he remembers. The ranch became the first grade-A goat dairy in Northern California, producing both milk and feta cheese. The brothers also spent their time playing in empty wine vats and picking

LEFT: Bruce Cohn's father, Sam, at the first Four Cohns shoe store in Chicago, 1927. MIDDLE: Bruce Cohn, his mother, Eleanor, and brother, Marty, 1956. RIGHT: Sam Cohn (looking through the slats) as Bruce and Marty milk two of the 115 goats, a chore they did twice every day of the week.

grapes, walnuts, and prunes to earn extra cash in the summer. Then, quite suddenly, Cohn's childhood was shattered when his mother was badly injured in an accident (a car going 100 miles-an-hour crashed head-on into her vehicle). She spent a year in the hospital and that hardship eventually forced his father to sell the dairy. The family moved to Santa Rosa, then to Chicago for six months, and finally returned to San Francisco where Bruce graduated from high school in 1965.

Both of the Cohn brothers attended the College of San Mateo, majoring in broadcasting and communications, and Bruce later continued his studies at the University of Colorado Boulder. In 1968 he returned to San Francisco, where his brother helped him secure a job at Channel 20, working nights as a television engineer. Thus, Cohn found himself in the center of San Francisco's cultural and musical explosion. Bands like the Grateful Dead, Creedence Clearwater, Santana, Jefferson Airplane, and Big Brother and the Holding Company were

becoming mega stars (he would eventually become friends with most of these artists) and Haight-Ashbury was the center of the hippie universe; altogether a vibrant and infectious atmosphere for a young man with Cohn's talent and drive.

While Marty worked in San Mateo as a recording engineer, the brothers opened a music rehearsal studio in a derelict warehouse on Third Street and Howard in San Francisco (which today is the Moscone Center). "I was working the late shift in TV, 4:00pm to midnight," recalls Cohn. "I had a Harley-Davidson and I used to drive down to San Mateo during the day, just to drive." (Motorcycles and restoring classic cars are other lifelong passions of Cohn's.)

"I was down in San Mateo when Skip Spence from Moby Grape brought in Tom Johnston and John Hartman, who wanted to cut a record," Cohn remembers. "Their band was called 'Pud' and they returned later with the other musicians to audition. Marty recorded a

Bruce Cohn, 1970.

About a year later, Warners dispatched Carl Scott to San Mateo to hear the Doobies play at Ricardo's Pizza. They were offered a recording contract and the chance to tour. The band realized they needed help, so they asked Bruce to be their manager and to tour with them. Though accepting meant giving up a secure (and hard to find) job in television, Cohn grabbed the opportunity, which of course proved to be a seminal decision in his career. If there is one absolutely true thing that can be said of B. R. Cohn—one true thing that has guided his life and made him the success he is today—he knows how to seize an opportunity when it comes his way.

Managing the Doobie Brothers has never been an easy job. Rock managers in the 1970s had to be hard characters, demanding payment before performance from promoters because of the high likelihood of never getting paid at all. "In the beginning we played for $100," Cohn reports with a laugh. "A few times we were paid by the Hell's Angels, who wanted to

demo." The Cohns liked their sound, which was a cross between rock, R&B, and fingerpicking, though the band's name had to go. So Pud became the Doobie Brothers and Marty sent their demo to Warner Bros. in Los Angeles.

LEFT: The Annual B. R. Cohn Charity Fall Music Festival, 2007. From left to right: MB Gordy, John McFee, Tom Johnston, Guy Allison, Cohn, Pat Simmons, Skylark. RIGHT: The Doobies and Cohn (with afro hair) at Warner Bros. in L.A., showing their gold records for "The Captain and Me," 1974.

Cohn (in orange jacket), the Doobie Brothers, and their crew on a private plane they called the Doobie Liner.
Overleaf: Since 1987, the B. R. Cohn winery has hosted 26 annual
rock music festivals and raised over $6 million for charity.

pay us in drugs. I told them we needed money for groceries, not drugs, and they said, 'Snort this and you won't need groceries.'"

The Doobies' first album was hardly a success. In fact, it landed in the recycle bin at Tower Records before the band returned home from their first national tour; without a hit they'd be doomed to obscurity. Warner Bros. gave them one last chance on a second album. It was a raging success: *Toulouse Street* (1972) sold over two million records, and

contained the first two of many hit singles to come, "Listen to the Music" and "Jesus is Just Alright." Suddenly, they were living in the fast lane—on the road over 200 days a year, travelling with a crew of more than 30 by private prop plane (dubbed the "Doobie Liner"), performing 150 shows around the world while simultaneously recording an album a year. (The group would eventually cut twelve albums in as many years.)

Because of Cohn's careful planning as their

LEFT: Olive Hill Estate in the 1970s when Cohn purchased it as a family house.
RIGHT: Today it is the home of the B. R. Cohn Winery.

manager, the Doobies would not suffer the financial disasters that felled so many other bands. "In 1972 I started a pension plan because I'd grown up with successful bands who ended up broke; pissed away everything with parties and limos 24 hours a day. I was afraid that would happen to the Doobies," says Cohn. "The band was only supposed to be around for five years. I had no idea they'd still be going strong 40 years later. My goal then, as always, was simple: plan for the worst, hope for the best. Whatever happened, I wanted to make sure everyone came out with something at the end. So I started this pension plan where we put in tax-free money and I bought commercial real estate all over the Bay Area. I had a full-time real estate broker working on it. When the band broke up in the 1980s, we sold everything and that (along with record royalties) was how the guys could live for the next six years without working."

Managing the Ranch

Early on, the hectic pace of touring and managing the band began to take its toll on Cohn. "After about a year on tour, I realized I'd probably

burn out," Cohn explains. "I was on the road about seven months a year and I was booking all the tours and managing the band from random hotel rooms. (There were no cell phones back then.) I was living in San Francisco and my wife was pregnant with our first child. I wanted to get out of the city when I wasn't on the road and raise my children the way my dad raised us. I wanted to rejuvenate between tours and work from my home. So I started looking to buy land in Sonoma. It took me two years to find this ranch."

Cohn had no idea he'd be venturing into winemaking when he first moved his family to Sonoma. "The place I bought was a closed dairy," he explains. "The 46 acres had been planted for hay and pears but was pretty much fallow except for fourteen acres of grapes; half Cabernet and half Pinot. The vines were four years old and they were half dead. I thought it was because of a frost problem, but then I learned the land was dry farmed (meaning without irrigation). I later discovered this was a frost-free ranch because of the geothermal hot springs, though I did not know that then. I saw that the land had an artesian well that was pumping out 25 gallons a minute. My dad had taught me the value of having a good well on a ranch because we'd had a hand-dug well on the goat dairy that sometimes ran dry in the summer. Of course, when I bought the place, I didn't know a thing about grapes, but the dairy had come with a contract for the grapes, so I had to quickly learn as much I could."

It was just the kind of challenge at which B. R. would excel. He began reading about grapes whenever he could find the time. "I purchased books on viticulture from U. C. Davis and was reading them while flying from gig to gig on the Doobie Liner," he laughs. "I was trying to figure out why my grape vines did not look like the pictures in the book. I discovered the pruning was wrong, and there was no irrigation. There was so much to figure out."

He named the property Olive Hill Estate Vineyards after the grove of 100-year-old Picholine olive trees on his property, replanted the dead vines, brought in new vines, and installed an irrigation system. Stan Berde, a friend and colleague who was also a wine collector, introduced him to Charlie Wagner, the legendary winemaker/Cabernet producer of Caymus Vineyards, who would become Cohn's mentor and have an enormous impact on the direction of Olive Hill.

"Between 1974 and 1984, I was selling grapes to August Sebastiani from the Sebastiani Winery," Cohn begins a favorite story he often tells at wine-tasting events. "August would mix my Sonoma grapes with truckloads of grapes from the Central Valley. Sebastiani made lots of wine. At the time, in the early 1970s, there were only about 30 wineries in the entire Napa/Sonoma area—today there are hundreds—and, for the most part, wineries were only producing jug wine, hearty red Burgundy. People were just starting to make varietals.

"Charlie told me that because August didn't separate the grapes, no one knew the quality of mine. He told me to bring him [Charlie] some of my grapes." The offer presented Cohn with a dilemma. "August was tough and I didn't want him to know I was bringing grapes to someone else," he remembers. "He might get mad and cut me off from my contract."

So Cohn turned the delivery into a covert operation. "Charlie told me that farmers are in bed by 7:00pm so if I brought him the grapes at night, August would never know. I loaded my truck in the evening and drove the long way over the mountain to avoid passing by Sebastiani Winery; the 20-minute trip took me 2½ hours and I burned out my brakes on those roads. Charlie was mad because it was 10:00pm and long past his bedtime by the time I got there."

Six months later, Bruce went to taste the wine Charlie made from those grapes delivered in the middle of the night. "I was 27 and had no palate," Cohn admits. "Mostly, at the time I was drinking Tequila and beer with the band. Charlie poured me a glass of Pinot, which was good, I thought. And I liked the Cab. But Charlie said it was the best Cab he had tasted from Sonoma County. He advised me to get August to keep my grapes separate and label them with an Olive Hill Estate Vineyards designation. When I called August to suggest this, he said he didn't have tanks small enough for just my grapes and, anyway, he didn't do vineyard designates. Then he hung up."

However, two famous properties, Ravenswood (renowned for their single-vineyard Zinfandels) and Gundlach-Bundschu (a respected Cabernet and Chardonnay producer), agreed to make "Olive Hill Estate Vineyards" an officially designated wine, labeled as such on their bottles. Immediately, both wines won awards. In fact, the 1980 Gundlach-Bundschu Olive Hill Cabernet received the honor of being selected by Ronald Reagan's White House and 200 cases were sent to China as a gift.

Cohn began looking for his own winemaker. In 1984 he hired Helen Turley, who was a cellar assistant at Gundlach-Bundschu at the time. Now famed for producing some of the most in-your-face, powerfully styled Cabernet Sauvignons and Zinfandel wines to appear from California to date, Turley built her reputation making B. R. Cohn Olive Hill Estate Cabernets in the mid-1980s. She set an impressively high standard for the winemakers who followed at Olive Hill, including Mary Edwards, who created Special Selection B. R. Cohn Olive Hill Estate Cabernets in the mid-1990s, and Tom Montgomery, who was Cohn's winemaker from 2004 until 2015.

The amphitheater on the grounds of the winery has been used for annual musical festivals and plans are in development to add a canopy to the viewing area.

The Valley Floor vs. the Mountainside

B. R. Cohn's 90-acre property lies on rolling hills along the valley floor rather than on the higher mountainside vineyards that surround the estate. Not surprisingly, Cohn is a firm believer that in the growing season, the warmer temperatures at the lower elevation suit the Cabernet grape better than the cooler temperatures above the fog line. His property benefits from underground natural hot springs that run about 1½ to 2 miles under his vineyard, warming the soil, which results in an earlier bud break, an extended growing season, and an earlier harvest. (Cohn can harvest his grapes two weeks earlier than other Cabernet vineyards in the valley.)

We should note that there's a serious difference of opinion over the viticultural benefits of the valley floor versus the rugged high altitude of the mountainside. This was a subject that popped up with every winemaker we interviewed in Napa/Sonoma, usually brought up by the winemakers or owners themselves. The winemakers on the valley floor, like Cohn, argued the benefits of their property while those high up in the mountains looked down on valley grapes, both literally and figuratively.

In our opinion, mountainside fruit produces more mineral-driven wines, as the vines virtually have to drill through rock. Elevation and diurnal temperatures also provide better balance and higher acidity, which we feel these California fruit-drenched wines absolutely require for freshness due to the added mineral structure and increased acidity. Grapes grown in the valley tend to show a more lush, softer character due to the more fertile soils but, as mentioned above, this is a controversial subject that, like the taste of wine itself, can be argued from many different viewpoints.

The Olive Hill Estate Vineyard has naturally drained, gravelly loam soils that suit the production of ripe, healthy Cabernet Sauvignon grapes. Varying soil depths and exposures to sun throughout the vineyard provide the grapes with added flavors and give the resultant wine, in turn, better depth of fruit.

Olive Hill Estate's 61 acres of vineyards are planted mostly with Cabernet Sauvignon, along with small amounts of Petite Sirah, Pinot Noir, Zinfandel, Cabernet Franc, Petit Verdot, and Malbec grapes. This is quite a big operation however (even though Cohn labels the estate a boutique winery, it's what we would call a "medium to large" boutique winery) and thus grapes are sourced from vineyards all over wine country, from Napa to Sonoma to the Russian River. Some wines, like the Pinot Noir, are made solely with fruit from the Russian River, while others, such as the Silver Label Cabernet Sauvignon, are a blend of grapes partly from select North Coast Vineyards and partly from the Sonoma Olive Hill Estate. Some cuvées, like the entry-level Classic Car Cuvées, are made up completely from brought-in grapes.

Olive Hill's eight individual blocks are farmed as unique, separate vineyards, as each has its own strengths and attributes. When the juices of each variety are blended together, traits from each vineyard can be detected in the final blends. The original vineyard sits right at the entrance of the estate. These two blocks are grafted primarily on old St. George rootstock and utilize two-wire trellising and 8 by 12-foot spacing. Cane-pruned, they produce the Special Selection Olive Hill Estate Cabernet, the finest and most prized cuvée in the entire portfolio. The more recent blocks,

B. R. Cohn's line of specialty olive oils and vinegars were bestsellers from the moment they went on the market.

which were planted away from the road between 1997 and 1999 utilizing viticulture techniques such as steel stakes, closer vine spacing, and vertical trellising with Cabernet Sauvignon (clone 4, Mt. Eden clone, and French clones 15 and 337), are planted on 420A and 101–14 rootstocks.

Each row within each block of the vineyard is worked separately, utilizing the practice of thinning both the canopy and crop depending on the vintage conditions, with the aim of ultimately achieving optimum berry development and concentration within the fruit. In past vintages some blocks were picked row by row, taking into consideration the differences of terroir in relation to the wine's final taste. The winery practices a non-interventionist approach, successfully letting the terroir of the Olive Hill Vineyards shine through the ripe sweet fruit flavor.

Another Lucky Break

Finally, we should add a note about the magnificent olive trees that grace the property. The trees, of course, had already been on the property for more than 100 years when Cohn first bought the dairy, but they'd been ignored and neglected for years. The previous owner had let them grow wild and only kept them because they provided both shade and protection from street noise. Cohn might not have done anything to the trees either, except that in October and November the falling fruit would form a solid carpet around the property. "I had four kids running around outside," explains Cohn, "and every autumn they'd track in the olives, making big black stains on our carpets. My wife at the time said that either I had to pick up the olives or buy her new carpeting for the house."

In 1990, he decided to pick up the fruit and haul it over to the one guy in the Central Valley who was then pressing extra virgin olive oil. "The Mediterranean diet was not yet popular," Cohn explains, "and vegetable oil was what everyone wanted." To his surprise, Cohn discovered he had the only grove of rare French Picholine trees in Sonoma County (all the other olive trees were from Italian or Spanish plantings). Thus, the olive oil from these trees was also unique to the area. The oil he bottled sold extremely well from the very first and soon he also developed a successful line of flavored olive oils. In fact, today the B. R. Cohn olive oils are almost as popular as the wines. Later, he added a line of vinegars that were equally successful. "Like everything else, it was a lucky break," says Cohn with a shrug.

Call it luck, or fate, or destiny, the olive oil business was yet another example of the way B. R. Cohn managed to spin gold from what was right in front of him. And like so many other opportunities he seized and worked hard to develop in his career, it has flourished and thrived.

What's New at B. R. Cohn?

Since that first visit to B. R. Cohn in the summer of 2010, much has changed. The biggest surprise, which we learned upon our return to the winery in 2015, was that B. R. Cohn had been sold to Vintage Wine Estates, a col-

The tasting room of the winery used to be home of Bruce Cohn and his family.

lection of family wineries based out of Santa Rosa, California.

Vintage's principal owner and managing partner, Pat Roney, has been instrumental in building a strong collection of family wineries as far west as the Sonoma Coast and across the Napa Valley. In addition to the B. R. Cohn Winery, the portfolio includes Cartlidge and Browne, Clos Pegase, Cosentino Winery, Girard Winery, Ray's Station, Swanson Vineyards, Sonoma Coast Vineyards, Viansa Sonoma, Windsor Vineyards, and the Wine Sisterhood.

Bruce himself has retired as a full time participant in the day-to-day operations, though he is still active as a spokesperson for the wines and olive oils he created. And he is still involved with and committed to music, both at and outside of the winery. The annual rock music festival that Cohn initiated at the winery in 1987 to raise money for charity was moved off-site this year for the first time to downtown Sonoma and renamed the Sonoma Music Festival. However, plans are in the works to bring other music events, both large and small, back to the winery where they began. Other changes on the horizon include renovating the barn and expanding the on-site facilities for special events such as weddings and private parties.

The winery looked different from when we first visited. Many of Bruce Cohn's pet decorations were gone, such as the vintage cars and the playful metal sculptures that used to dot the driveways. Memorabilia from the glory days of the Doobie Brothers are now celebrated in a dedicated rock 'n' roll room. Though it feels a bit less personal, at the same time, the winery also seems more focused on, and committed to, the actual business of making and selling wine.

From what we could see, the changes at B. R. Cohn were positive. We did indeed notice a new mood in the atmosphere at the winery. The tasting room had an air of invigoration with a staff of people who were more helpful, knowledgeable, and enthusiastic than in almost any other tasting room we visited in northern California. The website has been updated and enhanced. In all, the winery feels like it has reinvented itself.

Most importantly, we were thrilled to discover that the wines have vastly improved, as detailed in the following tastings.

The general store, adjacent to the tasting room, offers B. R. Cohn's vast assortment of olive oils and vinegars, along with many other products. PAGES 136–137: Picholine olives being harvested.

PORTFOLIO

The B. R. Cohn portfolio is vast and stylistically impressive with color-filled imagery and a sense of "playfulness," something frequently absent in the world of wine. (In Germany, for example, the wine labels can often resemble a legal writ.)

A great aspect of the portfolio is the price points—there's a wine for everyone, whether you want to spend $15 or $80 or more.

Stylistically, the wines are all clean and well made, with medium levels of concentration and sweet, lush, valley-floor fruit attributes. The tannins are generally soft and sweet, making the wines on the whole immediately accessible. The house style has definitely changed since the days of Helen Turley and her heady, super-rich concoctions. When she was in charge of the winemaking, however, two of the winery's flagship wines, the 1985 and 1986 Special Selection Olive Hill Estate Cabernets, were ranked among the top 10 in America and top 50 in the world by *Wine Spectator* magazine, which gave each a rating of 94 out of 100. (No doubt she was doing something right.) The 2003 vintage was rated 93 and the North Coast Petite Sirah was one of two red "sweepstakes winners" at the prestigious 2007 San Francisco Chronicle Wine Competition. (We, unfortunately, saw no Petite Sirah on the tasting sheet.).

Among the most interesting characteristics of the wines is a gentle but wild array of subtle complexity of flavor over power—the Pinot Noir and Sonoma Chardonnay are both good examples—capturing all sorts of light aromas and flavors such as wild herbs, minerals, and spice that zip across the palate to hold your attention. This clear attempt at achievable complexity, something that can be captured and combined with the newer, less obvious, previously powerful style, can be found in the bigger-scaled wines such as the Cabs and Zinfandels. Once again these wines mirror the qualities of their maker. In a way they have a lot of B. R's characteristics: they are ambitious, busy, well controlled, broad-shouldered, and bold, yet still retain a sense of elegance.

Obviously, some cuvées work better than others and these tend to be the Olive Hill Estate wines, especially the Cabernets, which are smooth and show relatively more concentration than the wines from brought-in grapes. The wines do show a nice restraint of new oak (barrels are used for two years); nonetheless, this being California there's no doubt it's an influencing factor, especially in the Special Selection Cabernet and the Reserve Chardonnay. The estate also makes a Cabernet Port and, interestingly, a Kosher Cabernet Sauvignon from the Trestle Glen Estate Vineyard in Sonoma.

For years the winery has been heavily involved with charities, ranging from veterans' to children's causes. Along with an annual golf event, the B. R. Cohn winery has raised many millions of dollars for charity.

Pinot Noir, Russian River Valley, 2008

An absolutely beautiful Pinot Noir that combines complexity with drinkability. So lush and pleasantly fruity one could drink this all day. Light ruby color. Plenty going on; the nose bursts with clean, sweet aromas of perfectly ripe and gently crushed red and black fruits such as raspberry, strawberry, and red and black cherries. A light waft of spice, minerals, earth, and light sweet oak accompany the fruit. In the mouth this wine positively floats across the mid-weight palate with different sweet fruit flavors touching all parts of the tongue and then seems to dissipate softly before making a reappearance with perfectly judged acidity, light tight-grained sweet tannins, and hints of earth, flowers, and spice, giving the wine good complexity.

Special Selection Cabernet Sauvignon, Olive Hill Estate, Sonoma, 2007

This is the estate's flagship wine and all the grapes for this cuvée are sourced from the original vineyard, which sits at the entrance of the estate, and other, newer plantings. This was my favorite of the Cabernet selections on offer, not because it was the most concentrated and powerful (although it was) but because it was the most complete, showing complexity, freshness, balance, and ageability. Very Californian in style but with a certain Bordeaux sensibility, it displays a fine, expensive French oak element that doesn't overpower the fruit but works with it. A medium-dark mahogany color is followed by a complex bouquet that showcases black cherry, currants, plum, anise, and mint aromas accompanied by new sweet vanilla oak. Youthful and a touch tight in the mouth, it expresses fresh, black fruits, vanilla, and wet earth. It is medium- to full-bodied with medium tight-grained tannins and light acidity that leads to a decent finish. This will last ten years in the cellar.

Chardonnay, 2013

This wine has a shiny, youthful, bright medium-gold color. Bold and ripe on the nose with powerful warm-climate citrus and tropical fruit aromas of ripe lemons, pears, peaches, and mango. Light notes of hazelnuts, honey, and jasmine add complexity. Medium-to-full bodied in the mouth with excellent levels of ripeness, this is a powerful, rich, warm-climate Chardonnay with solid white fruit flavors wrapped in creamy oak. Good acidity and a floral, jasmine note lift the palate from becoming blousy and one-dimensional. This excellent example of California Chardonnay has an exceptional stretchy, full mid-palate that leads to a rich lingering vanilla oak-infused finish.

Pinot Noir, Russian River Valley, 2013

An absolutely superb and unabashedly Californian Pinot Noir. I rated this my fa-vorite wine of the entire new portfolio as it has every quality you could hope for: expressiveness, ripeness, great balance, and, most importantly, it was serious yet also exceptionally fun to drink. Its color is a medium-light garnet with bright vio-let hints and a youthful pink rim. Pungent on the nose with a mélange of super-ripe black fruits such as black cherry and plums intermingled with raspberries, red cherries, and strawberries. A waft of powerful new oak and hints of damp earth also rise from the glass. Juicy, full, and bouncy on the palate with bright but light mouthwatering red lush fruits and an overlay of dark black-cherry-like fruit. Excellent levels of fruit ripeness matched with the uplifting acidity give the impression that the wine floats across the palate. A blast of creamy vanilla oak and sweet small-grained tannins carry this Pinot towards a very long finish that begs one for another sip.

Special Selection Cabernet Sauvignon, 2010

One of the best 2010 Cabernets we tried on our recent visit to California. Clearly, there has been an enormous and noticeable improvement in respect to the top tier wines being produced at B. R. Cohn. This is a great example, especially considering the difficult cold weather conditions of the 2010 vintage. If this is any indication, the underground hot springs that run beneath the property have an obvious and noticeable effect. The wines are neither massively scaled nor opaque in color but reveal a new-found depth of fruit and concentration, which, combined with the suc-culent mid-palate, results in impeccable balance.

This wine shows a youthful medium-garnet color with violet reflections. Wonderfully pure and clean briary nose. Classic Cabernet and Merlot aromas of weedy cassis and succulent black cherries mingle with secondary more complex aromas of mint, coffee, small currants, scorched earth, and well-judged spicy new oak. Powerful, rich, and ripe, the wine displays good delineation in the mouth with well-defined structure and attack, a broad succulent mid-palate, and a long back end. After an initial burst of cassis from the Cabernet, plumper flavors of black cherry from the Merlot enter the picture and fill out the mid-palate, until finally the Petit Verdot arrives, adding a touch of spice to the long vanilla-tinged finish. Additional fine complex aromas of chocolate, spice, and earth accompany these juicy, almost brawny, dark fruit flavors. The excellent levels of ripeness and concentration are without the usually perceptible "cool vintage" note of austerity often found in both the 2010s and 2011s. There has been an improvement in quality since previous recent vintages of this wine were tasted.

Cabernet Sauvignon, Select Block 3, 2011

The first of two excellent new "single block" offerings from the estate really demonstrates the seriousness of the new venture and showcases the real potential of the old estate vineyard. Procured from over 50-year-old vines on the estate's North Vineyard, this (and the Block 7) are very serious, age-worthy wines. Again, they are not overly colored or opaque but rather reveal a classic crimson old Bordeaux-like color with transparent cores (this however is not an indication of power). It has a superb dusty Cabernet-dominated nose with deep cassis and black currant aromas bathed in sweet vanilla oak. The wine is very direct and structured on the palate, exhibiting powerful (a little tough) tannins, good levels of acidity, and an excellent depth of fruit. There are also some serious notes of complexity hiding in the rear—shoe polish, mint, and sous bois. The wine's dark, dense, concentrated, very ripe mid-palate picks up a long thread of acidity, and fine tannins drive the wine to a chocolate-speckled finish. Again this shows only a small hint of austerity (maybe due to the property's thermal hot-springs) from the cold vintage, however a touch of narrowness can be found that should broaden out with some well needed short-term bottle age. I preferred the Single Block 3 to Single Block 7 as it revealed better depth and inner concentration of fruit. I'd like to re-taste these from a riper vintage in the future. Allocation through the wine club or vineyard purchase only.

Cabernet Sauvignon, Select Block 7, 2011

As mentioned, this was produced from the very cold 2011 vintage and this bottling does show some austerity, less obvious concentration, and less overt fruitiness. Though I preferred the above bottling to this Select Block 7, it's nonetheless still a high-quality wine that could do with some additional bottle age to soften its edges. Stylistically the Block 7 differs from the Block 3, perhaps reflecting more of a cool site on the property, but taste-wise and structurally they are similar. There is no doubt the Block 7 is concentrated and does have a lengthy finish but comparatively, at the moment, the Block 3 is singing. Allocation through the wine club or vineyard purchase only.

ESTATE GROWN

KAMEN

2008

Cabernet Sauvignon

SONOMA VALLEY

Robert Kamen

KAMEN ESTATE WINES

Sonoma

A Bona Fide Winemaking Nut

On our trip to Northern California, we met many winemaking celebrities who were in the business to make money (sometimes for charity) or to highlight their profile (or so-called brand) for personal reasons. Some were in it for vanity or the glory of being able to serve a wine with their name on the label. So in comparison, it was an unexpected joy to meet a celebrity who was also a bona fide winemaking nut. We don't mean someone who takes an interest when the vintage rolls around or final blends are being made. We mean someone who makes wine for the sheer love of the process.

Screenwriter Robert Kamen was, by far, the most personally dedicated and obsessed celebrity winemaker we encountered. One of the most successful screenwriters in the industry, he even confessed that though he loved writing movies (and being able to support his family with his writing), the other true passion in his life is his winemaking venture. And winemaking—especially in the Kamen style—is not exactly inexpensive. Though he earns a small fortune from each screenplay (many written in collaboration with French filmmaker Luc Besson), a huge part of his earnings are poured back into his vineyard. He will gladly and enthu-

siastically pay millions of dollars to jackhammer new vines into his rocky mountainside.

Kamen Estates sits just above the fog line and is almost impossible to find unless Robert escorts you personally up the mountain, which is exactly what he did for us. We had arranged to meet just outside the Cheese Factory in downtown Sonoma. We were waiting in our rented car, a light rain falling on the windshield, when Kamen screeched to a halt behind us and beckoned us into his red Jeep. We then proceeded to drive slowly upwards, winding through various unpaved, unsigned muddy roads.

Up in the mountains, the soil is markedly different than in the valley. Huge lumps of exposed lava, broken shale, and *galet*-style small boulders cover the ground; it's mindboggling that the vines can actually bore through this formidable barrier.

We went up and up into the clouds until we rolled into a driveway at the top of Kamen's mountain, where we discovered a small but beautifully designed little house with 180-degree views of his property. This is where he writes while constantly surveying his lands. His highest vineyard lies at 1,450 feet and can just be seen shrouded in fog in the distance. Even at this elevation, and from more than 40 miles away, San Francisco Bay can be glimpsed through the trees. It's a beautiful, peaceful spot—the perfect retreat for a writer— surrounded by his wildly undulating 50 acres of planted vineyards. Clearly, Kamen adores his property and treats it as if it was a living, breathing organism (which of course it is). He thinks of himself as a caretaker to this amazing property. "I'm king of my fiefdom," he says. "That's my eagle, those are my rabbits, that's my tree." He takes pride in everything that lives and breathes on his mountain.

Screewriter Robert Kamen atop his mountain vineyard in Sonoma.

The Zen Master

Small and wiry, short in stature and youthful in looks, with bushy untamed hair and piercing blue eyes, Robert Mark Kamen possesses boundless levels of energy. By his own admis-

sion, he only sleeps four hours a night. He appears to be someone who is comfortable in his own skin, exuding an almost Zen-like aura. However, he is also absorbed and restless; this is obviously a man who needs to work. "My entire life is lived on instinct," he says. "There is no calculation by me whatsoever; it is all of the moment."

The man who wrote *The Karate Kid* is a spiritual soul who excels (unsurprisingly) at martial arts and practices meditation. He has an eagerness to connect with and respect the earth; in the truest sense, he is a real hippie. He's also a firm believer in organics, biodynamics, and letting nature take its course in a non-interventionist fashion. Very opinionated yet not condescending, Kamen has his own vision of winemaking and the style he wants to achieve, driven completely by his personal taste. His vine tending and winemaking style is nothing new; in fact, it's based in large part on history and tradition. He hates manipulated wines that are created in the winery—for him it's the whole expression or sense of place that guides and dictates his winemaking and the ultimate character of the wines he makes.

Everything begins and ends with the grapes. "You can make bad wine from good grapes," he says, "but you can't make good wine from bad grapes."

Without a doubt he is a "terroirist," letting the elements that surround him take precedent as they have done for centuries in Europe. Perched on top of his vineyards, Robert is literally king of the hill, with an intimate knowledge of every vine, boulder, and animal that surrounds him. "This is my obsession; I can't even call it a passion. I know every rock on

Kamen's piece of the Mayacamas Mountains.

this property," Kamen says with an enthusiasm that can't be faked. "To make great wine you have to have tremendous focus and dedication; it takes decades."

A Bronx Boy in Afghanistan

Inside Kamen's house, we took off our shoes and sat in a comfortable circle, sipping tea as we listened to him tell his story. He seemed open and eager to answer all of our questions.

He grew up in a housing project in the rough Bronx district of New York City and attended NYU, where he received a BA in literature. An invaluable grant earned after college changed

his life, allowing Robert to see the world for the first time and gain an introduction to new cultures, even if the circumstances exposed an alternative agenda. "I received a grant to follow and record the daily activities of the Bedouin people who lived on the border of Afghanistan and Russia," he says. "I found out later that the grant was funded by the U.S. government in an effort to learn how the Bedouins were making their way across the border during the Russian occupation. So, I was basically a spy and didn't know it," he adds with a shrug and a grin.

Shortly after returning from his trip in 1972, he wrote a novel called *Crossings* about a group of college students and their

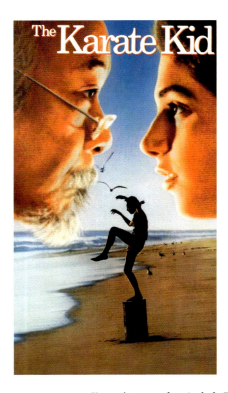
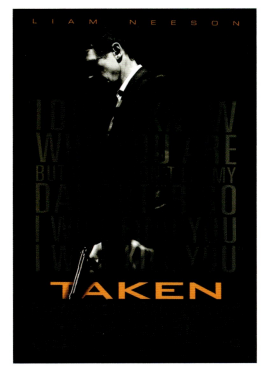

Kamen's screenplays include *The Karate Kid* (1984) and *Taken* (2008).

experiences in Afghanistan. The novel was published in 1975. He then adapted *Crossings* into a screenplay, which he sold to Hollywood and in 1980, received a check for $135,000, a significant amount of money in those days. To celebrate his sudden good fortune, he went hiking with a friend through the Mayacamas Mountains just north of San Pablo Bay and just west of the Napa County line. While on the hike, the two friends came across a beautiful and sensual piece of property for sale in the rugged Mount Veeder district.

Kamen remembers sitting on the mountain and feeling an immediate connection with the land. "I just knew this was the place," he explains. "Sometimes you feel an immediate bond, that you should be here." Without hesitation or a second thought—a trait for which he would become notorious in both business and life—he and his friend walked down off the mountain and into a local real estate office in Sonoma. Though he was unshaven and unwashed, he had that big check in his pocket and he turned it over as a down payment on the property. He hadn't even bothered to open a bank account or deposit the check. With that one impulsive act, he sealed his fate.

He went on to earn a doctorate in American studies from the University of Pennsylvania and then proceeded to become one of the most successful screenwriters of his generation, writing such films as *Taps, The Karate Kid* series, *The Fifth Element*, *A Walk in the Clouds*, *Leon*, *Transporter* and its sequels, *Taken*, and *Colombiana*. Yet despite all his success, he is about as far from the prototype of the successful Hollywood screenwriter as could possibly be imagined. Ask him about

working with Brad Pitt or Harrison Ford and, within seconds, the conversation veers back to his one true fascination: winemaking.

Tremendous Potential

In the 1980s, Kamen's property was overgrown, extremely rocky, and almost completely remote—with few roads and no electricity. Although it seemed isolated and wild, Kamen always felt it held tremendous potential for growing grapes. He hired Phil Coturri, a now famous viticulturalist and biodynamic advocate and pioneer—though, according to Kamen, "he prefers to call himself a farmer." The mountainous terrain was no easy place to cultivate, but Kamen and Coturri took up the challenge and immediately started to dig wells, build roads, and install electricity.

Today the estate is planted with 40 acres of Cabernet Sauvignon and three acres of Syrah. The budwood for the Cabernet was sourced by Robert from his neighbor, the famous Louis Martini's renowned Monte Rosso Vineyard. The vineyards ride the contours of hillsides that often exceed a 40% grade, which is very steep indeed.

Kamen's vineyards, on the southwestern slopes of Mount Veeder, actually sit on a spent lava flow made up of four different types of crumbly basalt rocks. The land has enough fractures so that the vines can squeeze their roots far down into the steep mountainside. This shattering of the lava only occurs when the flow is exposed to water and air, quickly cooling the sheet and fracturing the rock. At least four ancient lava flows have resulted in the numerous soil types and exposure angles that produce complex, mineral-flavored grapes.

ABOVE: Planting vines in the rocky terrain at Kamen Estates is unbelievably difficult and requires jackhammering. RIGHT: But the results are well worth the effort for Kamen. PAGES 150–151: Kamen's view of his vineyard.

The soils are so diverse that growing conditions can vary significantly even within a single row: this adds to the complexity of the fruit harvested. Yields in the vineyards never reach more than a microscopic 1½ tons per acre due to the extremely rocky environment and the viticulture practice of dropping slightly damaged or fully ripe fruit to assure maximum flavor and concentration of the grapes that are used.

Hallmarks of the weather during the growing season are cool, foggy mornings followed by hot afternoons. This microclimate—classified as a mid–region III in the U. C. Davis Heat Summation Scale—also benefits the vineyards, creating an environment in which wine grapes seem to thrive particularly well, providing for an even ripening of the grapes. The unique weather zone can now be monitored and managed by computer; if a row of vines needs more or less water, just that row can be activated or deactivated by the push of a button.

Born from Fire

The first grapes at the estate were harvested in 1984 and much of the fruit was sold to the top wineries in Sonoma. Then, in 1996, a devastating fire tore through the property. The cause of the fire was blamed on the Pacific Gas and Electric Company, which had failed to trim eucalyptus

Robert Kamen signs his bottles with famous lines from his screenplays such as "I will find you. I will kill you," from *Taken* (2008) and "Wax on, wax off," from *The Karate Kid* (1984).

trees surrounding their power lines. A sudden flare-up sparked the fire, which destroyed Kamen's house and half his vines. An ensuing lawsuit was eventually settled out of court.

In one of those strange cases of life imitating art, two years before the fire, Robert was working on the screenplay for his 1993 film, *A Walk in the Clouds*, which starred Keanu Reeves as a young winemaker in Northern California. Kamen was having trouble coming up with an ending for the film, until he had the idea of writing about a fire that would ravage the main character's vineyard.

In addition to being a freaky yet prescient accident, the real fire caused Kamen to reevaluate his vineyard, as he had to rebuild from the roots upward. He had a major shift in his vision for the property, with the new aim being to produce small quantities of mainly Cabernet Sauvignon wines from organically and biodynamically grown estate grapes. He believed that though production would be small, this would create intensely flavored wines.

Robert's new direction was fueled by his desire to plant the highest quality Cabernet Sauvignon with the lowest yields, utilizing the ripest fruit available. The 1999 vintage was the first produced at the estate, and in 2003 Kamen chose Mark Herold (whose former clients included Merus, Buccella, Hestan, and Kobalt Wines) to be head winemaker and work beside Coturri. New selections of Cabernet clones, different rootstocks, and cutting-edge viticulture techniques were employed. The overall philosophy was to preserve the wildness of the place with little or no intervention. As a result, the soils of Kamen Estate vineyards have never been exposed to chemical fertilizer, pesticides, or herbicides.

Terroir Obsessed

Kamen is obsessed with terroir and all his personal favorite wines are based on that philosophy. He's a naturalist and a naturist and, if he could, would sleep in his vineyards and add its earth to his meals. He believes that what the terroir gives you is what you get. "I don't drink wines from sourced grapes," he insists. "My interest is a wine that has a 'sense of place' year after year without being managed and manipulated in the winery."

Somewhat ironically, Cabernet Sauvignon is his least favorite grape and Bordeaux his least favorite wine region. He adores wines from the Rhône and yearns to make more Rhône-styled wines, but is cautious that the public won't buy them as easily as a Cabernet, something with which they are more familiar. His "mountain style" winemaking is a mixed blessing as, in general, Sonoma is renowned for its Pinots and Chardonnays and not the Cabernets Kamen is carving out of his mountain. However, he has planted a few acres of Grenache and in the future plans to make a Châteauneuf-styled wine.

Kamen's wines certainly have a wildness to them yet also contain a pinpoint balance of acidity that provides the cuvées with freshness. They are light on their feet but deeply concentrated. And like all the estates we visited in Northern California, these wines mirrored the characteristics of the person who made them. Rugged and direct, they told a story: a story reflecting where they came from and how they were grown and created—and, most importantly, a story about what nature provided to enable them to create their own unique taste.

Moon Mountain AVA

We revisited Robert Kamen in March of 2015 to discover that he'd been very busy in the four years since we first met—and we're not even talking about the three movies that have been produced from his screenplays.

The big news is that Kamen and his neighbors have succeeded in creating a new AVA called Moon Mountain. They did this because they no longer wanted to be associated with Sonoma, which is known for Pinot Noir and Chardonnay but not particularly respected for Cabernet or Syrah. By creating Moon Moun-

Robert Kamen's new tasting room in Sonoma.

tain AVA, this group of winemakers is working together to make the area as serious an AVA as Rutherford, with its own distinctive characteristics and terroir. They also get together once a month to talk about grapes and suitable sites for making the best wine in their own AVA, and bring along wines from all over the world to taste and share with each other.

Kamen also added a classy tasting room to the heart of historic downtown Sonoma. Right off the plaza, you'll discover a clean, modern storefront, minimalistic yet extremely inviting. At a gorgeous marble countertop, you can sample all of Kamen's wines and buy T-shirts printed with catch phrases from his films ("Wax on! Wax Off!"), cleverly packaged in film cans. Everything in Kamen's world is connected.

He asked us to meet him at his mountain-top work aerie and we were delighted to make the trip. "There's something up here I have to show you," he told us enthusiastically when we called.

Once in the clouds, as always, Robert only wanted to talk about wine. We jumped into his four-wheel ATV for the bumpiest ride of our lives, up to his lava block vineyard, high in the mountain, where his vines had been jackhammered into rock solid earth. Here the grapes are literally pushing out from fist-sized rocks and this is what Kamen wanted us to witness. Indeed, we'd never really seen anything like it at any other vineyard in the world.

These are Cabernet grapes and the advantage of planting them so high in the mountain is that prevailing winds prevent the grapes from suffering mildew or rot. This is definitely a place where grapes must struggle mightily to survive, making for extraordinary fruit and extraordinary wine.

After a tour of the fields, we returned to Kamen's oasis in the sky to talk more about wine. We wanted to know how Robert first developed a palate for wine and he told us a very interesting story.

Many years ago, when wine was only something he drank, not created, he visited a fancy wine store on Madison Avenue in New York City, where he was living at the time. He gave the proprietor $1,000 (a sizeable amount back then) to teach him about wine and educate his palate. Every month, Robert received a case of wine from the store. The proprietor started him on Burgundies and Bordeaux and then worked his way to Chianti and back. He admits they were not great wines but they helped him distinguish between vintages and understand wines stylistically. He learned about style of origin, terroir, and the taste of particular regions.

This was his introduction to wine and clearly it has served him well.

Robert Kamen has come a long, long way since he first hiked the Mayacamas Mountains with a substantial check in his back pocket. Since then, he has turned this wilderness into a wine-lovers paradise, spending his days going back and forth between his two great passions: making wine and writing movies. He travels so much for his screenwriting assignments that when asked where he lives, he replies, "Seat 6A on American Airlines." He's only half-joking. But he always returns to the mountain that he loves so much and cares for so well.

The past few years have been a busy and productive time for Robert Kamen and we can't wait to hear what he'll be coming up with in the future.

PORTFOLIO

The estate produces three Cabernet-based wines, a Syrah, and a Sauvignon Blanc. The super-cuvée Cabernet Sauvignon, called Kashmir, is only produced in extraordinary vintage conditions. This wine was developed after Kamen discovered that, in some years, certain blocks of vines within the estate exhibited a uniquely different character from the rest of the vineyard.

All of Kamen's wines are made in very limited quantities, with only 100 or so cases of the Syrah (very powerful and age-worthy) and the Kashmir released annually. The Cabernet Sauvignon cuvées are made from 100% estate-grown grapes.

At just over 1,000-case productions, Kamen Estate Vineyards Cabernet Sauvignon is allocated mostly to mailing list customers and exclusive upscale restaurants. The first release was in 1999. We personally found them to be the best-balanced wines showcased in the portfolio.

Stylistically these are super-concentrated wines that come from low yields and small, water-stressed berries. They have formidable structure and a noticeable mineral streak, a trait that runs through all the red wines. These are not the usual lush wines that Sonoma is renowned for; in fact, they most resemble a Napa mountain wine.

Syrah, 2008

Super concentrated, inky, powerful, and full-bodied, the Syrah showcases aromas of rich dark fruit, wild blueberry, and tea box with brambly undertones. These wines have enormous aging potential with 30 or more years of cellar sustainability. This was a great chance to see how Kamen's wines not only hold but also improve with age. This wine has not only become much more integrated but also obtained an extra dimension of complexity and this Syrah may be the best example of this Californian rarity that shines throughout in the Kaman portfolio. Besides the integration and softening of the wine's dense dark powerful structure the fruit has become much more savory. Combined with its intense minerality it showcases a very serious wine.

Syrah, 2012

Deep purple in color, this wine is inky with an opaque core and a broad pink watery rim. With an inky nose as well, it is deep and concentrated, releasing pungent complex aromas of ripe blackberries, taut black plums, cassis, raspberries, damp earth, minerals, white pepper, new vanilla oak, leather, sweet pipe tobacco, savory meat pies, and asphalt. Full-bodied and very dense in the mouth (small mountain berries) with ultra-concentrated black spicy fruits at the fore, the wine is rock solid but also smooth and sleek with an overriding mineral sheen. It is well-structured with powerful buried tannins and medium acidity that leads to a long white pepper finish. An excellent California-style Syrah with a distinct mineral quality acquired from the volcanic soils on Kamen's property. No reductive qualities noted. Maturation takes place in 50% new, select French oak barrels for sixteen months. Youthful at the moment, it will improve for at least ten years and hold for a further ten.

Grenache, 2012

Grenache grapes, sourced from a high half-acre vineyard that sits behind Robert Kamen's house, make up this unique cuvée, which had a tiny production of only about 25 cases. As a huge fan of the Grenache grape, I really took to this wine. The grapes were co-fermented with sun-dried Grenache stems. Light crimson with a wide watery rim, this is one fun wine to drink. Bright cherry fruits, raspberries, redcurrants, baking spices, well-judged vanilla oak, and orange floral notes soar from the glass. Positively sensual on the palate, the wine is expansive, bright, and ripe with mouthwatering acidity that holds up the lush Grenache fruit. With a lovely textured mouth-feel, the wine showcases bright red concentrated fruits, sassafras, spice, and sweet vanilla oak flavors. Great balance with high-ish acidity and sweet, smooth medium tannins; ends on a long mineral finish. Drinking well now, this will become more liquor-like over the next ten years.

Writers Block, 2011

A small batch of 250 cases of this 50% Syrah, 30% Cabernet Sauvignon, and 20% Petite Sirah blend make up this always impressive "proprietary blend." Made from the very cool vintage of 2010, style-wise it is quite Bordeaux-like. Highly aromatic with ripe blackberry, raspberry, dark cherries, restrained new oak, minerals, and an interesting savory note on the nose. On the medium-bodied palate the Cabernet plants the rich classic cassis flavors of the varietal whilst the two Syrahs shine through, filling out the mid-palate and adding a spicy element of varietal character. Medium-ripeness and high acidity due to the cold vintage conditions make this a very approachable wine that pairs especially well with food. Available through the wine club only.

Kashmir Cuvée Cabernet Sauvignon, 2008

To me, this garnet-hued wine boasted an array of oriental or Indian spice box aromas (hence, I suppose, the name). Powerful and floral, the wine is produced from select lots and then blended. Kashmir explodes on the palate with a velvety texture and is layered with notes of blackberry, currants, sweet oak, and tobacco. The wine is a seamless balance of delicacy and richness with vibrant acidity, smooth tannins, and a persistent finish.

Kashmir Cuvée Cabernet Sauvignon, 2010

Kamen's flagship wine has always been impressive and in great vintages can be as exotic as its name. The cool 2010 vintage has tamed the usually massively scaled proportions of this wine on the palate. I found the nose much more complex than usual. It is still a large-scaled wine with a saturated inky purple robe leading to a very expressive and complex bouquet of slick black cherry fruits, cassis, pencil lead, iron, tobacco, linseed oil, suede, chocolate violets, crushed rocks, and graphite, plus a unique, exotic, Moroccan spice box nuance. One of the best Californian 2010's that I've tasted, I actually prefer that it's not as flamboyant as the ultra-ripe vintages such as the '09. Great delineation on the palate, there's no disputing it is still definitely rich and powerful, but displays terrific elegance due to the vintage. Smooth and mineral-laden with fine-grained tannins, it's full-bodied and contains excellent acidity that lifts the fruit to a long liquid rock finish with lingering vanilla notes. Superb with food.

Silverado
VINEYARDS

2009

ESTATE GROWN

Cabernet Sauvignon

Napa Valley

ALC 14.5% BY VOL

Lillian Disney,
Ron and Diane Disney Miller

SILVERADO VINEYARDS

Napa

Anything But Mickey Mouse

Lillian Disney, the widow of Mickey's creator, along with her daughter and son-in-law, Diane and Ron Miller, founded Napa's famous Silverado Vineyards in 1981. They chose not to use their well-known name to sell their wines. And, honestly, their wine is so wonderful that it does not need a celebrity endorsement. This is wine that stands alone and stands apart. After several visits, Silverado easily proved to be the most impressive of all the estates we toured, especially in terms of modernization and innovation. It was apparent upon entering the grounds that it is a well-funded operation, designed and built to make serious wines that could compete with any other Napa winery and on an international level.

We arrived at the Silverado Winery on a cold and rainy February morning. (It never rains in California, *except* when it pours, to paraphrase the Mamas and the Papas.) Driving up a winding road, we admired the beautiful pale yellow building that seemed to combine old world charm, gracious living, and contemporary efficiency in one immaculate design. Inside, the airy tasting room boasted an extensive wooden

Sharon, Diane, Walt, and Lillian Disney aboard the *Queen Mary*, circa 1950s.

bar and a breathtaking view of the valley vineyard. Vines as far as the eye could see! Huge glass windows and French doors flooded the room with natural light, even on that overcast day. Simple yet elegant furnishings included comfortable chairs, a silver tea service, and tables overflowing with gorgeous coffee table books and assorted upscale accessories for the

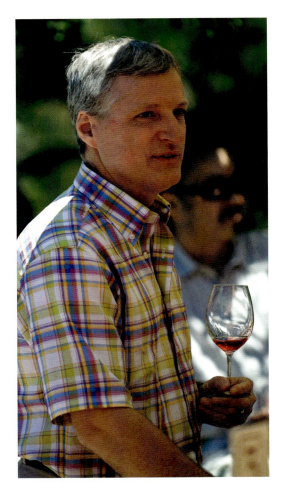

Russ Weis has been the general manager of Silverado since 2004.

wine lover. Everything about the place was inviting and well considered. Obviously, a great deal of thought and care went into the design and the upkeep of this place.

We introduced ourselves to the tasting room staff, including one woman with exceptionally white teeth who welcomed us with her high wattage smile. The general manager,

Russell Weis, was called and, within minutes, came down from his office to talk with us. A dapper man, movie-star handsome with sparkling blue eyes, Russell took us into an elegant private room and set up an extensive tasting of the best that Silverado had to offer. Few other wineries in Napa or Sonoma were quite so generous with their time, or made us feel so welcome.

A Bold Adventure in Napa

Although Silverado has the look and feel of a winery that has been around for centuries, it is actually quite new (at least in wine years!). We were fascinated to learn the history of this remarkable establishment. Anyone who has ever dreamed of starting a winery of their own (including us) would surely want their story to read as follows…

The Disney/Miller adventure into winemaking started in 1975 when Diane and Lillian visited the Napa Valley on a day trip from Los Angeles to look at two wineries that were for sale. At the time, Napa was just hitting the headlines as one of the up and coming wine regions in the world and the two women were contemplating the idea of investing in the wine business.

They toured various properties but returned home thinking that the most sensible way to proceed would be to find vineyard land as an investment rather than purchase a whole winery. They especially liked what they saw in the Stags' Leap district of Napa, finding it not only suitable as vineyard land but a particularly lovely place to perhaps live sometime in the future.

In 1976, a 90-acre vineyard owned by a man

named Harry See came up for sale in the Stags Leap district and the Disney/Millers learned that the property promised to be fantastic for growing grapes. "It was a beautiful property," writes Diane Miller. "The Napa River was the western boundary, the Silverado trail on the east. See's home was quite wonderful … a very masculine California ranch style, with heavy beams and lots of glass. A flattened pad on top of a small hill on the property was where See planned to build his winery. We made an offer, and it was accepted. During escrow, however, he changed his mind."

Terribly disappointed, the buyers soon learned that See's niece, who lived across the river from her uncle, was thinking of selling her property. She owned 80 acres that were already planted with Chardonnay and Gewürztraminer grapes. It also offered a charming old home where the niece had lived with her family. Ron Miller inspected the land and an offer was soon made. They quickly agreed upon a selling price. Then, in a strange twist of fate, Harry See's property was put back on the market. Without hesitation the Disney/Millers snapped it up as well, and combined the two parcels into one. "It was a bold investment," admits Diane, adding, "We've never regretted it."

Over the next few years the estate sold grapes, Chardonnay in particular, to Chardonnay specialist Mike Grgich of Grgich Winery. They also slowly replanted the vineyards with different varieties, especially Cabernet. This would prove to be a prescient decision as, over the next few years, the Stags Leap District became world-famous for Cabernet Sauvignon.

Richard Keith was the architect who designed Silverado.

From Growing Grapes to Making Wine

In 1981, the family decided to build a winery. "We chose Richard Keith as our architect," explains Diane Miller. "It would be built on the site that See had chosen." They also began looking for a winemaker. One day a young man named Jack Stuart called the architect from a pay phone during his lunch break. He was a winemaker and he wanted a job. The family agreed to meet with Stuart and ultimately liked his enthusiasm and confidence. He proved to be a brilliant choice as winemaker. "Jack made beautiful wine for us," according to Diane. "He'd actually picked some of the Gewürztraminer before it was ripped out and made some in his basement before the winery was built. It was lovely. We really enjoyed those few bottles." In addition to becoming the winemaker at Silverado (where he would remain until he retired in 2004), Stuart also agreed to take on the extra duties of general manager. In those days, the family was still living in Southern California, so having a GM on site was important to the operation. It would be a few more years before the family moved permanently to the Napa Valley.

Considerable deliberation went into naming the winery. The idea of naming it after a variation on the name Disney was contemplated. The Disney name was of French heritage, coming from Robert d'Isigny, originally De Isigney, meaning "from Isigney," a small village near Bayeux, in Normandy. (The Disney family had settled in England with William the Conqueror in 1066.)

Ultimately, the family decided on "Silverado," the original name of the vineyard. The name comes from the "Silverado Trail," which winds through the entire valley, starting in Napa and ending in the hills above Calistoga, at the mining ghost town of Silverado. It was also in the title of Robert Louis Stevenson's famous 1883 novel, *The Silverado Squatters*. The Disney/Millers would soon discover the truth of Stevenson's oft quoted line: "The beginning of vine planting is like the beginning of mining for precious metals: the winegrower also 'prospects.'"

Prospecting for Vineyards

Soon after committing to the winery, Diane and Ron Miller began searching for new vineyards to purchase. They looked at existing vineyards and uncultivated land, trying to figure out which would best serve Silverado. "We eventually wound up purchasing historic vineyard sites that needed redeveloping," explains Diane. "We acquired the Mount George property in 1988, which is now completely planted to red grapes, Cabernet Sauvignon, and Merlot, with small amounts of Cabernet Franc and, more recently, Malbec. In 1988, we also purchased the Carneros property that we now call 'Firetree,' which was partially planted to Chardonnay and we added more. Then in 1992, we purchased the beautiful Soda Creek property, which we planted to Sangiovese, Zinfandel, and later added Sauvignon Blanc. The olive trees on that property are the source of the oil we offer for sale. Another Carneros property, our Vineburg Vineyard, is our more recent and maybe final acquisition and is the source of our best Chardonnay."

Because the property itself is so diverse with various designated vineyards growing multiple varieties of grapes, Silverado produces a portfolio of many different red and white

The Miller family with matriarch Diane standing front row center (wearing a brown belt).
OVERLEAF: A view of one of Silverados's many vineyards.

wines. The individual cuvées are well scaled, ranging from easygoing to very serious and quite age-worthy. All are impeccably crafted and quintessentially modern-styled examples of Napa County winemaking. The philosophy is quality over quantity, with a marked emphasis on ripeness and balance. The six vineyards owned by Silverado are located in some of the best Napa growing areas, including the prestigious Stags' Leap AVA. Each bottling or cuvée is selected to present the best of what its individual terroir has to offer style-wise.

The Stags' Leap Vineyard is planted with Cabernet and Merlot (it's also planted with a California Heritage Clone of Cabernet, Silverado's very own UCD30 clone, one of only three Cabernets in California to be given this distinction). Miller Ranch, a mile or so south

from Yountville, is cooler and perfect for the production of white varieties such as Sauvignon Blanc and Semillon. The deep, gravelly down-slopes of an ancient volcano named Mt. George provide the vineyard of the same name with ideal conditions to grow Merlot.

Sparkling and Immaculate

From the spotless tasting room that overlooks the estate's sprawling vineyards, through the shiny new winemaking equipment, to the immaculately presented staff, the estate assumes the look and feel of a vast viticulture wonderland. To Disney fans, it might even seem like a castle that Walt himself would have created for one of his movies.

Silverado really benefits from the Disney/

Miller connection in terms of resources. Unlike some of the struggling wineries we've encountered, at Silverado there is almost no limit to what can be accomplished. "Our ability to take risks is phenomenal," says manager Russell Weis. "We not only have a family that is pushing us philosophically, but also have the means to go where we want to go and take some risks as we look for the ultimate in wine quality." The estate benefits from state-of-the-art equipment, which includes an electronic sorting machine that takes a detailed reading of every individual grape as it drops through the sorter. The machine can determine everything from the berry size to the skin's ripeness and surface smoothness. In a nanosecond, the machine uses the winemaker's input to decide what optimal fruit stays and what grapes it will blow onto the discard conveyer using its micro air jets.

Outside in the vineyards, Silverado uses another modern (albeit expensive) machine for harvesting specific vineyard blocks. With 1,100 tons of fruit at harvest time, it is not always possible to have the right amount of vineyard workers at just the right moment for optimal picking. So, using the machine avoids compromising quality. This high-tech version of a harvester travels above the vine, hugging each side. It then vibrates quickly and sucks only the ripe grapes off the vine onto dry ice, leaving the unripe fruit behind. It works so well that Weis considers it comparable to handpicking.

Also, the vineyards are illuminated at night so grapes can be picked after nightfall to retain natural acids and prevent oxidation. Special UV light machines are utilized in the winery to thwart TCA bacterial infections and the estate even has its own bottling line, a luxury for a winery its size.

The vineyards range from six degrees up to fifteen degrees of slope, making them well drained, ideal for producing small berries in the grape cluster so important for intense flavor. The Cabernet blocks are western facing with great exposure to the late afternoon sun, but really benefit from the diurnal temperature shifts that help the grapes retain their natural acidity. The soils are mainly rocky, with clay on the valley floor.

The whites are very competently made and released under screw caps, but it's the Cabernet

Map detailing the five plots of land that comprise Silverado vineyards in Napa.

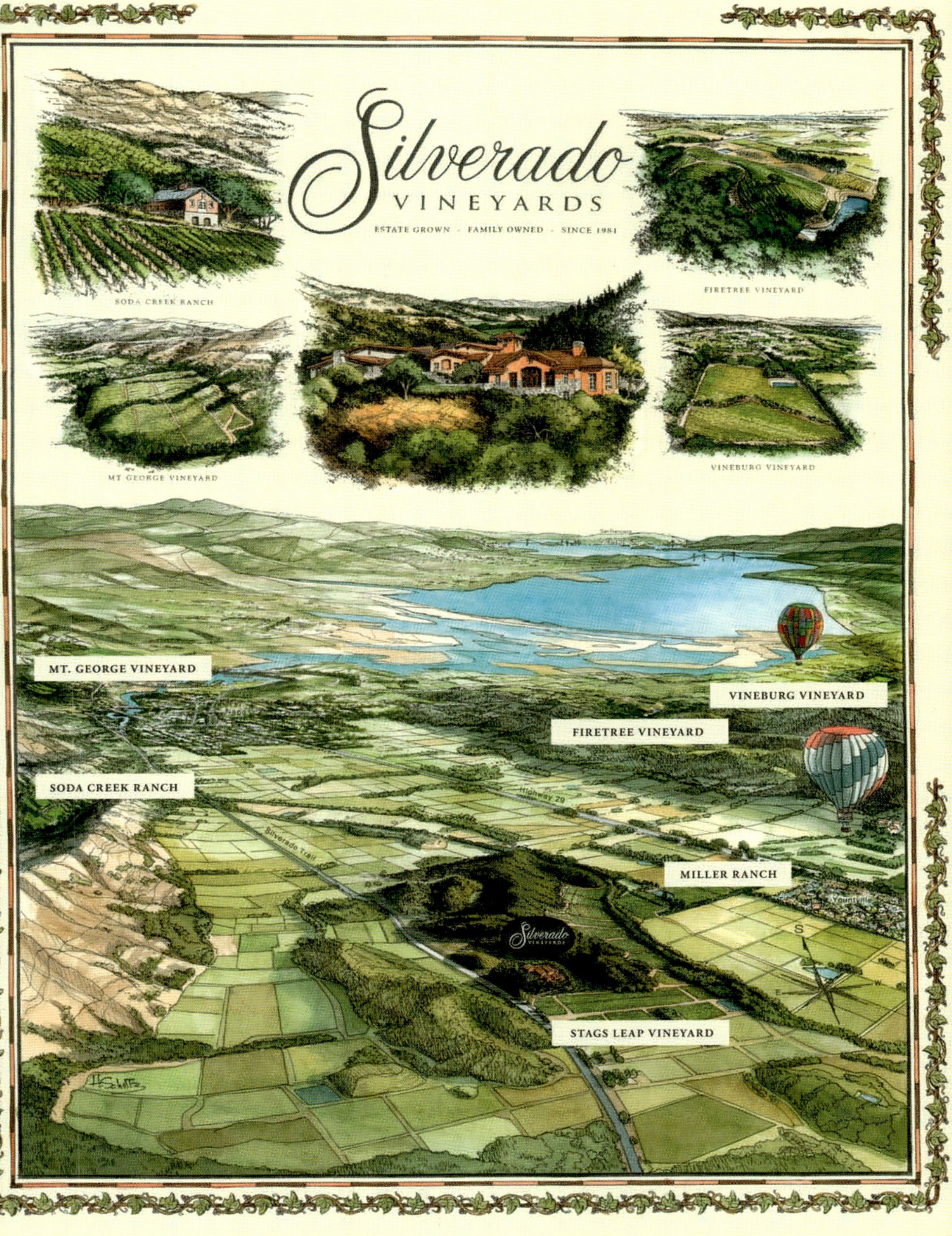
Silverado
VINEYARDS
ESTATE GROWN · FAMILY OWNED · SINCE 1981
SODA CREEK RANCH
FIRETREE VINEYARD
MT GEORGE VINEYARD
VINEBURG VINEYARD
MT. GEORGE VINEYARD
VINEBURG VINEYARD
FIRETREE VINEYARD
SODA CREEK RANCH
Highway 29
Silverado Trail
MILLER RANCH
Yountville
STAGS LEAP VINEYARD

Sauvignons upon which Silverado has really built its reputation.

How much is the family involved with the winemaking? "If I had to boil it down," says Weis, "they (the family) want a refreshing style of wine and for that we really require good levels of acidity. They set the tone for the feel and style they want to achieve." But do they actually get their hands dirty? "Oh, they are very involved," Weis insists. "They are always in the vineyards and we all get together twice a year with the whole family to see where we are."

The Legacy of Diane Disney Miller

When we wrote the first edition of *Celebrity Vineyards*, Silverado was one of our favorite wineries. We were dazzled by the elegance and unique style of their amazing tasting room and surrounding vineyards. The innovations were astounding and the wine was magnificent. Here was a stellar example of the very best in world-class refinement and modern technology that Napa has to offer.

We became good friends with general man-ager Russ Weis, who, from the very first, gave us his full attention and generously shared his enormous knowledge of wine and winemaking. We returned a few times and Russ even helped us with several tastings and events to promote the book when it was published. From the very first, Russ made it clear that almost every-thing special about Silverado came from Diane Disney Miller and his admiration for her was obvious.

Thus, when we returned to Silverado in 2015, it was with great sadness that we learned of the untimely death of Mrs. Miller, who suf-fered a fall in September of 2013 at her home in Napa and died three months later. Her pass-ing had a huge impact on the winery and on everyone who worked with and was inspired by her.

But somehow life goes on and Silverado continues to thrive, thanks in large measure to the legacy of Mrs. Miller. Russ was particularly excited to share GEO with us, a wine that is dedicated to the memory of Diane Disney Mill-er. It is quite an amazing wine and we think she would be very proud.

PORTFOLIO

The wines made at Silverado are unabashedly Californian in style, exuding ripe, concentrated levels of chunky black fruits while also retaining excellent balance between fruit, tannin, and acidity that gives the portfolio a literally refreshing feel. According to Weis, Silverado has always had a higher-acidic, more elegant style of wine.

The estate also has a number of unique bottlings and we think these cuvées are among the most interesting that Silverado has to offer. They can be single vineyard offerings, weird blends, rosés, or whatever takes their fancy depending on the vintage conditions of the year. All the wines, red or white, are suitably concentrated and all present a precise, clean, and fresh attitude towards winemaking. "We're very lucky," Weis concluded, "We have a family who absolutely loves wines and has serious focus."

When Silverado produces a Limited Cabernet Sauvignon, it has to be special. In the 1980s they only made two. In the 1990s (a good decade for red), they made seven. So far, in the 2000s they have made four. Vintage-driven, individual barrel selected, highly structured, and texturally rich, the Limited is the best of the best of the cellar. In 1993, the 1990 vintage of the Cabernet Sauvignon Limited Reserve was named the No. 3 wine on *Wine Spectator*'s Top 100 List. Rated 97 points, it was also the No. 1 Cabernet of the year in their annual Cabernet issue.

NICK'S TASTING NOTES

Cabernet Sauvignon Limited

Sleek and dark, medium-bodied with flavors of black cherries, plums, and bitter dark chocolate wrapped in sweet vanilla oak. Clean on both the nose and palate, it has a great balance of acidity to fruit. Smooth, rich mouth-feel with medium fine-grained sweet tannins and a touch of mineral; this is a serious wine. Long in the mouth and very drinkable.

SOLO Cabernet Sauvignon, 2009

Very dark color, almost opaque black. Bold solid nose of super-ripe plums, black cherries, pencil lead, earth, herbs, chocolate, and sweet vanilla. Very powerful, dense, and rich in the mouth, with a silky feel despite the high levels of extraction. Full-bodied and quite tannic (but fine-grained sweet tannin) with layer upon layer of fruit and a touch of umami on the long-textured finish. Good aging potential over the next ten years.

Sauvignon Blanc, Miller Ranch, 2013

Created from 96% Sauvignon Blanc grapes and 4% Semillon Blanc grapes that are grown high up on Silverado's Miller Ranch vineyard. Enjoying cool mornings and warm afternoons, the vineyard's grapes are imbued with good levels of natural acidity. It's pale lemon and youthful in color with an un-oaked bouquet that releases pure, vibrant, fruity aromas of white stone fruits, green apples, grapefruit, lime, and tangerine, plus a hint of mineral. Revealing a more tropical than herbaceous Sauvignon style, the wine is dry, yet also very ripe and juicy, giving it a silky, clean impression on the tongue. This light- to medium-bodied wine effortlessly glides over the palate with excellent levels of natural acidity. Elegantly lifting the fruit, it provides a long finish. Excellent quality, totally Californian in style, it's extremely drinkable, yet also a serious, consciously well-made wine that one could enjoy all day.

Chardonnay, Vineberg Vineyard, 2012

A lovely single vineyard Chardonnay from a very cool vineyard, this wine is pale gold and presents lively aromas of ripe Golden Delicious apples, white flowers, apricots, and citrus fruits. Clean, ripe, and pure in style, it is sleek and medium-bodied with unobtrusive oak and concentrated citrus and pear fruits. The lively acidity cleanses the palate on the way to a long and pleasing finish of star fruits and lemon flavors. Lithe, finer, and less obviously flamboyant than the Reserve Chardonnay, this wine possesses an overt European influence with a more mineral character.

Merlot, Mt George Vineyard, 2011

Besides being a high altitude site, situated in the foothills of an ancient volcano, Silverado's Mount George Vineyard lies on deep, gravelly slopes that are particularly well suited to growing the Merlot grape. This grape requires good drainage to achieve the optimal level of ripeness needed to create its signature plush texture and lush mouth-feel. At 100% Merlot, this wine displays a hearty crimson color and reveals powerful aromas of black cherries, black plums, and cassis, with restrained scents of vanilla oak and glimpses of such herbs as rosemary and mint. Though youthful, this wine is nonetheless beautifully balanced. Plump and fleshy in the mouth yet not at all thick or overdone, it is just about full-bodied with excellent levels of fresh acidity and fine strong tannins that provide structure. Good depth and purity, with concentrated black cherry and black plum flavors backed by earth and spice notes, this Merlot is finer and higher toned than the "Estate" Cabernet, revealing more elegance; it's velvety, svelte, and smooth, with a long chocolate-tinged finish. The wine will soften and become deeper with extended bottle age.

Cabernet Sauvignon, Estate Grown, 2009

Created from 94% Cabernet Sauvignon grapes and 6% Petit Verdot grapes this wine is an aged dark crimson color and reveals deep classic Cabernet fruit aromas of cassis, wild blackberries, and black cherry, plus notes of spice, mint, and damp earth. Because of the altitude of the vineyard, the wine possesses excellent uplifting acidity on the palate that definitely helps it age well structurally. The wine's medium-bodied palate has really filled out and deepened, giving it a rich and smooth mouth-feel. Aged with integrated tannins and a mild hint of new oak, the wine has gained deep aged nuances of dark chocolate, tobacco, pencil lead, and cedar. The tannins have become totally integrated and are now smooth and sweet. This wine has matured excellently, becoming a classic elegant Cabernet with a long lingering finish. Drinking well now.

GEO Cabernet Sauvignon, 2011

Here is a new cuvée that perfectly demonstrates the different styles of wine the Cabernet grape can produce through its terroir. The GEO makes a perfect counterpart to the SOLO's ultra-rich chocolate opulence and taps into a more mineral, red-fruit-driven style. Metaphorically speaking, the GEO could be considered the female counterpart to the SOLO's obvious masculinity. Very deep crimson in color, the wine's bouquet soars from the glass, releasing complex aromas of mineral-backed red and black fruits, red cherries, raspberries, and red currants slathered in sweet new oak, while a spine of black cherry provides a streak of structure. It's a very stylish wine containing excellent levels of concentration paired with powerful, fine, youthful tannins and well-balanced acidity. The wine is broad and ripe in the mouth, coating the palate with swaths of bright red and black fruits, sweet vanilla oak, minerals, and a touch of chocolate. Less obviously oaked than the SOLO and sourced from a high altitude vineyard, this wine is about pairing power with elegance. Achieving two very different dynamic examples of what can be done with Cabernet Sauvignon grapes grown in Napa adds an extra dimension and seriousness to Silverado's ambition to be ranked among the best in California. This wine was created in memory of the late Diane Disney Miller, considered by everyone who knew her to be the heart and soul of Silverado.

SOLO Cabernet Sauvignon, 2011

Darker in color and richer on the palate than the GEO, the SOLO is unabashedly Stags Leap. Powerful, lush, and dense it's much more full-bodied and lavishly oaked than the GEO, showcasing a black fruit profile and a richer depth of fruit. Full-bodied and silky with strong flavors of black cherries, cassis, and raspberries coated in dark chocolate, along with notes of coffee, licorice, vanilla, toast, and a strong nuance of bay leaf. Similar to all the Silverado wines, it reveals an excellent level of freshness and overall is quite elegant and Bordeaux-like, especially compared to many of their neighbors. If the GEO is very Left Bank in style, then the SOLO is definitely Right Bank, yet unbelievably 100% Cabernet. With excellent underlying structure, big-boned tannins, and good acidity, this is one of the few wines in the area that not only holds up but improves with bottle age and retains consistently excellent quality regardless of vintage conditions.

INGLENOOK

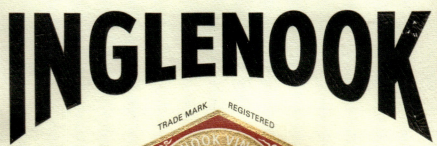

TRADE MARK   REGISTERED

NAPA VALLEY
RUTHERFORD
CALIFORNIA

2009

Rubicon

ESTATE BOTTLED

GROWN & PRODUCED BY INGLENOOK, RUTHERFORD, NAPA VALLEY, CALIFORNIA, U.S.A.

Francis Ford Coppola

INGLENOOK

Rutherford

The Godfather of California Wine

Francis Ford Coppola is certainly one of the most famous celebrities turned vintners in California, if not the world. An admired and controversial filmmaker, Coppola has won Oscars for writing *Patton* (1970) and *The Godfather* (1972), as well as three Oscars for *The Godfather, Part 2* (1974). His seminal films include *The Conversation* (1974) and *Apocalypse Now* (1979), among many others. As a vintner, Coppola's record is no less impressive; his extensive portfolio of California wines is distributed around the world.

According to Coppola, there is a strong connection between filmmaking and winemaking. "Winemaking and filmmaking are two great art forms that are very important in the development of California," he says. "They both start with raw ingredients—in the case of wine, the land and the grapes, and in the case of film, the script and the actors' performances. The winemaker takes these raw materials, ferments, blends, and creates. He says yes to one batch, no to another. The director does the same thing: a series of yes's and no's, from casting and costuming to edits and sound mixes. In both cases you have to start with top-notch raw materials—whether it's the land or a script."

Lights, Camera, Grapes!

Coppola makes films in Hollywood, but his wine is produced in the heart of Napa. The day we set out to find his vineyard in March of 2011, it was raining so hard that water streamed down the road in lapping waves. Totally blinded by the downpour and aquaplaning around corners, we cautiously pulled over to the side of the road. Just within sight and striking distance was Coppola's famous Rubicon Estate—as it was then known (in the

Publicity still from Coppola's 1997 film, *The Rainmaker*, based on John Grisham's best-selling novel.

summer of 2011, it was forever rechristened "Inglenook," it's original name). Encircled by perfectly manicured vineyards, the almost Disneyesque architecture boasts towers, pergolas, and an over-the-top Roman fountain that was spouting water despite the downpour. It was hard to believe this eccentric looking building once belonged to Gustave Nybom (later Niebaum), the rugged pioneer of Californian winemaking. Dodging the torrents of water that formed puddles in the parking lot, we dashed through the enormous, castle-like wooden doors that serve as the visitor entrance.

Winery or Movie Set?

The décor inside the castle was unlike any of the other innumerable wineries we've visited. The ornate and cavernous space resembled a movie set with plush, blood-red carpeting, crimson wallpaper, and highly polished wood. Examples of the estate's historical winemaking equipment are on view along with an ancient wine cellar of dusty bottles. A grand staircase leads to the upstairs museum. Even on that

The front door to the tasting room and the water fountain in front of the building.

The grand stairway and a detail from the elaborately decorated tasting room.

rainy, off-season day, the place was packed with visitors who all seemed eager to sign up for a pricy tour.

The well-tailored staff was on hand to arrange tours, tastings, and historical explorations of the estate. With careful individual pricing of all the activities, a trip to this vineyard can become quite expensive, as we later discovered for ourselves. Besides the massive gift shop selling everything Coppola, from books and films to clothing and cigars, there are two tasting rooms. One offers the basic cuvées from the main wine portfolio, while the other, more exclusive (meaning twice as expensive), room offers pours of their Estate Reserve wines from behind imposing wrought iron gates.

Coppola has art-directed this tourist haven into an entertaining combination of film set, museum, and winery. Yet hiding behind this over-the-top pomp and grandeur is one of Napa's most famous jewels—the Rubicon.

The Wrong Direction

A likable and accommodating neighbor, Coppola remains a popular—if ambitious—figure in Northern California wine country. While his filmmaking efforts have been dogged over the years by funding issues and occasionally a less than enthusiastic response from the public, these are not problems he has with his winemaking. Coppola's wines are popular, successful, and widely distributed throughout the world, from England to Australia. In fact, in the last few years Coppola has had to ramp up production to meet demand. His vast portfolio has grown even larger with new wines from Sonoma County. At the beginning of 2006, the director purchased the once highly admired Chateau Souverain in Sonoma's Alexander Valley.

Critics might think this acquisition is merely another moneymaking maneuver to expand into competent but rarely exciting lower-priced wines. However, according to the director, the real reason is quite the opposite. Over the previous few years Coppola had witnessed for himself the transformation of the Rubicon Estate from symbol to caricature and he didn't like the direction. "I never intended to have a Hollywood museum at what I still call Inglenook,"

he told *Wine Spectator* in 2006. He was also rightly concerned about the vast, complicated, and sometimes bewildering portfolio he'd built, with a price range that started at $30 for basic wines and then jumped to $145 for the Rubicon. The lesser wines were starting to take over the portfolio and the image and reputation of the unique estate wines, in particular the Rubicon, suffered from the consolidation.

The Chateau Souverain acquisition helped solve this problem. The new Sonoma winery, known as the Francis Ford Coppola Winery, now handles the lesser cuvées for the general public. To bring a more serious feel and ramp up the quality of the estate wines, Coppola scored a very public coup by prizing away one of the main winemakers at Chateau Margaux in Bordeaux.

Cabernet casks of wine in the Coppola cellars.

Born into Winemaking

In 1939, in Detroit, Francis Ford was born into a creative and supportive family environment; his father, Carmine, was a composer and musician, and his mother was an actress. The family moved to New York when Carmine became first flautist for the NBC Symphony Orchestra; they settled in Woodside, Queens. Growing up, Coppola was a self-confessed "lonely kid." At the age of eight, a bout of polio confined him to bed for a year, during which he spent his time studying science. "I was terrible at math, but I could grasp science," he says. "I used to love reading about the lives of the scientists. I wanted to be a scientist or an inventor." Instead, he discovered the screenplay for *A Streetcar Named Desire* and began making 8mm home movies. Though he had talent as a musician, he studied theater arts at Hofstra University, where he later decided to switch to filmmaking. He moved to California to attend UCLA, eventually going to work for Roger Corman, a job that would launch his filmmaking career.

By the early 1970s, he'd reached the pinnacle of success with his first *Godfather* movie and finally had the financial resources to buy property in Northern California's wine country. He had always had an affinity for wine. Growing up Italian meant that as a child his European parents allowed him a little wine mixed with water (although Coppola preferred adding ginger ale). They called wine at that level plain *rosso* and *bianco* (which, not coincidentally, are also the names of the current entry-level wines made at his Sonoma winery). But it was not until 1975, when he was 36 years old, that he was able to purchase the former home and adjacent vineyard of Gustave Niebaum.

Gustave Niebaum and the Inglenook Vineyard

Gustave Niebaum was born in Oulu, Finland, in 1842. After attending maritime school in Helsinki, he was commissioned by the Nautical Institute to map Alaska's coast. By the end of the 1860s, he was the world's leading fur trader. He was appointed Consul of Russia in the United States in 1867, and helped promote the purchase of Alaska. He married well and lived in San Francisco. Highly educated and cultured— he spoke five languages—he was interested in the wines of Bordeaux and decided to create a vineyard that could compete with, and indeed one day surpass, his favorite European wines.

He discovered the Inglenook vineyard in Rutherford. Originally planted by bank manager William C. Watson in 1871, its

A 23-year-old Coppola, a student at UCLA, won a $2000 first prize in a creative screenwriting contest and is given a check by producer Sam Goldwyn, May 10, 1962.

Coppola directs John Cazale (Fredo), Marlon Brando (Don Corleone), and Richard Conte (Barzini) on the set of *The Godfather*, 1972.

name was derived from a Scottish expression meaning "Cozy Corner." In 1880, Niebaum (who had by then Americanized the spelling of his name) finalized the purchase of the 78-acre Inglenook Estate, plus an additional 124 acres of nearby farmland, for $48,000. He took to the task of winemaking with uncommon zeal. He understood the demands of climate, aspect, and soil in growing successful grapes and is considered the forefather of what we nowadays call "terroir" in California. He bought vineyards, planted the same Cabernet Sauvignon and Chardonnay grapes being grown in Bordeaux, and built a winery designed by architect William Mooser that

was considered futuristic at the time. (In many respects Niebaum was well ahead of his time: in 1883 he began a six-year battle with the Board of State Viticulture commissioners to work out a plan to combat the devastating Phylloxera root louse, a problem that continues to this day.)

Inglenook's first vintage under Niebaum produced 80,000 gallons of wine. His was the first Bordeaux-style winery in the United States and soon, to increase production, he purchased another 712 acres of surrounding vineyards. Within ten years, Niebaum's wines were world-renowned, even winning gold medals in the World's Fair in Paris in 1889.

Engraving of the original Inglenook vineyards in Napa, California.
Portrait of Gustave Niebaum, proprietor (1842–1908).

After he died in 1908, all winemaking ceased for three years at Inglenook. Then, in 1911, Niebaum's wife took charge and revamped the estate, hiring Benjamin Arnhold, a well-respected winemaker, to run the winery operation.

"Pride Not Profits"

In 1919, Prohibition arrived in the United States and production at Inglenook ceased until 1933 when Carl Bundschu (who would later run his own famous winery) supervised the winemaking. When Mrs. Niebaum died in 1937, ownership went to her nephew, John Daniel, Jr., who would tolerate absolutely no compromise in the quality of the wine. His motto was "pride not profits" and he often refused to bottle vintages or vats that didn't meet his standards.

The wines under his stewardship have historically been considered the best ever produced from the estate. (The 1941 Inglenook Cabernet Sauvignon was rated a perfect 100 points by *Wine Spectator* in 1990 and named one of the top wines of the century.) Unfortunately, Daniel's admirable aggressiveness got the better of both him and the estate. Profits dropped drastically and in 1964 the conglomerate Allied Grape Growers bought the Inglenook brand name, the chateau, and 94 acres from Daniel, who barely managed to keep the mansion and 1,500 acres of vineyards.

Just before Daniel died in 1970, the estate once again changed hands when Heublein Incorporated purchased a majority interest from Allied Grape Growers. The quality of the wine sank ever further and the property was marginalized.

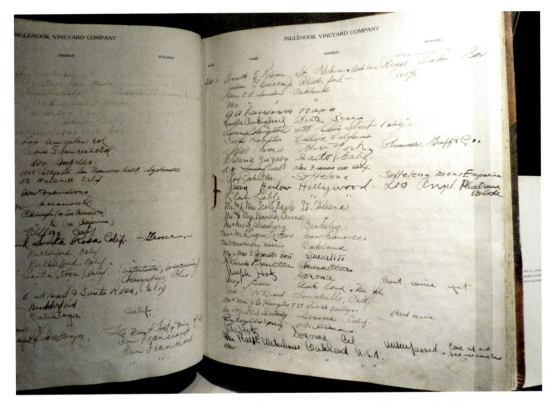

On display are the signatures of Jean Harlow and Clark Gable from an old guest book of the winery.

The Move to Rutherford

In 1975, Coppola and his wife Eleanor bid on the Niebaum Estate. For reasons that no one could explain, big companies like Seagram and established winemakers such as Mondavi had passed on the opportunity to buy the property—or even test the land for suitability. Eventually, 1,560 acres of the estate were sold to the Coppolas. In the French tradition the new owners linked their name with Niebaum's and created the Niebaum-Coppola Winery.

The Coppolas had purchased the land to make a family home, not start a massive winery. They planned to grow a couple of acres of vines to produce a small number of bottles, using the ancient foot-crushing method of Coppola's grandfather. "I could pretend I was my grandfather," the director once said. With this in mind, he planted some vines, which produced about four barrels of wine in 1977. The family came together to stomp the grapes barefooted, a tradition still celebrated at the estate when the Coppolas invite the neighbors, do a stomp, and then drink the wine at a big annual harvest party.

Roman, Eleanor, Francis, and Sofia Coppola in Rome
for the premiere of *Youth Without Youth*, directed
by Francis Ford Coppola, 2007.

Searching for something a bit more sophisticated, Coppola tried to hire winemaker André Tchelistcheff, a Russian émigré who'd arrived in Napa in 1937 and is considered the father of modern day winemaking in California. (He famously coined the term "Rutherford Dust" as a taste description for the wines from the area.) Coppola was smitten with Tchelistcheff's European vision of traditional Bordeaux-styled wines made in California. Eventually, after some minor difficulties (Coppola had to borrow the money to pay Tchelistcheff and rent the winemaking equipment), Coppola persuaded the modest vintner to join the estate.

Tchelistcheff stayed with Niebaum-Coppola until 1990 and is considered the innovator of the Rubicon, the now famous Cabernet Sauvignon Bordeaux blend that became the estate's flagship wine. First produced with Tchelistcheff in 1978, the wine would become the gold standard for quality California Cabernet Sauvignon in the '70s and '80s. Today the 1979 vintage fetches $500 a bottle.

In 1990 Coppola had the estate's grapes genetically tested, establishing that they are the

A 2000 print ad for Robert Mondavi wines,
featuring an endorsement by Coppola.

original vines Gustave Niebaum brought back from France in the 1880s. This clone is now patented as Rubicon Estate Heritage Clone #29. At present, Inglenook has 2,000 acres of certified organic vines and now concentrates exclusively on the estate-grown wines that consist of the Cask Cabernet, Blancaneaux, Edizione Pennino, RC Reserve, and, of course, the Rubicon.

Financial Dilemmas

A lot of press was given to the financial crisis that plagued Coppola in the late 1970s, midway through production of *Apocalypse Now* in the Philippines. Coppola was forced to mortgage the estate to raise the $25 million he needed to keep the project afloat. Then, when the winery was having financial difficulties in the 1980s, the proceeds from the last film in the trilogy, *Godfather III*, helped save it. In 1995, money from *Bram Stoker's Dracula* allowed Coppola to buy the remaining Inglenook vineyards. In 2002, he built on the original winery site, enlarging and improving the property.

In comparison, the Sonoma estate is much less serious in style, wine quality, and atmosphere. While Inglenook remains a major player in the production of quality Cabernet, the Francis Ford Coppola Winery in Sonoma is being run as a destination for fun and family games. Thus it features a pool, cabins for rent, and a movie gallery to entice the public. "I'm a movie director so I need a theme," Coppola said to James Laube, wine critic and writer for *Wine Spectator*, in 2006. "I have one philosophy about business: I've always wanted to give the public value. The theme for the Sonoma property is life. I want to create a happy Italian feeling!"

Update

When we returned to Inglenook in the spring of 2015, we discovered that the wines had improved in leaps and bounds. We learned that Coppola had been disappointed with the stylistic turn the wines had taken and wanted to revitalize the overall direction *backwards*, more toward the characteristics that originally defined the winery, including age-worthiness, site specificity, and deep-seated concentrated flavors achieved by the superb terroir.

With the introduction of Philippe Bascaule, former winemaker for Margeaux, the wines showcase a much more precise, clean winemaking style and achieve better levels of fruit concentration, structure, and complexity. Most importantly, though, the wines have newly acquired a sense of place with the Rubicon reverting back to its original name of "Inglenook" as a sign of Coppola's new desired approach.

PORTFOLIO

Coppola's vast portfolio includes easy-going cuvées of Cabernet Sauvignon, Chardonnay, Syrah, Merlot, Sauvignon Blanc, Sparkling, Bordeaux-style Blend, Viognier, White Dessert Wine, Zinfandel, Red Dessert Wine, Pinot Noir, Riesling, Petite Sirah, Alicante Bouschet, Pinot Grigio, and a Rosé. The range is simply mind-boggling and is constructed in a sort of pyramid, both of quality and typicity. Similar in style to a French appellation, each level denotes a particular style and focuses on the district in terms of category of wine. Most follow some sort of stylistic thread such as basic Chablis-styled, un-oaked Chardonnay or classic three-varietal Bordeaux.

All the cuvées, especially the new ones, are beautifully designed, with quite striking, painterly labels. The wines are made from grapes sourced all over California and blended at the Sonoma winery. We had the opportunity to sample selected wines ranging from the basic to the estate wines in a private tasting. As the portfolio is so large we have only included the estate wines that interested us. For the most part the wines were competent and densely fruited.

Blancaneaux 2008, 2009 & 2012

We were quite excited to taste the Blancaneaux, as not much is produced and it is rarely seen. It is modeled on the white wines of the South of France—particularly white Châteauneuf du Pape. Created in 1995 as a partner to Rubicon, Blancaneaux is produced each year from a mere six and a half acres. The Viognier is grown at the Saddle and Apple vineyards, where both receive great morning sun, but are fully shaded by mid-afternoon by Mt. St. John. Early vintages included small percentages of Chardonnay, but today the blend is usually 43% Roussanne, 38% Marsanne, and 19% Viognier. The wine is fermented and matured in stainless steel vats.

There were 870 cases of the 2008 made. Pale straw in color, the wine reveals a marked mineral quality and rich palate. Very perfumed on the nose, with soaring aromas of white acacia flowers, vanilla, citrus, and creamy oak, accompanied by hints of minerality and orange rind. Rich and dense, off-dry with a sweet impression and lowish acidity. Medium- to full-bodied with ripe fruit flavors of pears, lemons, and lychees melded to creamy oak. Medium-long length.

There were 1,000 cases made of the 2009. It is similar to the 2008 but with better freshness and less residual sugar; more delicate with less body. Still exhibits very low acidity but a similar floral nose with a lick of new paint. The oak is more restrained, with a medium-length finish.

The 2012: Sourced from the six-and-a-half-acre Saddle Vineyard, this white wine is a blend of Marsanne, Roussanne, and Viognier grapes. Many find this stylistically close to white Bordeaux Graves. However, for me it was more like a very concentrated, ripe, top-quality white from the Rhône (not a surprise as it uses white Rhône grapes). The wine is very pale yellow, almost watery white in color, with a warm nose that displays juicy, mouthwatering white stone fruits such as pears, citrus, peaches, and apricots enveloped in minerality. Additional complex secondary notes of orange blossom and cashmere also make an appearance. The wine is weighty in the mouth, dense with clean, fresh, concentrated white fruits as on the nose, minerals, floral accents, and a hint of ripe oranges/apricots. The wine has an excellent dense and full mid-palate that leads to a very long pear-infused finish.

The Rubicon 2007

The Rubicon is a blend of Cabernet, Merlot, Cabernet Franc, and Petit Verdot grapes. It is fashioned in a classic Left Bank Bordeaux style (a large percentage of Cabernet Sauvignon compared to the more Merlot-based wines typical of the Right Bank). The grapes are sourced from the Garden, Gio, Creek, Cask, Lower Cask, Apple, and Walnut vineyards, all of which are 100% organically farmed. The percentage of Cabernet Sauvignon in the blend has slightly increased over the years. The grapes are hand-picked, de-stemmed, and fermented in five- and six-ton Taransaud oak tanks for one to three weeks depending on the vintage. Once fermented, the wine is then put in typically 90% to 100% new 225-liter French oak barrels for an average of 28 months.

The 2007 is a great vintage boasting a very dark, red-purple color with a youthful wide rim. Great nose; it's obviously a Bordeaux blend with ripe dark currant aromas covered by a sheen of new French oak. Fantastic nuances of tobacco, leather, and fresh earth. Rich, compact, and very concentrated on the palate, this wine obviously needs some bottle age but reveals an excellent mouth-feel, with black cherry and black currant flavors sitting on a medium-bodied palate. Excellent balance of fruit to acid and the tannins are fine, ripe, and powerful. Lots of extract is harnessed in this wine, which is young but has excellent potential. Oak is well integrated and the finish is long and concentrated. Drink in ten years.

Inglenook, Rubicon, 2009 & 2011

The 2009 is a very good upgraded Cabernet Sauvignon, made from grapes grown at the front of the Inglenook Estate and comprised of 85% Cabernet Sauvignon, 12% Cabernet Franc, and 3% Merlot.

The wine shows a very dark, youthful crimson color with an opaque purple core. This is a quintessential Californian Cabernet from Rutherford. Earthy and quite briary, it reveals small black currants, cassis, and black cherries topped with vanilla and eucalyptus aromas on the nose. Full-bodied and Moorish, it reveals decadently sweet, ripe, dark flavors of black currants, cassis, fine milk chocolate, earth, and sweet vanilla oak in the mouth, with supportive acidity. The wine finishes long and plush with a whisper of red crunchy fruit on the back end. Due to very powerful tannins, this cuvée will age well in the short term and then hold for another ten years.

The 2011 is a classy and solid wine produced from a very cold vintage; shows more red fruits than usual and a slight bit of cold austerity. [Unfortunately, we were unable to taste the ripe 2012 to compare.] As in past vintages it's a deeply colored wine but more restrained than usual on both the palate and the nose due to the cold conditions of 2011. Still, it's an excellent wine releasing powerful complex aromas of black cherries, cassis, small black currants, briar, red cherries, coffee beans, dark chocolate, vanilla, leather, and a distinct dusty (Rutherford Dust) note.

The palate is medium-bodied, sleek, and concentrated with lashings of new vanilla oak (22 months new French oak) coating the almost malty black and red fruit flavors. The acidity is high; the wine is well delineated and structured with powerful tannins for the future.

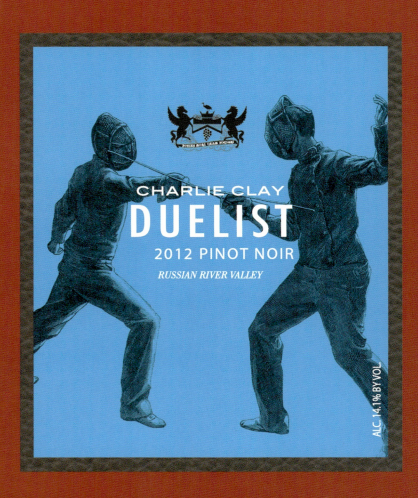

CHARLIE CLAY
DUELIST
2012 PINOT NOIR
RUSSIAN RIVER VALLEY

ALC. 14.1% BY VOL

Charlie Palmer

CHARLIE CLAY WINES

Healdsburg

Come North and Make Your Own Wine

Northern California—particularly the regions of Napa and Sonoma—is far removed from the typical European winemaking districts, even compared to the more famous, but still very gray, industrial regions of Bordeaux and Champagne. Very few people have ever settled in Champagne as an ideal place to live. In contrast, California is not only an awesome place for winemaking, it is also a drop-dead gorgeous and very much in demand area to both visit and live. The combination of consistently excellent weather, immense beauty, wealth, gastronomic innovation, and superb growing conditions for grapes has enabled California to emerge and develop differently than any other winegrowing area we've ever visited.

If there is one region in the world that can indulge the part-time vintner, it is Northern California. Here the amateur can experiment in his or her own backyard with growing, buying, or selling grapes, making 200 cases of Cabernet and 60 cases of another wine from a variety that originated in Italy over 200 years ago. Want to make your own barrel of Pinot? Then just visit a custom crush facility—a sort of winemaking co-op—and you are on your way. Northern California is an utterly unique

Charlie Palmer in the kitchen.

place where the world of winemaking is yours for the taking.

Of all the celebrities we interviewed for this book, there is no better example of someone who is seamlessly integrating the business of winemaking into his personal and professional life than the all-American chef Charlie Palmer. Here is someone who represents a new breed of chef, who excels with both an acute culinary and business sense.

Charlie Palmer's Dry Creek Kitchen in Healdsburg, California.

Pigs & Pinot

We first met Charlie Palmer at his restaurant Dry Creek Kitchen on a rainy afternoon in March 2010. Located in the center of Healdsburg, a small gastronomic enclave of Northern California, the restaurant itself is connected to Palmer's modern-styled boutique hotel. People milled around the hotel lobby, some waiting for spa treatments, others for tours, but the following day's festivities, namely the Pigs & Pinot event, took precedence. Guest chefs were arriving and the hotel was quickly filling up with visitors. The restaurant smelled, tantalizingly, as if 100 pigs were being roasted in the back room, which was actually what was happening.

We were sitting in the back at a large table with two glasses of water and one bad hangover between us—the inevitable result of spending so much time in the Napa/Sonoma region. We watched the rain that had followed us since San Francisco crawl down the immaculately polished glass windows.

Suddenly Palmer appeared stage left. He is a formidable presence at over six feet tall and is built like a battleship, with hands the size of butcher's blocks.

Sans his famous moustache but clothed in his chef whites, Palmer strode over to us in the dining room mumbling and pointing to various defects of each service station, which needed to be remedied before guests started to arrive for lunch. From the start it was obvious that he's a no-nonsense man with little time for fools. He was already multi-tasking. His eyes were continually darting from one side of the kitchen into the dining room and out the window to waving acquaintances. Friends and fellow chefs who were arriving for the weekend event stopped at our table to make dinner plans with Palmer.

Since that time, Pigs & Pinot has become an annual ritual. The most recent event in March of 2015 marked its tenth anniversary. "This was truly the culmination of ten amazing years of pork and pinot," says Palmer. The yearly celebration has raised over $600,000 for charity and local scholarships, while providing a weekend of fabulous entertainment to sold out crowds of wine lovers.

Family Roots

Charlie Palmer was born in 1959 and brought up on farmland in the rural town of Smyrna, in upstate New York, a gorgeously wild and rustic area. His family members were firm advocates of eating and growing fresh produce; they kept a well-tended and varied vegetable patch behind their house. Charlie in particular loved the garden and was soon preparing dishes from the available produce.

After high school, Charlie followed his love of cooking to the nearby Culinary Institute of America (or CIA), considered to be the best cooking school in the United States. He was hired to cook at the legendary New York City French restaurant, La Côte Basque, working under the tutelage of Chef Jean-Jacques Rachou.

Three years later a vastly more experienced Palmer was helming the kitchen at the Waccabuc Country Club in Westchester County. It was a comfortable job, yet ultimately unfulfilling. Feeling it was time for a change and more of a challenge, Charlie set his sights on France, the

ultimate gastronomic destination. Undeterred by the fact that he couldn't speak a word of French, Palmer was soon on his way to the best training the world had to offer a young chef.

He landed at the famous Georges Blanc Hotel in the renowned Loire region in northern France. For the next two years, Palmer trained under a fiercely opinionated chef, Alain Chapel. "My time spent at Georges Blanc in France, where one artisanal producer would bring all of his perfectly made goat cheese to the doorstep of our kitchen, had a strong impact on me," Palmer says. This is where his appreciation for regional ingredients was nurtured.

Progressive American Cooking

In 1983 Palmer was back in New York after being recruited as executive chef by Michael (Buzzy) O'Keefe, the chef-owner of Brooklyn's famous River Café, a gastronomic hotspot with a growing reputation. The pair developed a signature house style of classically cooked French dishes with a delicate modern twist.

By 1985 the restaurant was smoking hot, reservations were hard to come by, and the lucky patrons and critics who managed to eat there on a regular basis expected new and more exciting dishes every week. "I called it Progressive American cuisine," Palmer says, "because every time I stepped into the kitchen, I felt things moving forward." He soon earned a prestigious three stars from the New York Times, ensuring the success of the restaurant.

"I realized American cuisine was in its infancy and I spent a lot of time thinking about what the idea of American cooking

really meant to me," Palmer says. "I began to research my own small American producers and support them in an effort to use the best raw products available—it inspired my creative juices and helped to mold my style." Regional sourcing of all his meats, fish, fowl, and beef would ensure freshness and highlight locality. This was the beginning of a signature element that would be integrated into the development of Charlie's future restaurants and become a hallmark of his culinary style. At the time, he was well ahead of the curve on this now recognized trend in American cooking.

In 1988, at just 28 years old, Palmer made a landmark commitment to creating regional American dishes when he opened Aureole in an historic townhouse off Madison Avenue in Manhattan. Leaving the River Café in its prime was a gutsy move that caused a lot of speculation in his world, but the risk paid off. Aureole (which has since moved to midtown's dramatically modern Bank of America Tower at One Bryant Park) is a three-star premiere restaurant that has been inducted into the Relais & Châteaux association of quality hotels and restaurants and has received a Michelin star every year since 2007. The stellar success, especially in a city where restaurant failure is often the norm, was the beginning of Palmer's meteoric rise.

Building a Brand

Palmer's brand continued to expand. In 1997, Manhattan became home to Astra, a café by day and hip catering location by night and weekends (now Upper Story by Charlie Palmer).

Charlie Palmer tasting wine, one of the jobs of any chef and restaurateur.

It was followed by Aureole at Mandalay Bay and the Charlie Palmer Steakhouse at the Four Seasons Hotel in Las Vegas. Now with three other Charlie Palmer locations (Washington, D.C., Reno, NV, and New York, NY) and a total of seventeen bars and restaurants to his name, Chef Palmer has a well-established footprint across the United States.

As Palmer's name started to brand well with the public, he felt the time was right for expansion into other aspects of the hospitality industry, especially in the small but exclusive boutique hotel sector. The concept was to marry Palmer restaurants with an intimate, friendly, ultra-plush micro-hotel. Our meeting place—the Dry Creek Kitchen at the Hotel Healdsburg—was his first combination hotel/upscale restaurant, and its success led to the emergence of the Mystic Hotel and Burritt Room + Tavern in San Francisco and the Harvest Inn by Charlie Palmer and Harvest Table in St. Helena.

Today Charlie Palmer's empire includes restaurants across the country, a growing collection of food-forward wine shops, award-winning boutique hotels, and five top-selling cookbooks. Inducted into the James Beard "Who's Who of Food & Beverage in America" in 1998, he appears regularly on TV as a frequent guest on NBC's *Today Show* and a celebrity judge on *Top Chef*, among many other programs.

Palmer's astounding success has not interfered with his love of cooking. Even today, he steps into the kitchen with innovation in mind. "Without a doubt, people eat with their eyes long before they put fork to food," he says. "So I continue to look for a playful yet respectful way to create excitement on the plate."

The Palmer Style of Relaxation

The path that led to Palmer's involvement with wine and winemaking had little to do with empire building, making money, or garnering fame: it seems to be much more personal. For him, it's all about relaxation and family.

What is relaxation for most people? For some, it's a six-pack and a football game, poker with friends, watching a great film, or being outdoors. Restless people—those who are the most driven—seem to look for more existential pursuits for relaxation; rather than self-indulgence, for them, the act of learning becomes a pleasure. Palmer is clearly one of the rare breeds who possess an insatiable thirst to learn, experience, and forge boldly forward. Not surprisingly, the people who are willing to take great chances in life are the ones who succeed. That's not to say Palmer's never failed, but he's obviously someone of character who's never failed to try again. This brings us to how he came to be a winemaker.

As we sat talking in his spotless dining room, three factors about Palmer and wine became clear to us. First, he was immensely knowledgeable about winemaking, not just about what happens after the grapes hit the vineyard sorters, but also about everything in between—from clonal selection, row spacing, and vinification techniques to final maturation and even bottle packaging. Second, his expertise is a natural extension of his vast sensory abilities as a chef. Lastly, yet most interesting of all, is what he, Charlie, personally achieves from making wine.

By his own admission, he has a huge cellar of hundreds of immediately drinkable high-quality wines. For over 30 years he's had the

The elegant Aureole Bar in New York City.

opportunity to taste many of the world's most famous wines. Yet, for all this intimate knowledge, Palmer rarely speaks about wine and has little patience for collecting wines that require extended bottle age. No, for Palmer the most exciting aspect of the world of wine boils down to its most basic factor—bringing people together, namely, in this case, his family.

When we asked what's the most fun he's achieved from making wine, Palmer's eyes widened as he described working with his sons in the vineyards. He and his four sons worked side by side creating the first few vintages of Charlie's Pinot Noir; from picking to punch-down to sticking labels on bottles, these were clearly special moments for Palmer. Not only was it fun getting purple with the kids, it was also educational, unusual, and memorable. One day, sometime in the future, each of his boys will get to taste the first vintage they made with their father.

Wine Preference

Being a chef, Palmer is naturally drawn to sensory pursuits, and wine is packed with endless

explorations of sensation—aromatic, visual, or gustatory. For a chef it's an absolute requirement to hone all these sensory perceptions into a fine art; appreciation of wine is crucial for all modern chefs.

The pairing of wine and food is a tricky and difficult skill to master, but good chefs usually have the inherent capability to learn the craft quickly. Dealing day to day with sometimes bizarrely clashing flavors in dishes and, even more specifically, interpreting the integration and combination of wildly different flavors into an exciting and palatable creation is the reason why most chefs are gifted tasters of wine. It is curious that there are not more chefs in the wine trade, as they obviously have a clear sensory advantage over others.

In terms of wine preference, Palmer has always been enamored with the Pinot Noir grape and the wines it can produce. "On the whole they are more versatile with food," says Charlie. For serious red wine lovers the Pinot Noir grape can rarely be topped. Considered a bastion in fine red wine appreciation, Pinot Noirs can prove almost transient on the palate. Many love the overt richness of Cabernet Sauvignon or the fiery excitement of a powerful Shiraz, yet, when it comes down to the basics, as all art inevitably does, elegance, refinement, complexity, and infinite nuances are truly the domain of the Pinot Noir grape.

Not usually the most concentrated of wines (yet it can be), the appreciation of Pinot Noir is mostly cerebral. A common French expression is that Cabernet Sauvignon wines (Bordeaux) represent the man—sturdy in character, hearty, and masculine. Conversely, the Pinot Noir wines of Burgundy reflect much more of a feminine style—delicate, complex, and almost ethereal in nature and composition. ("Bordeaux for the heart" and "Burgundy for the mind" are expressions heard quite often at wine tastings.) As a grape, Pinot Noir is notoriously fickle to grow; its thin skins easily expose the flesh to rot and are quick to oxidize in the winery if not cared for with immediacy. But for wine lovers, there's no doubt that great wines made from the Pinot Noir grape represent the Holy Grail in terms of complexity and nuance.

Charlie and Clay

After many years in New York City, Palmer and his family moved to the ultra quaint, charming, and friendly town of Healdsburg, California. There, Palmer met many ambitious winemakers who frequented his wine-friendly restaurant. One of them stood out from the others—a young man by the name of Clay Mauritson.

The Mauritson family had been growing grapes in the Dry Creek Valley AVA since 1868. Clay's great-great-great-grandfather, S. P. Hallengren, was a grape-growing pioneer in the Rockpile region. He first planted vines in 1884, shipping wine back home to his native Sweden. The family's Rockpile homestead and ranch grew to 4,000 acres. In the early 1960s, all but 700 ridge-top acres were acquired by the Army Corps of Engineers in order to develop Lake Sonoma. Hence, many of the vineyards became underwater plots and, for the next 30 years, the Rockpile property served mostly for sheep grazing. By the mid-1990s, Clay had returned from college, began working the vineyards, and was ready to release his inaugural

Family portraits of Charlie and Lisa Palmer and their four sons in 2010 (Above) and 2015 (Below).

Mauritson Dry Creek Valley Zinfandel in 1998.

Today his family's operation is vast, spreading across Dry Creek Valley, Alexander Valley, and the Rockpile Appellations. Mauritson Wine Estate sits on the elevated, dusty Mill Creek Road, just off River Road in the heart of the Dry Creek Valley, with additional grapes sourced from over 2,000 acres of excellent vineyards. Palmer became a silent partner in this impressive operation and privately owns a smallish vineyard exclusively planted to his favorite grape, Pinot Noir. His selective plot produces 3 to 3½ tons of fruit per acre.

Clay and Charlie began their winemaking collaboration after a journey to France's famed wine country. "It all started on a trip to Burgundy in December, 2005," recalls Mauritson. "Chef Charlie Palmer and I were traveling with some friends to the Hospices de Beaune, one of the most famous wine auctions in the world. The now infamous 2005 vintage had just been put into barrels, and we were fortunate enough to taste what can only be described as perfection in a glass. Inspired, Charlie decided that he wanted to make Pinot Noir. Though Charlie owns a beautiful Pinot Noir vineyard, it is less than two acres. It was time to call in some favors. After countless phone calls and much begging, we were able to get our hands on fruit from some of the greatest Pinot Noir vineyards in the Russian River Valley, and Charlie Clay was born."

Always eager to immerse himself in a new project, Palmer took to the various tasks of winemaking with gusto. He's keen to learn and is adept in both the vineyard and the winery, involved with everything from vine spacing in the vineyard to juice-racking opinions and the percentage of new oak utilized in final maturation (it's about 40% New French). These various methods of expertise extend from age-old techniques such as light refraction to gauge grape ripeness to more cutting-edge methods such as reverse-osmosis of grape juice to increase concentration by eliminating excess water.

Charlie's passion within wine appreciation, however, is for red Burgundy, but he has come to accept that making it from the land he purchased may not be a realistic goal. The ground is much more fertile than he had hoped, the deep loamy soils so far preventing the vines from striving for the mineral depth required to capture real complexity within wine. "It's never going to be Burgundy, nor should it," says Palmer with wry smile. "All the vines are organically farmed, but they need more," he shrugs. "It's something we're working on."

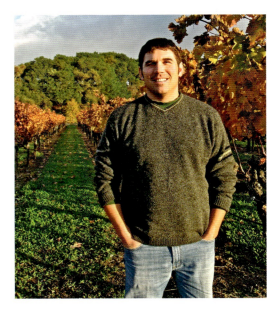

Clay Mauritson, Charlie Palmer's partner in winemaking. OPPOSITE: Aureole Las Vegas; Palmer's restaurants feature extraordinary wine lists and brilliantly designed storage towers.

The Future

Being a restaurateur, Palmer has always had a burgeoning interest in sparkling wines, particularly those made using the traditional Champagne method. Because of their inherent high acidity, these wines work notoriously well with food, especially light California-style cuisine. In the past, Palmer experimented making cuvées with famous estates such as Iron Horse Vineyards—specialists in Russian River sparklers, which come the closest to the original Champagnois style, yet originate in Northern California. Technically speaking, carrying out double fermentations in the bottle is a particularly difficult craft to master, making it (no surprise!) something Palmer is personally keen to pursue in the future. We have no doubt that if anyone can make it happen, it will be Charlie Palmer.

PORTFOLIO

Working together, Palmer and Mauritson have produced two cuvées of Pinot Noir wines. The first is a blend of four vineyards consisting of three of Clay's best Pinot sites and Charlie's own prized vineyard. Each of the chosen vineyards produces around four tons of fruit to add to the blend. The cuvée is called Charlie Clay in honor of the two men responsible for bringing it to the table.

The second wine is a powerful single blend of Pinot from Charlie's vineyard, called the Duelist, which has only been made twice to date.

NICK'S TASTING NOTES

Pinot Noir, 2008

Taste-wise the wines are unabashedly Californian in style, ripe and lush with silky red and black-berried fruits, unobtrusive oak, moderate levels of fruit concentration, and, most importantly, a fresh uplifting wave of natural acidity that elevates the fruit flavors and provides an overall sense of elegance that can often be missing in warm climate wines.

Pinot Noir, Duelist, 2007

As a single-vineyard wine, the Duelist has a slightly denser, more solid structure than the brighter and more lively Charlie Clay cuvée that showed a fresher core of red-oriented fruits (which I somewhat preferred). Both wines are stylishly packaged with painterly front labels that complement each other. (This wine is not currently available.)

Pinot Noir, 2013

This Pinot presents a translucent youthful ruby hue with hints of crimson leading to an energetic bouquet of lively, mouth-watering, ripe red summer fruits such as raspberries, red cherries, and cranberries, bound to sweet vanilla and cola aromas. On the palate, at the moment, it contains a medium-bodied concentration of taut bright fruits as found on the nose. It's high-toned and structured with brisk acidity and chewy medium tannins. The wine reveals a succulent, juicy core of mineral and red fruits that provides a fine, textured impression on the palate. All the components are here for the future, and the wine, well balanced with a good purity of fruit, definitely needs some additional bottle age to soften, lengthen, and fill out. Elegant, refined, and well delineated, this cuvée is very Côte de Beaune in style compared to the darker, more Nuits-like Duelist.

Pinot Noir, Duelist, 2012

Purposely created to be food friendly both this and the Pinot above are styled to be subtle, refined, and slightly austere. Made so as not to overpower, but rather let the food shine through, they definitely come into their own with a meal, revealing lovely subtle nuances that enhances the flavors of the foods they compliment rather than take center stage. However, this doesn't mean they aren't seriously made wines. As with Burgundies (which Charlie Palmer has an affinity for) they need some cellar time to integrate, flesh out, and reveal their inner complexity. The Duelist is the more powerful, concentrated, and structured of the pair. Deeper colored, the Duelist unleashes a mélange of black fruits that includes black cherries, cassis, blackberries, and taut, unripe black plums. Loamy and medium-bodied with high levels of acid to bolster the smooth, spicy black fruits and fine light oak. The wine at present exhibits some impressively strong tannins that should resolve themselves and sweeten out with bottle age.

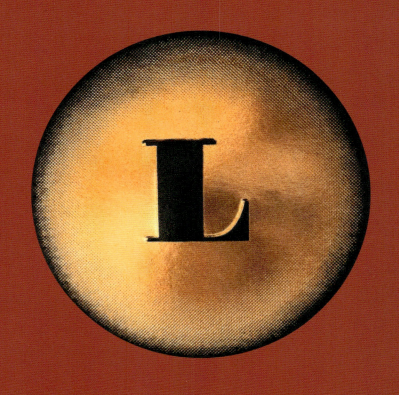

Randy Lewis

LEWIS CELLARS

Napa

Out of the Way Winery

The first time we visited Lewis Cellars, the winery was not open to the public. Since then, things have changed. Visitors are now welcomed, though by appointment only. You must call ahead and reserve a space. This is not one of those walk-in tasting rooms that sells tons of tourist goods in addition to wine. No, this winery is special and really only for those who truly enjoy sampling some of the best wines to be found in the Napa Valley.

Situated just outside the city of Napa's northern boundary, Lewis Cellars is not an easy place to find. On our first visit, and despite our GPS's insistence that we'd arrived at our destination, we had to drive up and down Big Ranch Road several times looking for the winery. Finally, we spotted an unassuming building adorned with the letter L on the side. We drove up the long driveway before we were convinced we were in the right place.

We were thrilled to arrive at last. Though Randy Lewis started his career behind the wheel of a racecar, he has certainly excelled in his second chosen profession as a winemaker. Lewis Cellars wine has an almost unprecedented reputation for consistently superb quality and since actual production is relatively small

Randy Lewis in the barrel room at Lewis Cellars.

(under 10,000 cases a year) this wine is not easy to come by. Sold mainly through their mailing list and to finer restaurants, whatever goes into the marketplace usually sells out quickly. Thus, we anxiously anticipated the private tasting Randy had generously arranged for us.

On and Off the Track

Born in Charlotte, North Carolina, on July 18, 1945, John Ransom Lewis III is better known to the racing public as Randy Lewis. In his youth Lewis dreamed of becoming a doctor. However, after witnessing an awe-inspiring professional car race as a teenager, he decided to try his hand behind a wheel. Soon he was gaining a reputation for being a star on the track, winning SCCA race after race and swiftly graduating to Formula Atlantic. It would be an understatement to say he was an adept driver; even early on, it was obvious he had a natural gift. The young Lewis felt it too and, intoxicated by the raw excitement of the track, he decided his future was in racecars.

Lewis went to Europe in 1971. His first race was on the legendary Monaco track with 127 other cars as a prelim to the Formula One race. "They ran four or five different qualifying sessions because of all of the cars," Randy told *Autoweek* in December 2008. "I remember qualifying very early in the morning, just because there were so many entered. I qualified 12th and finished in the same position. I started off pretty good." His competition was unbelievable, including such drivers as James Hunt, Alan Jones, Jochen Mass, and Danny Sullivan, all of whom would later be recognized as some of the best in the sport.

For the next three years, Lewis raced on the Formula Three circuit, where it certainly wasn't five-star hotels and charity dinners for the young driver. "I was living out of my van," Randy says with a laugh. He was also towing his own racecar on an open trailer behind the van and, after the races, performing all the mechanics on the car himself. But it was still exciting and proved important for another reason, for it was here that Lewis first became fascinated with wine. "I was single, and between races," he recalls, "I'd stop in these little villages throughout Europe. I'd buy some of the local wine, and that's really where I developed my love of the fruit."

By 1974, Lewis had returned to the States,

where it was difficult to get sponsorship. Eventually backed by Cribari Wine and Wrangler Jeans, he competed in Formula 5000 and Can Am and landed an IndyCar ride in 1983. He competed in his first oval race in 1987 and remained in IndyCar racing until the early 1990s. On the track, Lewis soon garnered a reputation for pushing himself and his car in pursuit of podium glory. For over 23 danger-filled years, Lewis raced cars on both international and national circuits, and was one of the sport's most popular drivers throughout the 1980s. (By the end of his racing career he'd qualified for the Indy 500 on five occasions.)

After more than two decades behind the wheel, it became clear to the veteran that equipment and car performance was becoming more crucial than the drivers themselves. "I took a long look at my surroundings and I knew I wasn't getting the best equipment with which to compete," explains Randy. "That fact also affected the sponsors who put up the money for the racing teams. I finally decided it was time to do something else I truly loved."

The Road to Napa

After retiring from the sport in 1991, Lewis decided to pursue a new dream and start his own winery. He took a trip to the winegrowing district in Northern California to explore the possibility. "At the end of my racing career, my best friend bought a vineyard and he wanted us to make some wine together," explains Lewis. "So we made a few hundred cases, from 1989 to '91, during the last three years I was still racing. When I quit at the end of the '91 season, my wife, Debbie, and I started Lewis Cellars with the 1992 vintage."

Autographed photo of Lewis on the track during one of his many races.

As anyone contemplating winemaking will acknowledge, there are three ways to start a winery. Option one, the obvious choice, is to buy an existing property and its accompanying vineyards. This, however, requires a great deal of money. Another method is to create a vineyard from the ground up, which, of course, also requires a huge financial investment—and extensive prior knowledge. Finally, one can start small by sourcing grapes from selected vineyards. Lewis picked the last option, though perhaps it was not really a *choice*. "We didn't

have the financial resources to buy a vineyard," he admits, "which we would've loved to do back then. However, it turned out perfect in the end." And this is what made visiting Lewis Cellars and talking with Randy one of the most fascinating experiences we had in Northern California. His operation was unique among all the winemakers we interviewed.

In the wine world, especially in California, making wine from sourced grapes is considered inferior to growing your own fruit. Most estates only use sourced grapes for their

basic cuvées—the mass-produced grapes are usually cheap because they are sourced from big machine-picked vineyards where quantity rules above quality. Lewis, however, approached the situation from a different perspective. "What if you convinced people with great vineyards to sell part of their crop, just enough to make small cuvées of your own intensely flavored and concentrated wines?" he asked, turning the concept of sourced grapes upside down. Lewis took this idea even further. Did he really need to buy a winery? Why couldn't he rent space and save himself an enormous expense and hassle?

Lewis put both ideas into practice. "We don't own lots of vineyards," he explains. "We don't own an expensive winery. We lease the building." Of course, the concept model behind Lewis Cellars is not exactly new. In Bordeaux, they've had so-called garagiste wines for over

Lewis rents his winery and sources his grapes, which makes for intense and exciting winemaking.

twenty years. But, in the 1990s in Northern California, Lewis Cellars was something of a maverick operation. (Today, however, Lewis's approach has become increasingly popular among vintners and even celebrity winemakers such as Yao Ming.) Part of the success of the operation is keeping production manageable. "We didn't have enough money to make a lot of stupid decisions, and we only grew as quickly as we could grow," Randy says. "We've been the same size now for over ten years."

Each cuvée or bottling in the Lewis portfolio begins as numerous small lots of fruit classified by vineyard block, varietal, clone, and rootstock. It's intense and exciting winemaking. Lewis had the good instincts to understand that if a winemaker is sourcing grapes to make wine, then he has to get the best grapes and make a plan for the future. So Randy created long-term contracts with phenomenal vineyards.

Another smart approach was to seek the expertise of some of the best winemakers in the business. In 1996 Lewis hired the cult winemaker Helen Turley, a move that was to prove extremely beneficial. Turley consulted on vineyards and helped decide what fruit to plant. Fruit was sourced from the finest vineyards in Pritchard Hill, Calistoga, St. Helena, Rutherford, and Oak Knoll for red varietals and from exceptional plots in Oak Knoll, Carneros, and the Russian River Valley for whites: all are well known throughout the world as prime grape growing areas.

In addition to Helen, other brilliant winemakers who worked with Lewis include Paul Hobbs, Robbie Meyer, and Pat Sullivan. With so many famous winemakers, and so many different signature styles, one would imagine the wines would taste different from year to year, from winemaker to winemaker, but Lewis makes sure that doesn't happen. "I've tried not to have winemakers change our style even though I've had a number of them," he says. "I think we've been successful in that we're making the same kind of wine as we did in 1996 with Helen. These are still big extracted wines, but they are balanced. They're not low-alcohol, but they're not over the top. They're not sweet. We use a lot of new oak that's well seasoned and toasted so it's not oaky. We've been successful for almost twenty years now, and we don't need to re-invent ourselves." This does not mean that Lewis Cellars is static. "We want to remain at the forefront so we still experiment with new techniques, new barrels and vineyards, and such," Randy adds. "Even though we're very happy with our wines, we are always looking for ways to improve."

The Craft of California Winemaking

We wanted to know how Lewis was able to become so knowledgeable about the art of winemaking and grape growing, two incredibly difficult crafts that can take years to master. "I did take some classes," says Randy, "but really the way I learned was I hired the best people in the business, and then I asked them a million questions. I watched everything they did, and tried to understand the why and how so I could take the general concepts a little further."

The aim of the Lewis style of winemaking is to produce big, powerful, opulent, lush, and forward wines with soft, round tannins. Though they are certainly not cheap, these award-winning wines are continually highly rated (scoring regularly in the mid- to high-

90s) and win high praise from prestigious publications such as *Wine Spectator*.

Every year since the first release the portfolio has improved in quality at an unbelievable rate; these are seminal examples of the region's best wines. Totally and unabashedly Californian, they uniquely express a personal vision. The wines mirror their producer. Like the 5-foot 10-inch Lewis, who stays fit by cycling 2,500 miles a year, the wines are similarly broad shouldered, sleek, precise, lush, and powerful. They display an opulent glycerin immediacy, yet also have the capacity to age well due to the powerful but sweet tannins in the top cuvées—and they're so damn drinkable.

Grapes for Lewis Cellars are sourced from some of the best vineyards in Northern California, including the Barcaglia Lane vineyard.

Bottle Age

Many serious wine lovers believe that California's heavily extracted, very ripe style of winemaking creates wines without potential for additional bottle age. There is some truth to the fact that these wines will not age like the wines of Bordeaux, picking up the typical small nuances and subtle secondary and tertiary aromas. We asked Randy how he thought his wines aged and if he'd recently tried his older vintages. "Well, the '94 Reserve Merlot is still tasting terrific," he said. "I haven't had the '92 in a while, but I should probably try that sometime soon, just to see. I think if you look at the wines around the world, from Burgundy and Bordeaux for example, the best vintages were those that showed early on. The best vintages were great when they came out, so obviously they were going to get better. The things that make a wine last are the same things that make it fun to drink early. You need mature tannins, not green tannins; you need fruit—not tutti-frutti fruit but a serious mouth-coating feel. All of our wines have good acidity, so that's not an issue."

Lessons Learned on the Track and in the Fields

Are there similarities between the art of winemaking and the dangerous sport of car racing? Lewis has always thought so. "What I learned from racing is that you need the best equipment to succeed. If you had a great car, you had the best chance to win—simple as that," he explains. "In making wine, you need the best grapes to succeed. You also need the best

Randy Lewis and his wife, Debbie, have named some of their cuvées after their grandchildren: Alec, Ethan, and Mason.

team, the best winemaker, and the best crew. In racing, you take chances. The best drivers get it right in terms of how far to push it without crashing, although we all crash occasionally. I think it's the same in the wine business. You make the best wine by taking chances, but if you just go for it, you're going to mess up. Having the patience to wait—maybe longer than everybody else does to pick the grapes, for example—is one of the most important lessons I learned from racing. In both racing and winemaking, in any business really, you need to focus your attention on the details, surround yourself with the best people, and know when to go for it."

Lewis's attention to detail was obvious on our tour of the winery. Parts of the operation felt like a science lab where lots of experiments were being conducted. The winery boasted the most current and best equipment available and was the most organized and well-kept one we visited on our entire trip to Napa. All the wines were aging in 100% new top French oak barrels and each cask was carefully positioned and identified. The entire plant was spotlessly clean. It's something one might expect from a former driver with pit lane diligence and an awareness of the importance of order and cleanliness.

Update

We revisited Lewis Cellars on a recent trip to Napa in March of 2015 and were delighted to spend some time with the ever-cheerful and ebullient Randy Lewis. We had a wonderful conversation and enjoyed catching up with Randy, who always seems to be travelling somewhere exciting. We also tasted some amazing wines.

Lewis is still making stellar wines, among the very best to be found in all of Napa, which is saying a lot. We discovered that the only real change to his operation is that the Lewis Cellars tasting room is now open to the public, though on a limited basis as tastings are by appointment only.

We think anyone who is seriously interested in wine and winemaking should make it a point to visit Lewis Cellars while in Napa. We are absolutely certain you won't be disappointed. And if you are lucky enough to be there when Randy is in town, raise a glass for us.

PORTFOLIO

The estate's total production is less than 10,000 cases of wine per year from thirteen different wines: four Chardonnays, a Sauvignon Blanc, a Merlot, two Syrahs, Alec's Blend, and four different Cabernets, amounting to a meager 120,000 bottles in total. "Each winery has its own level of comfort," Lewis explains. "It's really the point where you can totally control your product with what you have on hand. At Lewis Cellars, we do everything ourselves in a manner we have found works best for our wines. To increase our production even a little would be difficult for us to do correctly."

The Sauvignon Blanc is whole cluster pressed, fermented, and barrel aged in French oak and stainless steel for nine months with zero malolactic fermentation—a technique that produces a style of Sauvignon Blanc called Fume Blanc (*fume* refers to the flavors and bouquet the wine attains from the barrel maturation). The estate currently produces four Chardonnays: 1,200 cases of a Sonoma Chardonnay that is a bit crisper and well balanced; 1,500 cases of a Napa Chardonnay exhibiting ripe fruit and toasty oak aromas with flavors of cinnamon-laced pear and stone fruits; 400 cases of Reserve Napa Chardonnay with rich, forward tropical fruits, a nice balance of minerals, and a creamy finish; and 450 cases of the single-vineyard Barcaglia Lane Russian River Chardonnay from the Dutton Ranch, which is strikingly aromatic and shot through with honeysuckle and hazelnut spice with a lively citrus-laced finish.

As for the reds, even the entry-level wines are made in very limited quantities. Only 100 cases of a wild, spicy-tasting Syrah are produced. Over the course of our trip to Northern California, we tasted very few Syrahs that we thought could compete against their European or Down

Under counterparts. So why do so many Californian vintners continue to produce it? The simple answer is that they love wines from this varietal. Was this the reason Randy decided to make one? "Yes, exactly," he replied. "We not only like wines from the Northern Rhône, we really liked Australian Shiraz. I did the first race down in Surfer's Paradise in Australia, so Debbie and I visited different wine regions before the race. A few years later we went back and I became a big fan of Australian Shiraz. Ours is certainly not a Northern Rhône–style Syrah, but that was our impetus."

Even more rare than the Syrah is a 100-case cuvée of Merlot, smooth and elegant in style with hints of sandalwood, cedar, clove, and oak spices, wrapped in a core of wild berries. There is also a trio of small and unique boutique-styled red cuvées named after the Lewis's grandchildren: Alec's Blend varies every year but is generally 70% Syrah, 20% Merlot, and 10% Cabernet Sauvignon; they also produce a Syrah named after Ethan and a Cabernet named Mason.

But Cabernets are really the estate's masterworks, considered not only some of the best in California, but some of the world's finest examples of what this grape can achieve.

The regular but extemporaneous Napa Cabernet showcases several small hillside vineyards from Rutherford, Calistoga, and Oak Knoll. Each vineyard contributes a unique element, whether it is minerality, spice, or structure; 1,400 cases of this wine were released in 2010. The Cabernet Reserve achieves a very high level of quality indeed. Here is an extremely concentrated wine, with an obvious use of small mountainside berries. Demand is great for this high-quality, reasonably priced wine; it usually sells out quickly in the marketplace.

The jewel in the family's crown, however, is the very rare and powerful Cuvée L, which is made only in exceptional harvests (which thankfully are not all that uncommon in Northern California). The Cuvée L is rich and concentrated, yet also manages to retain elegance and a good sense of place. "We only make Cuvée L in years we feel our product is truly superior," explains Randy. "With the marvelous fruit of the 1997 vintage, we decided to give it a try. The resulting wine was incredibly well received and represented a major breakthrough for our operation. Once it was finished, most of the people involved felt we could compete with anybody in the valley with respect to quality." While previous vintages have included Cabernet Franc, recent blends are 100% Cabernet Sauvignon. It's a massively endowed wine with layers of dense blackberry, cedar, clove, and oak flavors. It coats the palate and ends with hints of vanilla bean and espresso on the finish. Voluptuous and sinewy, it can age well. There are usually only 150 cases in production.

And, if the Cuvée L were a car, we asked, what car would it be? It didn't take Randy Lewis more than a moment to answer. "A 458 Ferrari Italia," he said with certainty.

Reserve Chardonnay, 2009

The wine has a deep lemon-gold color. It's a little closed at present but very Californian in style with tons of sweet cream, vanilla, and super-ripe aromas of citrus, pineapple, green apple, green figs, and lemon curds. Light touch of minerals but it's mostly full forward in style. Rich, broad-shouldered, and medium- to full-bodied with impressive concentration of silky white fruits. Totally dry, but a sweet impression and medium acidity insure easy drinkability. Quite light on its feet and has a great sense of elegance for such a concentrated wine. Lush, sweet fruits such as apricots and pineapples mingle with firmer stone fruit and citrus flavors that lead to a long vanilla- and marshmallow-tinged finish. Very Californian in style but lush, silky, and very drinkable. Exceptional balance. The grapes are sourced from and utilize the Dijon 96 and Old Wente Chardonnay clones.

Reserve Cabernet Sauvignon, 2008

As high quality as the Reserve Chardonnay, this wine exhibits a ruby-black color and an explosive nose of super-ripe dark fruits—black cherry, black currants, and blackberries intermingle with classic Cabernet aromas of pencil lead, India ink, dark chocolate, earth, new vanilla (French in both), and oak, with some red fruits in the background. Full-bodied on the palate, with a great mouth-feel but not heavy at all, exhibiting as in the Chardonnay, a pinpoint balance and good linear direction. Some structure accompanies the rich, powerful fruit with super-fine, tight-grained, medium-strong tannins ensuring some bottle age. This complex, high-quality wine holds interest and displays a long, lush, juicy black fruit finish. Grapes for both these wines are bought from some of the best vineyards in Northern California.

Reserve Chardonnay, 2013

Sourced from some of Randy's favorite vineyards within the Sonoma and Russian River AVAs, this wine clocks in at 14.5% alcohol. The vineyards were chosen personally by Randy to deliver maximum levels of concentrated exotic ripe fruit while still managing to maintain a modicum of elegance and serious inner complexity. An intense gold color edged with deep green reflections and a slow, warm-climate swirl introduces this wine. Expressive yellow plum, citrus, flowery jasmine, and butterscotch notes intermingle on the nose. This is a rich, ripe, oaky unabashed California-style Chardonnay; big and concentrated. Buttery citrus nose reveals a cornucopia of secondary aromas including hazelnuts, marshmallows, yeast, white poached pears, and minerals. Immense in the mouth, seriously concentrated but also so drinkable and creamy. Flavorsome and silky on the palate, this wine is full-bodied and very rich but has no problem handling its sheer weight as it's perfectly balanced by an uplifting acidity that supports the dense oaky juice. Wonderfully textured with layer upon layer of different citrus fruits, it's a plush, hedonistic, and extremely long wine. Lewis utilizes wild yeasts and the finished wine is matured in 100% new French oak. The wine will cellar and age well, but why wait, as it's so delicious.

This ripe 2013 vintage has produced a wine with fat, opulently textured layers of broad-shouldered fruit but also has provided just enough sherbet-like acidity to match the density of fruit. Make no mistake though: this leans towards the bigger scaled, heavily-oaked wines of Napa that are pushed to the maximum in every sense, an approach they love at Randy's house. Allocation through the wine club only.

Barcaglia Lane Chardonnay, 2013

If one is looking for a more restrained style of Chardonnay from Lewis Cellars, their Barcaglia Lane Chardonnay is perfect. Sourced from Dutton Ranch Fruit in Sonoma, it reveals a finer, more delicate style that's provided by the region's cooler climate. It has a golden apple color with a deeper golden core. A warm-climate citrus bouquet is coupled with secondary aromas of sour honey, honeydew melons, minerals, and lavish, creamy new oak. Lush, soft, and ripe in the mouth, the wine is medium- to full-bodied. It is less obviously concentrated and shows more minerality and finesse than the Reserve Chardonnays. Cut lemons and limes bounce along the palate backed up by a balanced acidity that leads to a fine loamy finish. Almost a European style of Chardonnay yet still undoubtedly Californian at heart.

Mason's Cabernet Sauvignon, 2010

Ruby black with an opaque pitch-colored center core and a youthful pink rim, this is a truly huge wine from a great warm vintage. Fun and bouncy, packed with super-ripe fruit on a very accessible lightly-structured frame, I can only surmise this wine is for lively, opulent parties. And what's wrong with that? Intense black fruit on the nose, packed with ultra-ripe black cherries and blackberry spice. Loose knit, with richly concentrated, almost syrupy fruit, echoing vanilla, dark chocolate, and creamy black cherries. Very primary at the moment, this wine's light tannins and low acidity obviously point towards an early drinker. This cuvée is named after one of Randy's grandsons. Allocation through the wine club only.

Ethan's Syrah, 2012

Striking dark violet-purple color, though not opaque, with a broad, watery, crimson rim indicating it's a young wine. Spicy black fruits leap from the glass; ripe blackberries, black cherries, new oak, and white pepper are all backed up with some light floral (violets), mineral, black tea, and tarry notes. A light blast of crunchy red fruits also make a fleeting but pleasant appearance. Not a huge wine in the mouth and by usual Lewis standards this has a restrained cooler-climate style. Nonetheless it is still very concentrated and ripe with sappy, spicy black fruit flavors similar to those found on the nose, with an overlay of new oak. It's just about full-bodied with a smooth linear mineral quality on the tongue. Obviously sourced from high altitude vineyards, this wine has natural uplifting acidity, powerful tannins, and a long peppery finish. It will hold for years but will also improve with age which is rare in California. Named after Randy's grandson. Allocation through the wine club only.

Reserve Cabernet Sauvignon, 2012

The flagship wine in the Lewis Cellars portfolio, the Reserve Cabernet is a hugely powerful wine that is also supple and graceful. This is a totally unabashed California Cabernet in style, with deep-veined concentration but no signs of jammy over-extraction whatsoever. In wider terms, this wine truly reflects a "sense of place." Created with fine-tuned precision, the Reserve always manages to easily meld its sheer density of fruit with a sensual elegance. This is top-class, incredible winemaking; consistently up there, in my opinion, with any of the best examples Napa has to offer.

A blend of 98% Cabernet and 2% Petit Verdot, it is sourced from the finest vineyards in Oak Knoll, Rutherford, and Calistoga with maturation for twenty months in new French oak. It is crimson purple in color with an opaque black core. A big waft of super-ripe cassis, black cherries, blackberries, leather, sweet new vanilla oak, small concentrated currants, toast, chocolate, and licorice, this wine is very complex despite being youthful, which indicates it can improve. Big, bold, and rich on the mouth yet streamlined, plush, and seamless with layer upon layer of multi-dimensional black fruits that caress the palate. Don't be fooled however, buried under this serious depth of fruit lies ever-so-sweet, tight vanilla tannins, and some well-needed natural acidity that makes this amazing wine seem to float to an endless mocha- and cassis-liquor-flavored finish. Exceptional and will hold, but will it improve? Most probably, but we adore it upon release. This is becoming a new classic. Allocation through the wine club only.

VERMEIL

Cabernet Franc

2007

Dick Vermeil

VERMEIL WINES

Calistoga

A Passion for Football

In a rustic little town in Northern California called Calistoga, we discovered Vermeil Wines, the namesake of Richard Albert "Dick" Vermeil. Among football fans, Vermeil is known as the legendary head coach for three of the top teams in the history of football: the Philadelphia Eagles (1976 to 1982), the St. Louis Rams (1997 to 1999), and the Kansas City Chiefs (2001 to 2005). His work as a coach to the Eagles was celebrated in the 2006 movie *Invincible*, starring Greg Kinnear as Vermeil and Mark Wahlberg as Vince Papale.

Ever since Dick Vermeil was a young man, he was captivated by the sport of football. A promising quarterback in high school, he showed an uncanny understanding of the game and its tactics. Both his mother, Alice, a housewife at the time, and father, Louis, an owner-operator of a garage, encouraged him to hone his talent at college. This led Vermeil from Napa Junior College to San Jose State University, where he began to learn the skills necessary to become a top football coach.

Vermeil spent four years coaching high school before shifting into the Junior College ranks. After two seasons at Napa Community College, he moved on to Stanford University for four years and then entered the NFL, where he started coaching for the Los Angeles Rams.

After four successful seasons with the Rams, Dick took over coaching at UCLA. In his second year, the UCLA team won the Pac-8 Championship and went on to beat Ohio State at the Rose Bowl in 1976. This victory led to a job offer from the Philadelphia Eagles. In his third season as head coach, the Eagles initiated a four-year consecutive-season playoff run that was highlighted by an NFC Championship in 1980 and a trip to Super Bowl XV.

Citing "burnout," Dick worked as a sports announcer for CBS and ABC for the next fifteen years. He returned to coaching with the St. Louis Rams in 1997. Under his guidance, in a mere three years the Rams transitioned from being the worst team in the NFL to winning Super Bowl XXXIV. Dick then announced his retirement and headed home to Philadelphia, his eleven grandkids, and his venture into winemaking.

The winemaking started quite small with 500 cases but, in time, grew to produce 2,220 cases of nine different wines and 2,200 cases of one particular wine, affectionately called XXXIV after Vermeil's Super Bowl win. (The XXXIV is 82% Cab, 2% Merlot, and 16% Cab Franc.) But

Zinfindel grapes from the Luvisi plot planted in 1908.

even between the family and the winery, Dick wasn't busy enough so his friend Carl Peterson persuaded him to join the Kansas City Chiefs as head coach in 2001. The wine business continued to thrive, as did Vermeil, until he retired (again!) in 2005.

Dick Vermeil currently spends his time travelling, lecturing, and selling wines across the country. He and his wife, Carol (his high school sweetheart), find themselves back in Calistoga several times a year. They are almost always around for the Louie Vermeil Classic (a sprint car race) and harvest.

Leadership

Vermeil will always be remembered for his emotional breakdowns during press conferences, even crying on occasion. These public displays have made him one of the most beloved football coaches in history.

The coach's success is summed up in "Dick Vermeil's Seven Commonsense Principles of LEADERSHIP," which is the foundation of his popular lectures on the subject. These guidelines apply not only to coaching football but also to excelling in almost any endeavor, including Vermeil's second career as a winemaker:

1. Make sure your people know you care!
2. Be a good example!
3. Create a working atmosphere in which people enjoy working!
4. Define—delegate—then lead!
5. Bring energy to the workplace!
6. Build relationships as you implement your vision, values, and process!
7. Be sincere!

One of Dick Vermeil's favorite stories about wine and football is when he bet a bottle of Bryant Family Cabernet Sauvignon (valued at around $500) to his kicker and fellow wine enthusiast Morten Andersen of the Kansas City Chiefs if he converted the game's winning kick. Andersen completed the kick and won the wager, but Vermeil was reprimanded as the prize constituted extra compensation and was therefore a violation of the NFL league salary rules. Anderson, however, did find a bottle of the Cab strategically (and anonymously) placed in his locker.

Meet Mr. Smith

Though passionately devoted to the winery, Vermeil spends a great deal of his time on the road, giving inspirational and motivational lectures and promoting his wines. Vermeil was travelling when we first visited Calistoga in the early spring of 2011, so we were fortunate to garner an interview with Paul Smith, who was then the head winemaker and vineyard manager at both Vermeil Wines and OnThEdge, a small boutique winery in Napa that specializes in the little known, but highly respected, Charbono grape. [When we recently revisited Vermeil in March of 2015 we discovered that Paul was no longer associated with Vermeil, having moved on to another winery.]

That initial meeting with Paul took place on a rainy, cold Sunday morning. It was in fact our very first interview with any winemaker so we were a bit nervous and arrived early for our appointment. We waited in Vermeil's Calistoga tasting room. [Recently, a second tasting room opened in Napa.] Then, as now, the Calistoga room was managed by the super energetic Mary Sue Frediani, who graciously guided us through various well-made wines as we waited for Paul to return from the vineyards. We soon learned that the Frediani and Vermeil families go back several generations, as documented by the fading black-and-white photos on the walls of the tasting room. It was obvious from these images that family connections and age-old friendships are the foundation of this operation.

We were looking at the photographs when a giant of a man lumbered towards us. A little wobbly with a slight stoop, Paul Smith wore the standard torn jeans and full beard of a Napa winemaker. Smith extended a huge, earth-colored hand, which was tough as leather. After introducing himself, he said it was unusual for him to be the subject of an interview and he was unaccustomed to, and uncomfortable in, the limelight. We laughed as we informed him that this was our first interview also and that seemed to set him more at ease. After a few minutes, he warmed to us and to the subject of winemaking, an art and science he has been practicing his entire career.

Smith earned his degree at Cal State, Fresno in enology-viticulture and has over 30 years' experience in the wine field. He's held technical and management positions with companies including Joseph Phelps Vineyards and Robert Mondavi. During Paul's seventeen years with Mondavi, he was responsible for the technical development, facility design, and project management of several internationally recognized, state-of-the-art facilities, including Opus One. He is also a teacher, a talent that became apparent to us very quickly by the knowledgeable and fascinating way he spoke about making wine. He was eager to show us the vineyard so we all trounced out to the parking lot.

Unlike Europe, in California it's not entirely strange for a winery to have a tasting room that's miles away from where their wine is made and/or from their vineyards. The reason for this is that many don't have an associated winery or their vineyards are difficult to reach by car.

Outside, rain was pouring down as we raced to the car. Paul drove a rickety white Saab and, like a platoon sergeant, he instructed us to pile into his decrepit beast. We were about to tour the vineyards; the torrential rain only seemed to encourage Smith as we skidded across the unpaved, muddy, pothole-strewn road. Smith pointed out the gnarly, ancient-looking, head-pruned Zinfandel vines, planted originally in 1956, which stood watch over the more delicate, refined, tidy, and cordon-pruned Cabernet and Syrah vines that grew by their side.

After our guided tour of the vineyard (where we miraculously managed not to get stuck in the mud), we returned to the tasting room to dry out and continue talking. Whenever Paul mentioned a particular wine, a bottle and clean wine glasses would magically appear in front of us as Mary Sue raced around the tasting room without ever letting her attention to her customers stray too far from us. It was something of a shock when we later realized we'd been talking nonstop for almost five hours.

A Unique Grape

Despite his work experience before Vermeil, Paul's vision was never to emulate the creamy smooth style expressed by Opus One or the Bryant Family. Smith had a deep passion for the unusual Charbono grape, which makes for a rustic, deeply colored wine with a distinc-

Irene Roux Wines & Liquors, Fillmore Street, San Francisco, was owned by Dick Vermeil's grandfather at the turn of the century. RIGHT: Gene Frediani at Frediani Vineyards.

Dick Vermeil's Italian great-grandparents at their summer home in Calistoga;
they owned half of Calistoga at the turn of the last century.

tive spicy, tarry edge. Similar in style to Petite Syrah, but not as powerful or complex, it has been used in Europe as a bulking agent to add color or body to lesser wines. The Charbono grape is not hugely popular in the U.S., mainly because it can't be labeled as Cabernet, Merlot, or Zinfandel. The grape itself is not well known either. Plenty of other fashionable grapes are much more profitable to grow, though that fact hardly impacted Paul's loyalty.

Like the Charbono grape he so admired, Smith seemed sturdy and reliable, as tough as boots. He is one of those rare people who says what he means and means what he says. His honesty could be disarming, as could his down-to-earth nature. Most winemakers in the valley drive expensive 4×4s, punting $200 bottles of Cabernet Sauvignon, but Paul was hardly an ordinary winemaker. It was no surprise to learn he was a Navy man in

Vietnam—a submariner, no less.

For many of us, the idea of being trapped underwater for months at a time would cause a claustrophobic shudder, but Smith enjoyed the enclosed atmosphere. He also realized that his time isolated deep under the sea gave him a definite advantage as a winemaker, as both professions require a fierce ethical dedication and extreme patience. Zen-like commitment is a must for the extended periods of seclusion, continual repetitive manual labor, and long hours his job required. Winemaking is a complicated business, especially when one man is wearing several hats—horticulturist, chemist, businessman, and gambler, with a splash of artist thrown in for good measure. Paul worked many hours both in the cellar and the vineyard with only one helper, which meant he did a massive amount of the work himself.

His days started at 5:00am and he would spend the next twelve to fourteen hours in a dark, damp cellar working with his grapes. Out in the fields, he possessed an almost spiritual connection to the earth. This is a trait he shares with Dick Vermeil, who still attends every harvest, racing around the vineyards in his old tractor, roaring advice and opinions to the crew as if they were players on the football field. "Wine is in Dick's blood," said Smith. "So many developers want a Napa Valley charm on their bracelet. With Dick, it's absolutely authentic. He's still got his soul here."

Family Ties

Unraveling the connections between the Vermeil, Frediani, and Smith families is a complicated piece of genealogy, but crucial in understanding the evolution of the vineyards and winery.

After emigrating from their native Tuscany around the 1890s, the Fredianis eventually landed in Napa Valley. Abramo Frediani (Mary Sue's grandfather) traveled over from the Sonoma Valley to the northernmost portion of the Napa Valley, and picked a property in the rustic Calistoga region, just

 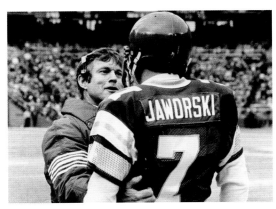

Dozens of action packed photos from Vermeil's football days hang on the walls of the tasting room in Calistoga.

221   Vermeil Wines

Promotional photo of Dick Vermeil holding a magnum of his wine.

off Pickett Road. The small, roughhewn, one-track lane still remains (now it is part of Frediani's property). Coincidentally, this dividing line between the two counties is also the inspiration for the Charbono bottling label, called OnThEdge, meaning it sits on the border between Napa and Sonoma.

The vineyards lie near the base of the Palisades and offer up a varied patchwork of soils. The Pleasanton gravels at the base of the hills are better suited for the production of red wines; the richer, heavier soils and the Bale clay loams sit lower down near the Napa River and are ideal for white varieties such as Sauvignon Blanc and Semillion. The vineyards enjoy warm days and cool foggy nights, which are the most important weather features of the Calistoga area.

Grandpapa Abramo Frediani was always interested in grapes and wine production. In their native village, north of Lucca, his family had farmed the land for generations. In the New World, he continued to work in various vineyard and winery operations. His oldest son, Eugene (Gene), returned home after the Second World War and with his bride, Jean, purchased a small parcel of land in Calistoga. Gene leased the nearby orchards and fields and turned them into thriving vineyards of high quality. At one point, the Fredianis owned over 250 acres and leased another 250. Gene's reputation as a quality grape grower grew quickly, and his fruit was sought after by many wineries. Eventually, he planted the world-renowned Eisele Vineyard, which is today considered one of the finest and most famous in Northern California.

The relationship between the Fredianis and Vermeils dates back to even before the marriage of Jean and Gene. Their families had summered together in Calistoga and remained close for generations. Even today, their long-forgotten connections keep surfacing. In 2001, two years after the winery was established, Mary Sue learned that the Frediani ranch (which had been purchased in 1972 and is currently used for Vermeil's JVL Cab) had once been owned by Vermeil's great-grandfather, Garibaldi Iaccheri. "Garibaldi had originally planted the vineyards and started the Calistoga Wine Company way back then," writes Mary Sue in an impassioned email. "So here we are, using fruit from a vineyard that was once in Dick's own family to make his wine!" Mary Sue, the family historian, also discovered that Dick's French great-grandfather, Jean Louis Vermeil, had a summer home in the same village near Nice where the Frediani's great-grandmother, Jean Cazeau Roux, was born and raised. "Talk about a small world," exclaims Mary Sue. "I say there are no accidents in life. Everything happens for a reason and the only reason we discovered all these connections is because of our making wine together, even though our families have known each other and been friends all these years."

PORTFOLIO

The estate produces five reds—a spicy Syrah and Zinfandel, an elegant Cabernet Franc, a supercharged age-worthy Cabernet Sauvignon called JLV after Vermeil's great-grandfather Jean Louis, and the tarry Charbono that's produced under the OnThEdge label. The white is a Sauvignon Blanc with light tropical notes and a light creamy finish produced from clay-rich soils.

As an overview, all the wines show good clear, clean fruit with a slightly rustic edge. Any new wood utilized is pushed to the background and the chunky black fruits sit comfortably on a spicy frame.

The style being achieved by Vermeil's wines are not like the usual Napa wines found in the valley. These are rough-and-ready, powerful wines packed with earthy fruit flavors and displaying a measure of refinement. There's too much dry extract to ever eliminate the rustic, earthy, dry character that runs like a pulsing vein throughout all their red wines. That doesn't make them undrinkable at all; quite the contrary, they are strongly flavored and dense but also accessible with good acidity and soft tannins that provide needed structure. These are "like them or loathe them" wines. The smidgen of elegance hiding in the background adds decent length. Most importantly, though, they have a sense of place and don't hide behind a sheen of new oak that's so frequent in California wines.

Vermeil's are honest California wines made with a certain ripeness and sweetness of fruit that can only be achieved in that climate. This makes them very drinkable. On the whole, the wines are improving as the vines mature, with a step up in elegance and refinement. However, these are wines that are never going to emulate the glossy, sleek style of Napa's most expensive cult wines or lose their unique rustic style. Nor, for that matter, do they or the owners want to. Will the Charbono grape ever become as popular as Merlot or Cabernet in California? Definitely not. Plainly put, they are just too challenging and rustic. However, having said that, Petit Verdot seems to have its admirers.

Vermeil's wines have changed noticeably since we last tasted them in 2011. Today they seem to have put on weight and become cleaner and more modern in style. The new "single vineyard" releases are excellent and indicate a much more serious approach to the whole Vermeil venture, pushing them ever closer to the top tier. Vermeil has certainly benefitted from the new direction in regards to the overall style of the wines across the whole portfolio.

"OnThEdge" Charbono, 2009

The Charbono grape produces a deep ruby-colored wine with an interesting bouquet that's packed with spice, blueberries, black plums, vanilla, earth, and a touch of tar. Interesting wine: smells like a Petite Syrah on the nose but on the palate it's much lighter and elegant, yet still retains a rustic feel to the profile. Good balance and excellent concentration with black cherry flavors. However, it's an acquired taste due to the rusticity. Acidity and tannins are of medium strength and provide needed structure. Good concentration but medium-bodied with a decent tarry finish. It's a well-made and good rendition of a wine from a little known and usually lowly regarded grape.

Cabernet Franc, 2007

Very darkly colored wine with an almost port-like nose that is obviously enhanced by the hot conditions of the area where it grows. The aromas of the wine are sweet but the wine has a totally dry palate that exudes white peppermill flavors with sweet vanilla oak lurking in the background. Plummy, with ripe black cherry flavors and cracked pepper nuances. Reasonable length and good acidic lift on the finish makes it pair well with meat dishes.

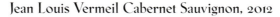

Jean Louis Vermeil Cabernet Sauvignon, 2012

The wines at Vermeil have dramatically improved over the last few years. They are noticeably cleaner, richer, fruitier, and are structured in a much more serious manner. In my view they have reached the next level of winemaking: the big leagues. The Jean Louis cuvée is a great reflection of their "new style." The grapes come from a single block of Cabernet sourced from the family's famous and ancient "Frediani" vineyard. The color is a youthful deep crimson with purple hints and a broad watery rim. Powerful dark aromas leap from the glass: ripe cassis, black cherries, earth and coffee, chocolate, and briar paired with a sweet dash of vanilla oak. Superb on the palate, smooth and generous with classic Napa Cab flavors of very ripe black cherries, small black currants, vanilla, and oak, with loamy notes. Liqueur-flavored red currants and red cherry also make an appearance. This wine exhibits superb inner richness and depth of fruit revealing very concentrated flavors, a broad, stretchy deep mid-palate, and an incredibly long finish. The wine caresses and coats the palate with its primary fruit; however, there is a serious tannic structure buried beneath. The tannins are sweet and the wine's juiciness is kept in check by adequate acidity. A complex high-quality wine that will age nicely over the next few years and hold for yet another five.

Integrity, 2011

This wine presents a deep crimson color with a youthful pinkish rim. Its refined nose offers up a mélange of primary ripe black and red forest fruits and high-quality new oak. Secondary aromas of lavender, thyme, spices, earth, and minerals can be found in the background. It's obviously a complex and serious wine. Expansive in the mouth, the wine is lush, fruity, and fresh yet is also well-structured and seriously concentrated with powerful tannins and good uplifting acidity. Seems to float on the palate with a wonderfully textured sweet-ripe mouth-feel. Initially the wine exhibits a classic cassis and black cherry kick from the dominant amount of Cabernet (71%) in the blend; red cherries, red currants, and green herbs from the Cabernet Franc (26%) appear mid-palate; and finally, a lingering hint of spice from the touch of the blended Petite Syrah (3%) adds interest to an endless vanilla-tinged finish. This wine has excellent balance and will age well. In my opinion, the best wine in their portfolio.

Rosedale Block Cabernet Sauvignon, 2012

The first of Vermeil's two new stellar single-vineyard wines releases. This "single block" vineyard is situated to the east of Calistoga in Cougar Canyon, a micro-climate that benefits from cooling fog at night, heavy breezes, and a virtually bottomless, free-draining Pleasanton gravel soil. The wine mainly has a dark fruit (cassis, black plums, and black cherry) profile but there is a small dash of crunchy red summer berries lurking in the background that adds interest and lift. The wine is complex on the nose with savory secondary aromas of Portobello mushrooms, dark chocolate, briar, and sweet vanilla oak. The flavors on the palate mirror the nose, and the weight is full-bodied with excellent levels of concentrated dark fruits. There is superb balance and structure to this wine, revealing excellent acidity and powerful tannins hidden beneath the wealth of ripe fruit. Long in the mouth, the wine ends with an uplifting blast of small frambois on the finish. Overall, this is a superb wine with a darker profile than the Pickett Road cuvée.

Picket Road Block Cabernet Sauvignon, 2012

I absolutely adore this wine. It has more of a red-fruit profile than the Rosedale Block Cabernet plus a lusher, more textured mouth-feel. As if in reverse of the Rosedale, this wine first showcases very ripe, red crunchy fruits then sweeps into the black fruits with a swish. Red cherries, raspberries, and red currants give way both on the nose and palate to cassis and black cherries swathed in vanilla. There are also notes of minerals and light spices. Soft and generous in the mouth, the wine is full-bodied, smooth, and broad. Despite being less tannic with lower acid levels this is slightly better balanced than the Rosedale with an exceptional, endless finish (over two minutes). A totally mind-blowing wine and easily one of the best wines in the Vermeil 2012 portfolio.

Fess Parker

Sta. Rita Hills
2010 Chardonnay

Ashley's

Fess Parker

FESS PARKER WINERY

Los Olivos

On the Trail

As we traveled by car from Sonoma in Northern California down through the fertile valleys lush with bright swathes of tall green and yellow grasses swaying in the wind, the terrain slowly gave way to a flatter, dustier, more arid countryside with noticeably higher temperatures. It was a long, magnificent drive. We eventually motored through the coastal Santa Barbara region, even though the maritime winds caused our big American car to shudder and swerve, reminding us why the county is so revered by grape growers and cult wine producers such as Ojai and Morgan. The hot, arid days and cool nights of the region provide excellent ripening conditions for the grapes while, at the same time, create fog that can cause the dreaded gray rot. Yet this unique powerful wind, the one that almost lifted our car off the asphalt, is also the perfect cure for the dampness, pushing it far into the Central Valley. As we streamed towards dusty Paso Robles, the latest hotspot

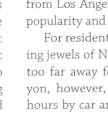

for the production of high-grade, thick-skinned Zinfandel and Syrah, temperatures rose even higher and the green gave way to dusty beige. Even so, the potential for grape production was obvious, especially as irrigation is widely accepted as the norm.

Along the way to the Fess Parker Winery, we stopped to check out two superb wineries: Tablas Creek and Justin. Even though they did not fit within the criteria for inclusion in this book, it was a joy to taste the amazing wines from these two excellent producers. Finally, we entered the quaint town of Los Olivos and hit the newly-in-vogue Foxen Canyon Wine Trail. Only a stone's throw from Los Angeles, this region has exploded in popularity and was packed with visitors.

For residents of Los Angeles, the winemaking jewels of Napa and Sonoma are a smidgen too far away for a quick escape. Foxen Canyon, however, can be reached within a few hours by car and has recently gained a stellar reputation for producing excellent wines. It is

Tiny coonskin cap toppers are sold in Fess Parker's winery.

obvious that Fess Parker and his family were well ahead of the curve when they invested in this valley. Wineries have popped up everywhere on the trail, and good ones to boot: fashionable wineries like Testarossa and Firestone have settled here and earned high acclaim not only with the public, but also in the press. But the only winery that is considered to be truly exceptional and historical on the trail is Fess Parker. Their wines regularly score above the 90s in the press and they produce numerous varietals of different grapes and superb single-vineyard Syrah offerings. And who is not a fan of Davy Crockett?

Movie Star Perfect

Packed with visitors and surrounded by immaculate vines, the iconic tasting room at Fess Parker was featured in Alexander Payne's popular 2004 film *Sideways*, and it is easy to understand why. It is a magnificent room with heavy dark beams, stone floors, comfy club chairs, and two long wooden bars set up for tasting. A distinctive Old West, cowboy feel floods the cozy room. With Fess Parker's trademark coonskin hats for sale and a huge lit fireplace, one almost expects buffalo to come stampeding out of the restrooms.

Fess Parker's tasting room was featured in the seminal wine lover's film, *Sideways* (2004).

The staff is friendly and knowledgeable about the various wines produced on the estate (and there are numerous varietals on offer). It's a very professional operation and, judging from the public's response, also a productive and commercial one. Before he passed away in 2010 at the age of 85, Fess Parker and his wife enjoyed greeting and even serving wine to their visitors. Fess didn't take any part in the winemaking process, but well understood the world of fine wine and apparently had an excellent palate. The winemaking was left to his son, Eli.

Eli Parker began in the family business as assistant winemaker in 1989. After several years of learning the craft at the side of renowned and accomplished winemakers, Eli took the reins as head winemaker with the 1995 vintage. Eli formally assumed the title and responsibilities of president of the win-

ABOVE: Dallas McKennon and Fess Parker in *Daniel Boone*. RIGHT: Parker and Dorothy McGuire in the Disney classic, *Old Yeller* (1957).

ery in 1996. Fess's son-in-law, Tim Snider, has been running the winery since 2010.

King of the Wild Frontier

Even though Fess Parker is well known as portraying two historic cowboys, Davy Crockett and Daniel Boone—the former being the proud wearer of the most ill-fitting headgear in TV history, he is rarely recognized as one of the original pioneers of modern California wines.

Fess Elisha Parker, Jr., was born on August 16, 1924, in Fort Worth, Texas, and grew up on a farm near the small town of San Angelo. It was a tough time in America, from the end of the Great Depression to the beginning of political tensions with Germany that would eventually lead America to join in the Second World War. As a young man in a remote town, there weren't many job prospects available to the young Fess Parker except the usual service enlistment. Like many boys his age, Parker joined the Navy with dreams of becoming a

pilot. But at 6 feet 6 inches tall, the lanky Texan was simply too large to fit into the cockpit of any of the fighter airplanes of the day and he found himself landlocked. However, he was delighted when he was transferred to the Marine Corps as a radio operator and eventually saw action in the South Pacific just prior to the end of the war.

After being discharged from the Navy in 1946, Parker enrolled in the University of Texas on the GI Bill and excelled at sports, where his big frame was an asset. However, after being stabbed in the neck by a drunken driver in a random, violent case of road-rage, he was deemed unfit to participate in sports. Fess graduated from the University of Texas in 1950. He then took drama classes at the University of Southern California and worked his way towards a master's degree in theater history. In the early 1950s, he auditioned at the studios in Hollywood, managed to meet various producers, and

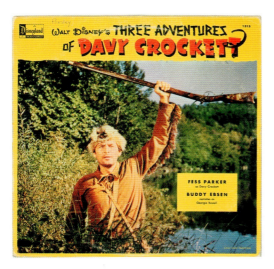

**Davy Crockett collectables include
this LP album from the 1950s. OPPOSITE:
Fess Parker and his son, Eli. Undated.**

landed a small part in a production of *Mister Roberts* with Henry Fonda.

Still, roles in the movies were hard to come by and he struggled to find work. That was until someone at Disney noticed him in the 1954 horror film *Them!*, where Parker had a small scene as a pilot put into an insane asylum after claiming his plane had been downed by giant flying insects. At the time, the Walt Disney Company was looking for an actor to play Davy Crockett on television. According to Parker, they originally considered the popular James Arness (who had starred in *Them!*) for the title role.

But apparently Walt Disney was impressed by Parker and invited the actor to an audition. With his guitar in tow, Fess met Disney, sang a song, and then promptly left. Several weeks later Fess was informed that he'd been chosen for the role of Davy Crockett, having been selected over Arness and several other actors including Buddy Ebsen, who eventually played Crockett's companion, George Russell.

Once knighted with his trademark fur cap, *Davy Crockett* was unveiled to the public and his success was immediate and immense. Fess Parker came to embody what some considered the definitive Walt Disney portrayal of the all-American Wild West hero. Parker became a household name in the States—a blessing and a curse, as the actor would eventually discover. The show attracted so many viewers that some consider it to be the "real" birth of television. It also created a huge market within the film industry, now known as "merchandising." Every kid in America wanted to be Davy Crockett, a fantasy that required the distinctive fur cap, and Disney jumped at the opportunity, pioneering a trend that is still in play today. From coonskin hats, popguns, and chewing gum to moccasin shoes, Disney hit a gold mine with the Crockett accessories.

Self-sufficient On Screen and Off

Much of the success of *Davy Crockett* was due to what Parker brought to the character: namely, himself. His interpretation of the self-sufficient outdoorsman was a hit with males and females, of all ages, but especially with the young. For a start, Parker was a tremendously handsome man, athletic and authoritative, both in build and character. Unlike the usual savage portrait of Crockett, Parker (who was always immaculately groomed) played him as a noticeably softer, more natural character. Part frontiersman, part congressman, and, of course, part tragic hero (he died at the Alamo), Crockett reflected the all-American values of bravery, determination, patriotism, and fair-

Fess Parker always wore his signature coonskin cap in *Daniel Boone*.

no one worried about Fess. Daniel Boone was another frontier character, unabashedly patriotic, and the ratings reflected his popularity. The show ran through the late 1960s, a time of adventure, travel, and personal freedom for individuals. America saw a noticeable increase in camping, trekking, and exploring, and a surge in the popularity of Boys and Girls Clubs among the young. Some people have speculated that, in part, Fess Parker (as a film and TV character) was a small, indirect, yet underlying factor that led to the hippie movement of the mid-1960s. We're not suggesting Fess Parker was a hippie icon, but it is true that a whole generation of kids who grew up on Crockett and Boone entered young adulthood and ventured far beyond their houses, hometowns, and even countries.

Seemingly confined from the start to the small screen, Fess made extensive guest appearances on TV, even composing and singing his own songs on various shows. He regularly appeared in Disney family classics such as *The Great Locomotive Chase*, *Westward Ho*, *the Wagons!*, *Old Yeller*, and *Light in the Forest*. Though Parker felt he was typecast, basically always playing the same role, Disney refused to give him any other kind of part, with a few exceptions.

Throughout his career Parker became increasingly more ambitious. He ventured into wildly different areas of business: buying real estate, including mobile parks, creating resorts, and, of course, growing grapes and making California wine. Starting a vineyard in Los Olivos may seem like a no-brainer today but, at the time, this was a bold and innovative move in an unproven area. We have to admire Parker's unnerving drive, vast appetite for knowledge, and unswerving self-confidence.

ness. He came to symbolize the fundamental American principle of "freedom for everyone," a privilege held sacred by every American, even to this day.

By the time Fess starred as Disney's Daniel Boone in the 1964 TV series, Americans feared a possible nuclear war with the Soviets and national patriotism was high. Blacklisting and censorship were sweeping the nation—but

Emerging Grape Production

By the early 1970s, Parker's acting career was all but gone and he devoted himself entirely to his other endeavors. It was during this period that wine production started to make an impact in Santa Barbara. Fess and his son, Eli, saw the emerging potential in grape production and decided to plant a small vineyard in 1987. At first they were going to buy a modest plot of land, 5½ acres, plant Riesling, and sell the grapes to other winemakers, but over the next few years the project expanded. Soon they were in control of a 714-acre ranch in Los Olivos in the center of the Santa Ynez Valley. As Parker's daughter, Ashley, explains, "Fess is from Texas, so he can't do anything small." The estate now owns and farms 110 acres and farms and purchases fruit from an additional 100 acres.

The Fess Parker wineries' inaugural harvest came in 1989, and to date has earned 90-plus points from the likes of *The Wine Advocate*, *Wine Enthusiast*, and *Wine Spectator*.

In tribute to his acting career, Parker's wine labels sport a logo of a golden coonskin cap; the winery is known for selling coonskin caps and tiny coonskin cap bottle toppers. The whole

The Santa Ynez valley is now fully cultivated but was barely developed when Parker planted a vineyard in 1987. OVERLEAF: The Fess Parker vineyard at sunset.

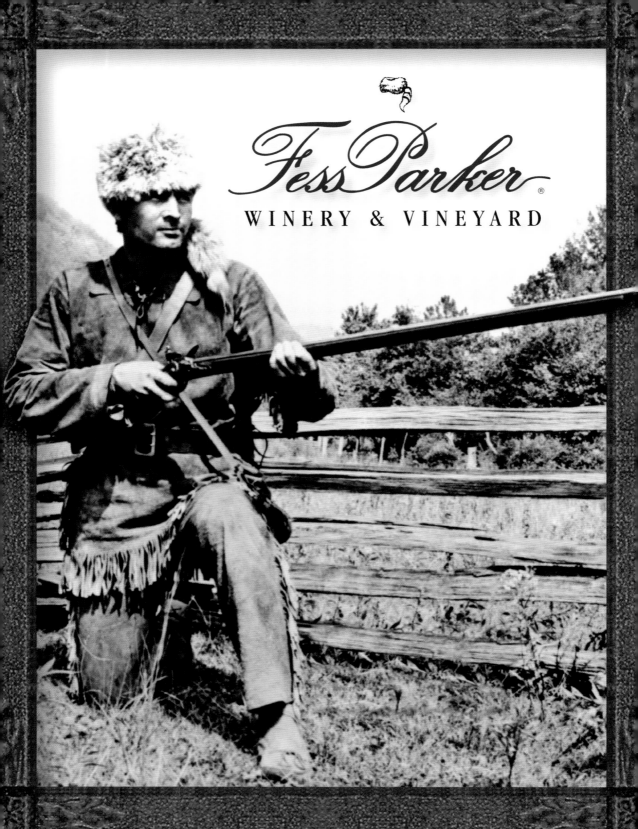

The Fess Parker Winery in Santa Ynez.
RIGHT: Eli Parker is now president of his father's
winery. OPPOSITE: Fess Parker built his career upon
his image as "the king of the wild frontier."

family is involved. In 1998, Ashley became Eli's partner, working on the public relations, sales, and marketing teams. The head winemaker at the estate since 2005 is Blair Fox.

In the entrepreneurial spirit that created the winery, Fess Parker's Doubletree Resort opened in Santa Barbara in the mid-1990s. In 1998 the family bought the landmark Grand Hotel in Los Olivos, which is now re-named Fess Parker's Wine Country Inn & Spa. Both are quite successful. Clearly, the spirit and popularity of Fess Parker continues to thrive with his fans—old and new—who celebrate the legacy of the Wild West, which is alive and well in a vineyard just north of Los Angeles.

Chardonnay, Syrah, and Viognier are among the varietals grown on the estate and, across the board, are all of high quality. The style achieved is fruit forward with layers upon layers of ripe, extracted fruit cradled in spicy, coconutty new oak. Without a doubt, though, the single-vineyard offerings of Syrah are the jewels in the crown of this winery. All are exceptionally rich, spicy, and sturdy, yet also lush and chocolaty. The Rodney's Syrah is especially superb and easily capable of five years of bottle age, but in my opinion best drunk when young.

The wines produced under the Fess Parker label have since been recognized for their style and quality, especially, as mentioned, the single-vineyard Syrahs. Reviews such as 90 points in *Wine Spectator* for the 1993 Syrah and the '93 American Tradition Reserve being named "one of the five best Syrahs in the world" by the *Boston Globe* ensued. The single vineyard 2007 Rodney's Vineyard Syrah was rated very highly by Robert Parker, Jr., in the 93–94 point range, and the 2007 Big Easy Syrah earned 91–93. Syrah is grown next to white Riesling and red Cinsault.

NICK'S TASTING NOTES

Rodney's Vineyard Syrah, Santa Barbara County, 2007

Inky blue-black color with a very interesting nose of black plum, blackberries, spicy vanilla, black cherries, and white pepper. Juicy, bold, and fresh. Background nuances of fresh-cut tobacco, anise, sage, chocolate, and savory meat juices. Rich flavors of spicy black cherries, chocolate, and spicy vanilla coats the palate. Medium to full-bodied, strong, firm, yet sweet tannins and a good, uplifting acidity note give this wine good length. Will last five years.

Ashley's Pinot Noir, Santa Rita Hills, 2007

Deep dark ruby color; fresh and enticing, yet dark Nuits style of Pinot with complex notes of dark plums, black cherries, damp earth, vanilla, and Asian spices on the nose. Rich and brawny on the palate, with an array of sappy black-fruit flavors accompanied by wilder notes of dried herbs, cinnamon, and chocolate. Lighter on the palate than the nose; on the palate it showcases lush red cherries, chocolate-covered raspberries, and spicy vanilla oak. Medium-bodied but very concentrated, quite serious, with medium structured tannins and decent sweet meaty tannins. Good modern-styled vanilla finish. High quality, weighty, yet light in the mouth. Drink now.

Ashley's Chardonnay, Santa Rita Hills, 2013

Exhibiting a shiny gold youthful hue, this wine is a stylistically archetypical Californian Chardonnay with lush, creamy citrus flavors backed up with nuances of bananas, ripe golden apples, pears, and minerals, plus a sweet overlay of powerful creamy vanilla oak. Medium-bodied with a medium concentration of ripe warm-climate fruits, this isn't a powerhouse wine and purposely exhibits a finer, more lively, almost jazzy character. It's flavorful in the mouth with hints of greengage, floral, and honeydew melon that add interest. Refined and very cleanly made.

Rodney's Vineyard Syrah, Santa Barbara County, 2011

The legendary Rodney's Vineyard Syrah could be considered the star of Parker's portfolio. Always a reliable pick, this is a great example of what Santa Barbara can achieve with great terroir. Produced from a cool vintage, this wine is a touch austere and closed at the moment, but nevertheless a serious and age-worthy candidate for future enjoyment. The wine possesses a very dark crimson color with a youthful broad pink rim. Smoky and spicy, warm-climate dark-fruit aromas wrapped in sweet vanilla oak rise from the glass. It's a pungent bouquet without a doubt, packed with dense feral aromas of spikey blackberries, black cherry, and vanilla-tinged cassis fruit, backed up with secondary aromas of liquid smoke, licorice, exotic spices, earth, white pepper, herbs, and blueberries. Complex and medium-bodied on the palate yet fresh and lively due to cool vintage conditions, it reveals a medium concentration of fruit, high but balanced acidity, and slightly chalky tannins, which will probably resolve and merge with bottle age. There's no doubt this currently very brawny wine has great potential with extended bottle age.

Clone 115 Pinot Noir, Santa Rita Hills, 2012

Parker's base for this wine is the reliable Pinot Clone 115, a regularly used, sturdy clone that usually provides the backbone in most "clonal" (same variety, different structure and taste) blends. It's a rare wine for the region with only twelve barrels produced every year. Taut, sinewy, and spikey, this is an unusual wine. Quite light in color, with an initial blast of red cranberry and raspberry fruit, the first impression betrays the wine's overall dark character—chunky, spicy, and brawny. Fresh and modern style in the mouth with good attack and a medium concentration of very toasty red and black vine fruits, the wine finishes with decent length and some stern tannins.

ANDRETTI

S E L E C T I O N S

Cabernet Sauvignon

C A L I F O R N I A

— 2011 —

ALC. 13.6% BY VOL.

Mario Andretti

ANDRETTI WINERY

Oak Knoll, Napa

For the Love of Wine

Mario Andretti didn't get into winemaking by accident or coincidence like some of our celebrity winemakers. He knows exactly why he became a winemaker: he wanted to have friends and family sit at his table for long, lingering meals and enjoy a wine that was reminiscent of his native Italy. Who can blame him? Wouldn't you love to tell your guests: "This little wine comes from our rear south-facing vineyards, which, by the way, is perfect for the production of top-grade Sangiovese. Please enjoy it!" Andretti certainly delights in being able to share his love of wine (and his own bottles) with the people he most enjoys.

But making wine will always rank second to his lifelong love of racing cars, a sport for which he is physically suited. Small and wiry but slightly stocky, Andretti's compact frame was meant to fit into and drive Formula One cars, which are fast, small, bumpy, loud, and

Mario Andretti with his two passions, a glass of wine and a Ferrari.

Eighty Ferraris parked outside the Andretti winery.

cramped. This is a very specialized and dangerous sport. Grand Prix cars have reached speeds of up to 230 mph on the track and are capable of going from 0 to 100 mph and back in less than five seconds. Being in the driver's seat is like piloting a rocket, and when they crash, as they often do, it can prove fatal. A Formula One driver has to be extremely fit, always operate at the very top of his game, and have nerves of steel. These characteristics are evident in Andretti: he's soft spoken, calm, and careful about choosing his words, speaking in a slow but deliberate voice. When asked about the dangers of racing, Andretti simply shrugged and explained it's part of the sport.

Speeding to America

Mario and his twin brother, Aldo, were born on February 28, 1940, in Montona, Italy (now Motovun, Croatia), to Luigi Andretti, a farm administrator, and Rina, a housewife. From his earliest days, Mario and his family were victims of the political strife raging through Italy at the time. In 1948, they landed in a refugee camp in Lucca, subsequently immigrating to the United States in 1955. With only $125 to their name, the Andrettis settled in Nazareth, Pennsylvania, in the heart of the Lehigh Valley. In 1964, Mario became a naturalized United States citizen, though to this day he retains his Italian accent.

Even as a young boy, Mario was fascinated with speed. By the age of five, he and his brother were racing wooden cars through the steep streets of Montona. "The first time I fired up a car," Mario wrote in his book, *What's It Like Out There?*, "I felt the engine shudder and the wheel come to life in my hands; I was hooked. It was a feeling I can't describe. I still get it every time I get into a race car."

In Pennsylvania, Mario and Aldo discovered a half-mile dirt track behind their house; roughhewn and curvy, the track seemed custom made for racing anything with an engine. The twins first revamped a 1948 Hudson Hornet Sportsman, modifying it into a stock car. Funded by money they earned working in their uncle's garage, the brothers started racing in the late 1950s. By 1959, after four races, the twins each had two wins. Near the end of their second season, Aldo was seriously injured in a crash. This did not stop Mario. He continued racing and, by 1961, had garnered 21 modified-stock-car wins in 46 races. His phenomenal potential on the track was obvious.

Andretti is the only racer to be named United States Driver of the Year in three separate decades (1967, 1978, and 1984). Incredibly, he is also one of only three drivers to win races on road courses, paved ovals, and dirt tracks all in one season, and it is a feat that he accomplished a staggering *four* times. With his final IndyCar victory in April 1993, Andretti became the first driver to win IndyCar races in four different decades and the first to win automobile races of any kind in five.

By the end of his career Andretti had 111 career wins on major circuits, including four IndyCar titles, the 1978 Formula One World Championship, and the IROC VI. To date he remains the only driver ever to win all three of the world's most prestigious races: the Indianapolis 500 (1969), the Daytona 500 (1967), and the Formula One World Championship (1967). Along with Juan Pablo Montoya, he is one of only two drivers to have won races in the NASCAR Sprint Cup Series, Formula One, and an Indianapolis 500. No other American has even won a Formula One race since Andretti's victory at the 1978 Dutch Grand Prix!

Italian Wine in Sunny California

This amazing career enabled Mario to travel the world, exploring different cultures and crafts. Winemaking was always a particular interest. However, it took some time for Andretti—a man brought up with lean Chiantis—to appreciate California winemaking. In fact, he was in his thirties before he developed a taste for the American style of winemaking.

"I was in Long Beach for the Formula One race in 1977, having lunch with an internationally diverse group of people," he remembers. "I selected a French wine. An Englishman at the table, who was a connoisseur of California wines, asked why we weren't drinking a California wine in California. Not long after that, I made my first trip to Napa, and the more visits I made to the region, the more fascinated I became with its wines. Here I cultivated knowledge, as well as friendships."

He began dreaming about making his own wine and Napa, with its welcoming atmosphere and ideal weather conditions, seemed like the right place to start.

Andretti didn't act on this dream until after 1994, when a commemorative California wine was produced in his honor. This small event proved inspirational and soon afterwards he decided to buy a vineyard. To accomplish this goal, he teamed up with his former colleague, Joseph E. Antonini, who as president, chairman, and CEO of Kmart, was one of Mario's major sponsors.

The two men found a 42-acre vineyard situated in the heart of the Oak Knoll appella-tion, a few miles south of Yountville, in Napa. As Mario explains, "What we found was a no-name winery that was already planted and the grapes were being sold to several wineries. We purchased the property and the permits, which were already in place."

A Different Grape

The Oak Knoll district is located toward the southern end of the Napa Valley, at a relatively low elevation on the valley floor. The district benefits from the climate-moderating effects of San Pablo Bay; cooling breezes and coastal fog provides for an exceptionally slow ripening of

The always exuberant winner, Mario Andretti.

the grapes, often extending the growing season for up to eight months. This is a much cooler climate than other famous Napa appellations, such as Stags' Leap or Rutherford, yet warmer than the Carneros region to the south, which is the coolest. Happily, for the commercial success of the region, after a decade of work by the growers and winemakers of this area, the Oak Knoll District has been officially recognized as a distinct sub-appellation of Napa Valley.

Even though Andretti claims to be a fan of California wines, his obvious personal preference has remained with the Italian Sangiovese grape and the wines it produces. As fate would have it, soon after purchasing the vineyard, a friend introduced him to a local winemaker named Bob Pepi, who had a reputation for producing fine wines made from the Sangiovese grape. From their first meeting, Pepi saw promise in the Andretti vineyard. "Bob Pepi had come on board with us in the first days," Mario says, "and what he liked most about our site was the vineyard and the possibility of growing Merlot and Chardonnay, as well as limited quantities of Sangiovese, Pinot Noir, and Sauvignon Blanc."

A Winemaking Heritage

Located on Big Ranch Road, Andretti is directly across the street from Lewis Cellars. (Isn't it ironic, we thought, that two famous racecar drivers, Randy Lewis and Mario Andretti, are making their own wines not a stone's throw from each other!)

The Andretti property is designed like a Tuscan villa, circa the 1970s. In fact, there's a touch of the '70s about the whole Andretti setup, from the ornate, gold-embossed family

Andretti's winemaker, Bob Pepi.

crest above the doorway to the paved courtyard. Surrounded by its impressive vineyards, the estate consists of a number of different-sized buildings painted in the traditional pinkish pastel and earthy tones so familiar in the Italian region. Small interconnecting palazzos are adorned with bubbling fountains, cypress trees, and fragrant yellow broom flowers, with twisting vines crawling up the colored walls.

The tasting room, to all appearances, is a mini-shrine to its owner. Pictures, awards, articles, and letters adorn the walls. Visitors seemed to be a mixture of racing fans (some of whom spend more time reading the walls than

tasting the wine) and people who are only vaguely familiar with Andretti's name.

Our first visit to Andretti Winery was highlighted by an interview with winemaker Bob Pepi. As Mario has freely admitted, he personally has little interest in actually making the wines—so if you want to know how the winery operates, you have to talk with Pepi, which is, we discovered, a rare opportunity to learn a lot about winemaking and grape growing.

Bob Pepi

Pepi is the son of the famous winemaker Robert Pepi, proprietor of the respected Robert Pepi Family Winery in Oakville, well known as being among the first to have commercial success selling wines from Napa. The family originated in Florence, Italy, before immigrating to the United States. The Pepis are recognized as early proponents of growing Italian varietal grapes in California.

As a young man, Bob developed his early winemaking skills at the family's estate and soon gained a reputation for pioneering and encouraging the cultivation of the Sangiovese grape in California's winegrowing districts.

Bob's mentor was the legendary cult winemaker Tony Soter, who now runs the Etude Winery. The pair originally worked together at the heavy-hitting Cabernet specialist Chappellet Winery, high on Pritchard Hill.

They made some groundbreaking, powerfully styled wines before going their separate ways and, in the process, Pepi garnered a stellar reputation. He is now a much sought-after

Andretti's winery is designed and painted in the Italian style of a Tuscan villa.

consultant in the States and abroad. He makes wines for various wineries, from the nearby Flora Springs in Napa to as far away as the Bodega Valentin Bianchi in Argentina, one of the oldest and most important wineries in South America. Bob Pepi also has a personal label, Eponymous, which produces small amounts of mountainside Cabernet, Chardonnay, and Pinot Noir from select vineyards in Napa.

The partnership between Bob Pepi and Mario Andretti began by chance in 1995 after a colleague of Pepi's suggested that he take a look at the new venture in town started by a famous Italian racecar driver. Rumor had it that Andretti was planting mostly Italian varietals, which piqued Bob's interest. The two proud Italians met and instantly hit it off.

Over the years, Pepi has been a huge asset to Andretti, who repeatedly remarked to us that if Pepi weren't involved with the winery and the winemaking, he (Andretti) would consider folding up the whole operation. It's obvious, when speaking with the two, that they make a good team and are good friends, talking about each other with fondness and respect. It helps that both are proud of their shared heritage and have a love of all things Italian.

Pepi eventually came on board as Andretti's winemaker and the two agreed on a European style for the portfolio. Pepi was and remains adamant about the vineyard being the most important factor in winemaking.

With Andretti's valley-floor vineyards, they were never realistically going to make a broad-shouldered, super-cult Californian Cab like Bryant or Pride. "It's like having a kid who wants to be a football player but you keep trying to make him a pianist, or vice-versa," Pepi explains with a shrug. "You got to

Winemaker Bob Pepi.

go with what you got." Their style was going to be bright, clean, juicy, and, most importantly, drinkable with food.

Babysit the Grapes

Pepi is a true man of the vineyard. Rangy and tall in frame with weather-beaten skin, he looks more farmer than famous vintner. He doesn't deny this; he says they were all farmers in Napa before the grapes took over. "It is totally like being a farmer," he admits, "but being a farmer with a little control.

"I'm glad I got my start in the vineyards, because that's where you make the wine," he says. "To me, if you're doing it right in the vineyards, then you babysit the grapes through the winery." Pepi doesn't have much interest in brix or pH levels; he places far more emphasis on personal feel and experience. The harvest date, for example, is decided by Pepi when he feels the grapes are ready, not by the numbers or arbitrary equations used by the more meticulous wineries, but by taste alone.

All the grapes on the estate are handpicked after two or three green harvests (handpicking out the unripe and unhealthy grapes from each bunch). They use cordon and cane training of the vines and are trying to be as organic as possible, but occasionally have to carry out some adjustments in unusual years.

The style of the wines follows Mario's preferences—European with a splash of Californian sunshine. They are not huge and fruity as some of the wines often produced in Napa, but rather molded in a more food-friendly style. They are immediate with moderate but ripe fruit and low levels of tannins, but also retain a decent acidic balance, which keep the wines focused and fresh. Of all the whites we tasted, the Montona Chardonnay impressed us much more than the other somewhat ubiquitous white varieties. As for the reds, the lightly fruity but ripe and succulent Sangiovese took the top marks over the more expensive Montona range. All the wines are reasonably priced.

Andretti produces a rather large portfolio of wines.

PORTFOLIO

The Andretti Winery produces roughly 10,000 cases of wine a year, from whites such as Riesling, Sauvignon Blanc, Pinot Grigio, and Chardonnay to such reds as Merlot, Zinfandel, Syrah, Cabernet Sauvignon, and, of course, Sangiovese. The estate vineyards are planted with Cabernet Sauvignon, Pinot Grigio, Chardonnay, and Merlot.

The portfolio is divided into four levels of quality and is somewhat confusing: the first is the California Selections series, in which all the wines are from grapes sourced (bought in) from across Napa and Sonoma. These are easy drinking, soft wines in the inexpensive bracket. The Selections series include a Fume Blanc, Chardonnay, Merlot, Zinfandel, and a Cabernet Sauvignon. The Villa series is a step up. The grapes are still sourced from various appellations but are mostly picked from individual vineyards. The Napa Valley series is the next level and Bob Pepi sources all the fruit contained in these wines from vineyards carefully chosen for their specific characteristics.

Finally, the Montona Reserve series, named after Andretti's Italian childhood home of Montona, Italy, is the highest quality level in the portfolio. These select wines are produced exclusively from estate-grown grapes and other premium Napa Valley vineyards. For each vintage, Bob Pepi uses the best handpicked fruit; the wines are produced in limited quantities and include an Estate Reserve Chardonnay, Estate Reserve Merlot, and Napa Valley Reserve Cabernet Sauvignon. These are more expensive and can be hard to find in most shops.

When we returned to the winery in 2015 we discovered that the two new Montona offerings we tasted show that Andretti has the ability to compete with the big boys in Napa. These wines display a serious side to Andretti's winemaking and presently include a Cabernet Sauvignon, Chardonnay, Merlot, and a terrific Super Tuscan. Produced in very limited quantities, these wines are in high demand and are first made available to wine club members and then sold exclusively through the winery or on the website.

NICK'S TASTING NOTES

Sangiovese, Napa Valley, 2008

Very typical medium-deep color, with the sour red cherries and earthy aromas of classic Italian Sangiovese and a twist of California sunshine. As Pepi explained, they are not trying to achieve blockbuster wines but a more drinkable, European style that can be enjoyed immediately and goes well with food. The wine achieves a good balance of medium-to-high acidity, sweet red ripe fruits, and light approachable tannins on a very medium-bodied frame. The style is more Chianti than Brunello. There are the typical bright red cherry and earthy flavors with a whack of sweet vanilla oak that pairs with the sweetness of the fruit. Medium concentration and of decent length, this wine is drinking well.

Montona Reserve Chardonnay, 2007

A lemon-colored wine with some evidence of creeping age on the rim. Very creamy on the nose, with notes of sour cream paired with a combination of exotic and cool-climate fruits such as pineapples, Cox's apples, pears, grapefruits, and citrus fruits. On the almost off-dry palate there are hints of spice and a strong buttery overtone. Clean and focused, medium-bodied, it's well balanced—not a huge mouth-feel but adequate—with uplifting acidity on the medium finish. Drink now.

It was a wonderful opportunity to try an aged Reserve Andretti Chardonnay side by side against the recent cuvée bearing the same name (below). The color of this aged wine is darker gold and the wine overall is more savory on both the nose and palate. It is plainly obvious that this wine's separate components have now jelled and come together with additional age and the wine has developed a seamless quality.

Montona Reserve Chardonnay, 2012

This Chardonnay reveals a youthful light gold color with bright reflective hints. A clean, fresh, juicy nose releases scents of ripe white stone fruits, such as lemons, limes, peaches, and white pears soaked in well-judged sweet vanilla oak. Hints of white flowers, minerals, and grilled nuts can be found lurking in the clear background. Medium-bodied, the wine reveals a tight mineral style, however it's finely concentrated with a good depth of silky, warm-climate citrus-like fruit flavors, especially on the mid-palate, that coat the mouth. Fine-tuned levels of high acidity accompany the laser-like bright citrus flavors that drive towards a delineated, mouthwatering finish. The oak on the palate is very restrained (spending twelve months in new oak) and lets the vineyard fruit shine through the wine. A Californian Chardonnay made with deft precision and a European restraint.

Montona Reserve Cabernet Sauvignon, 2012

This is Andretti's Californian rendition of a Super Tuscan; a blend of the estate's very tasty, lip-smacking Sangiovese with a dollop of Cabernet Sauvignon, added in an effort to produce a wine with better body, color, and, most importantly, mid-palate depth.

The wine's color is a youthful, clean, and bright medium ruby red. A cornucopia of red- and black-fruit aromas wrapped in toasty new oak soar from the glass with ripe scents of red and black cherries, red plums, spice, and vanilla oak. Again, this is a very precisely made wine with all components finely tuned on the palate; tightly wound levels of uplifting acidity, well-judged sweet oak, and currently very powerful tannins create a sturdy structure for the fruit. An interesting and very well-constructed wine that's a touch angular at the moment but should broaden and soften with some extended bottle age.

Raymond Burr

ESTATE PORT

SONOMA COUNTY

2 0 0 9

ALC. 18.5% BY VOL.   500ml

Raymond Burr

RAYMOND BURR VINEYARDS AND WINERY

Healdsburg

At Home in the Vineyard

Though we believe in the adage that one should never judge a book by its cover, still, it's hard not to form a first impression of a person by the look of their home. The same is true for a wine estate, especially after visiting hundreds of them around the world. The assumed value of the land, the design of the buildings, the up-keep of the vines, and many other factors form a visitor's perception of the type of person who works and oftentimes lives on the property.

For example, the meticulously groomed Silverado Estate (owned by the descendants of Walt Disney) positively sparkles, echoing the Disneyesque vision of the fantastic, while the Kamen Estate reflects the rugged, singular, and all-encompassing passions of its owner, Robert Kamen. Visiting the Andretti Winery is akin to stepping into Italy, complete with Tuscan palazzos emblazoned with the earthy orange tones of the Adriatic region, while the artful boulder gardens and amazing flora at Chappellet reflect the imaginative design aesthetic and artistry of Molly Chappellet. Then we come to the Raymond Burr Estate in Dry Creek, Sonoma, once owned by the popular television star.

After winding up the rough drive we parked under a tree, as there's no formal parking lot. It was raining and in the foggy afternoon, the estate resembled a fading farmhouse complete with worn porch and creaky screen door. Although Burr died more than two decades ago, his presence can be felt almost everywhere on the grounds. There are the cracked greenhouses still used to grow his beloved orchids, the well-worn, roughshod wooden decking overlooking the slightly untamed and overgrown vineyards, and, of course, the array of pictures and memorabilia—indoors and out—of the man once known to the public as Perry Mason.

Burr spent most of his later years on the estate and though we immediately sensed that wonderful times were enjoyed there, there was also a palpable feeling of loss and sadness in the many shrines to his memory. Clearly, it wasn't just a place to grow grapes and make wine like, say, Silverado, where they attempt to pump out the finest, most concentrated yet elegantly modern styled wines. No, the Burr Estate was obviously built around the enjoyment of nature, place, and good living. It is comfortable and rustic, welcoming and inviting, making any visitor feel like a long-lost friend and cher-

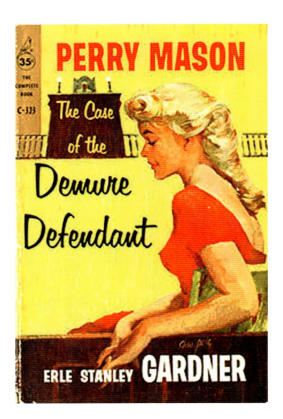

The popular TV show was based on
books by Erle Stanley Gardner.

ished guest. And so it was no surprise that the estate reflected the loving kindness and fond memories of its elderly proprietor and Burr's longtime partner, a lovely, soft-spoken Father Christmas lookalike named Robert Benevides.

Memories Last a Lifetime, and Beyond

In the tasting room, we also met Francisco Baptista, supervisor and event planner for the vineyard. Both he and Robert were wearing worn dungarees and seemed to be slightly suspicious of our request for an interview. Though we had made an appointment weeks earlier, we couldn't help but wonder if they had wanted to either cancel on us or, at the least, not be very forthcoming. We'd already spent some time pondering whether or not we could ask Benevides some rather personal questions without offending him. We understood that he might be reluctant to share information with us, as recently there had been some controversy about issues both personal and professional.

We asked for a quiet place to talk and were ushered into a small office, crammed full of metal file cabinets. Two desks were jammed into the room and papers, file folders, and invoices covered every surface. There was barely room for our tiny digital recorder. It was just Robert and us packed into the room and no one seemed sure of how to proceed.

After a few initial tense questions, Benevides began to relax (and so did we). He leaned back in his chair and folded his hands behind his head. We refrained from asking questions about his personal relationship with Burr until he seemed more forthcoming. Soon, though, he opened up, reminiscing about his old friend and the joyous times they shared together. We began to sense that he was enjoying his trip down memory lane and it was obvious that his deep-rooted feelings for Burr had not dwindled over the decades. For Benevides, the property is a living tribute to Burr. Everywhere we looked there were pictures of the burly actor, bottles he'd signed, posters of his films and TV shows.

It was painfully obvious how much Benevides still missed his partner. He talked about the trips they often took to their beloved Portugal, Burr's fondness for cooking, and the languid, peaceful

Raymond Burr and his partner, Robert Benevides, who now runs the vineyard.

times they spent drinking wine while looking at their vineyards from the porch. His eyes welled up as fond recollections came flooding back.

A Secret Life

Born in 1930, Benevides had always dreamed of becoming an actor, and moved to Hollywood in his late teens to break into the big time. He was a stunningly handsome young man and easily found bit parts until finally landing a role on a TV crime series called *Perry Mason* in the mid-1950s. He became increasingly good friends with Raymond Burr, the star of the show, whose portrayal of a sympathetic and uncannily prescient lawyer was to become his defining role.

A serious relationship developed between

The tasting room is a shrine
to the life and career of Burr.

the two men, a relationship that would last more than 30 years. However, it was not a time when homosexuality was considered acceptable. In fact, any hint of homosexuality in the '50s and '60s could absolutely destroy an actor's career. In 1963, after having been together for about three years, Benevides gave up acting. Eventually, he would become a production consultant for more than twenty *Perry Mason* made-for-TV movies and the executive in charge of production for *Ironside*, another long running TV show starring Burr.

The Life of Raymond Burr

The Canadian actor was born on May 21, 1917, to a concert pianist mother and an Irish father who was a hardware salesman. Part of his childhood was spent in China; he moved to California when his parents divorced. He attended junior college in Long Beach and took some courses at Stanford. His acting career started in 1937 at the Pasadena Playhouse before he became a contract player at RKO. From 1946 to 1957, he appeared in more than 60 films, usually playing the heavy, and frequently worked in both television and radio. Perhaps his most well-known movie role was as the suspected murderer in Alfred Hitchcock's classic thriller *Rear Window* (1954).

His breakout role, of course, was as the gruff but brilliant lawyer, Perry Mason, in a show that ran from 1957 to 1966. By the end of his life, he'd garnered two Emmy Awards for his work in the series. His second hit was as the wheelchair-bound investigator Robert Ironside, which earned him six Emmy and two Golden Globe nominations.

Burr was a guarded but intriguing man. On screen he embodied the rough and tough determined fighter of crime. In reality he was a sensitive, gentle, and generous man who liked to cook and drink all day (when not working he would have his first of glass of wine while cooking breakfast as he started heating the pans, remembers Benevides). He generously donated to many charities, becoming a well-known philanthropist.

However, throughout his life, he was haunted by personal demons. He had worked hard to build a career and was constantly terrified by the threat of losing everything if his secret life was ever discovered. In fact he was so concerned about his image that he rarely, if ever, spoke of his private life in interviews. To combat and subdue his ever-increasing fears, he bizarrely became an imaginative fantasist, making up stories whenever the whim struck him.

Burr played the villain in Alfred Hitchcock's *Rear Window*, 1954.

At one point he claimed to be a war hero at the battle of Okinawa; another time he told reporters he had been married three times.

He claimed his first marriage was in 1942, to an aspiring actress named Annette Sutherland, whom he had met while working in London. He said she died in 1943, when her plane was shot out of the sky while she was travelling to Spain with a touring theater company. Burr then insisted he married Isabelle Ward, but this relationship ended in a quick divorce. Finally, Burr said he had settled down and married Laura Andrina Morgan, who died of cancer in 1955. He added that his son, ten-year-old Michael Evan Burr, died of leukemia in 1953. Years later, a newspaper exposé could only verify that a Raymond Burr had indeed married an Isabelle Ward; the rest of his stories could not be documented, including his war escapades and the birth and/or death of a son.

Surprisingly, Burr was never outed during the course of his long career (a feat that would be practically impossible today). Years later, in a *People* magazine interview, Benevides finally admitted to Burr's homosexuality, something the man himself would never do during his lifetime.

Making Wine and Growing Orchids

In 1976, as the nine-year *Ironside* series was drawing to a close, Benevides began thinking about fulfilling a lifelong dream of living on a working farm. "I wasn't thinking about making wine when I came here," he explains. "I had read *The Good Earth* by Pearl S. Buck when I was a kid and I'd always had this dream about owning land."

Benevides had grown up on a farm and asked his elderly father, who lived in Sonoma, to find a property for sale in the area. One day the senior Benevides called to say he had found the perfect place, in Dry Creek Valley, just north of Healdsburg. Burr and Benevides went to check it out.

"When my father showed us this place, it was eight acres with nothing on it," remembers Benevides. "I mean, nothing. It was only Manzanitas and rattlesnakes." Even so, Benevides and Burr fell in love with the land and purchased the property. They were both into the cultivation of orchids and this seemed the perfect place to continue their hobby. Not long after, they purchased an adjoining property that included a house and a barn. By

Burr appeared on Jack Benny's TV show in 1961.

1980, both men had sold their homes in Los Angeles and moved to Sonoma to live fulltime.

"At the time, the valley was mostly prunes, walnuts, and apples," according to Benevides. "The agriculture was diverse, unlike today." Around this time, the early '80s that is, the Dry Creek Valley AVA was just beginning to be recognized as prime terrain for the growing of Cabernet Sauvignon and Chardonnay grapes. Eventually, the entire valley would be a monoculture dedicated almost solely to grapes.

Even before winemaking, Burr and Benevides were interested in the cultivation and hybridization of orchids. Their hobby turned serious when they started a company devoted to orchids called Sea God Nurseries, which eventually had a presence in Fiji, Hawaii, the Azores, and Southern California.

One of their orchid growing schemes, however, did not pan out. "We were in the Azores, visiting relatives," explains Benevides with a smile. "Raymond noticed that the Pan Am flights were going back empty so he came up with a scheme to grow plants in the Azores and transport the flowers back on Pan Am. We brought people over to Sonoma to show them how to grow the orchids in the Azores." The idea might have worked out brilliantly except for one unexpected turn of events: Pan Am went out of business before the orchid scheme could take hold. Still, this did not deter the two partners from continuing in the orchid business. In fact, their partnership within the orchid world was responsible for the cultivation of hundreds of new orchids being added to the worldwide catalogue including the "Barbara Hale," which Burr named after his *Perry Mason* co-star. (A gorgeous example of one of Burr's orchids adorns the wooden table in the tasting room; we learned that orchids could live forever.)

First Vintage

It was Burr who first wanted to cultivate grapes. "Back then it cost about $35,000 an acre to plant grapes. Mostly, people were growing Zinfandel but Raymond didn't like Zin. We had to restructure the land and put in drains and so forth," Benevides explains with a shake of his head. The first grapes on the estate were planted in 1986: Cabernet Sauvignon, Cabernet Franc, Chardonnay, and,

Barbara Hale (AKA Della Street) was Burr's co-star and close friend right up until his death in 1993. Burr cultivated a Barbara Hale orchid in her honor.

especially for the proprietors, a small section of Port grape varieties—the bare-root stocks imported from Portugal.

In 1990, the beautiful south-facing vineyards below the house produced their first vintage. Carefully handpicked, they were carried down to the Pedroncelli Winery where John Pedroncelli, a second-generation winemaker, made the wine for the two men. After spending eighteen months in French and American oak cooperage, the wine was bottled in November 1992 and finally released in 1995.

By 1992 the vineyards were in their prime—but Burr's health was failing; he had been diagnosed with kidney cancer. At a time when he could have legitimately retired to "watch his garden grow" he made a decision to take on a grueling schedule of shooting four more two-hour *Perry Mason* television films that each involved six weeks of shooting, a testament to his commitment to, and love of, acting. (He would only live to film two of them; four others were filmed without him as a series called *A Perry Mason Mystery*.) Burr found time to taste from barrels the 1992, and a few days before his death, to watch the harvest. By some coincidence, and not a little skill, the 1992 Raymond Burr Cabernet Sauvignon is very much like the man: big, full of gusto, complex, and jubilantly alive.

Burr passed away on September 12, 1993, at his beloved Sonoma country ranch. He was 76 years old. "I was left here with all these grapes," says Benevides sadly. "We had just started producing wine. I had never planned on running a winery or getting involved with this at all. It just happened."

Though Burr bequeathed the bulk of his estate to Robert Benevides, the will was

Raymond Burr, Barbara Hale, and Robert Benevides at the vineyard, shortly before Burr's death in 1993.

challenged by his niece and nephew, Minerva and James, the children of his late brother, James E. Burr. The tabloids estimated that the estate was worth $32 million, but Benevides' attorney, John Hopkins, countered that the claim was ridiculous. According to Robert, Burr was both generous and frivolous with his money and died practically broke. Benevides won the claim and now owns 100% of the estate, which is certainly what Raymond Burr would have wanted.

"He was such a humble man, he did not want the vineyard named after him," Benevides says. His original plan was to name the vineyard *A Quinta dos Dais Amigos*, a Portuguese expression that, translated into English, means "The Farm of Two Friends." But after much soul searching, Benevides concluded that, in this case, the link between the man and his wine could not be separated. "I finally decided it should be called Raymond Burr Vineyards," Benevides explains. "He didn't want it, I know

Robert Benevides samples wine in the tasting room with vineyard supervisor and event planner Francisco Baptista (LEFT).

that. We had talked about that possibility and he didn't like that at all, but we're making great wines now. It's a memorial to him, to his ideas, and I think it deserves to be named after him." In some ways, the estate is not so much a memorial to Raymond Burr as it is a symbol of his living, breathing presence.

Today's Winemaker for Raymond Burr

At the beginning of the 2006 grape harvest, Benevides hired an up-and-coming winemaker, Phyllis Zouzounis. "It's been proven that women have a better palate," Benevides says with authority.

A charming sign welcomes you to the Raymond Burr winery.

It took Zouzounis two weeks to decide to take the job, claiming it was the terroir that drove her to the spot. She had begun her winemaking career working at nearby Dry Creek Vineyard in 1980, and after fifteen years there she moved on as winemaker and general manager of another Dry Creek winery just down the road, Mazzocco Vineyards. In 1987 Phyllis and her partner, Jim Penpraze, started their own Dry Creek winery, Deux Amis, making award-winning Zinfandels.

The 100% estate-grown vineyards at Raymond Burr offered Zouzounis a new challenge—to single-handedly produce great Cabernet Sauvignon, Cabernet Franc, and Chardonnay wines. "Great wine starts in the vineyard with quality grapes. The Raymond Burr vineyard is a good example of this," says Zouzounis. "Because it is an estate vineyard winery, this allows Raymond Burr Vineyards to create and preserve the quality in the vineyard first and then follow through to the finished wine." Zouzounis, like all great winemakers, is a believer in balance. "My focus is balance," she says. "Balance of the vine, balance of the fruit, and balance in the wine."

PORTFOLIO

The wines made at the estate have a style that is unique to Sonoma. Both Burr and Benevides considered themselves to be Europhiles. Virtually every holiday was spent somewhere in Europe, usually Portugal. They were entranced by the European traditions of art, diversity, drink, and, of course, food. They loved the long lunches, siestas, and the relaxed and accepting culture of their private lives in Europe.

They were fascinated with how the elements of European culture worked together, especially the synergy between food and drink, and they soon began to question the American creation of "Coca-Cola" wines, that is, wines that were so big and lush that they could happily be enjoyed without food. With food, however, these wines didn't work so well and seemed all too often to swamp the flavors of the food. Eating was something that Burr took very seriously. Together they made the decision to create European-styled wines in the heart of a wine growing area—the Sonoma Valley—renowned for producing the plushest examples of sweetly fruit-packed wines in California. This doesn't mean that they wanted a fruitless, austere portfolio of wines; it was more about restraint.

Raymond Burr wines do not knock you over the head, nor are they rustic; in fact they have quite a lot of finesse. They do have higher levels of acid than any of the other vineyards we visited, and they certainly don't possess the opulent, lush feel so common to the wines of the area. They are very dry wines, sinewy at the core with solid tannic structures that make them very food friendly, with earthy flavors. They won't win a lot of show medals, but will complement the dinner table better than most of the wines we came across in Sonoma.

NICK'S TASTING NOTES

Chardonnay, 2008

Medium-bright gold color with aromas of ripe Bosc pears, green apples, orange blossoms, and creamy vanilla oak. Quite sensual with a soft, clean mouth-feel, combined to good medium-bodied concentration of ripe white fruits on the nose. Fresh and bright on the palate, not too oaky, and with excellent balance of citrus and light earthy flavors and a long, cream-tinged finish. Restrained and direct, it has a cool-climate feel and is long in the mouth. Drink now.

Estate Port, 2009

Though the Port was originally intended just for family and friends, it has somehow found its way onto the *cartes du vin* of a couple of upscale San Francisco restaurants, and in 1996 the Port took Double Gold at a wine fair there.

Produced from estate-grown Tinta Cao, Tinta Maderira, and Touriga Nacional grapes (traditional port varieties), this is strangely fortified with Germain-Robin Cognac (instead of traditional neutral grape-skin spirit) and aged in French oak. The Cognac makes for a unique fortified wine with a hint of light orange rind flavor that I found very appealing. Very dark ruby, almost black in color, with interesting and complex notes of dark chocolate, plums, and black super-ripe cherries steeped in alcohol. Sweet and caressing on the palate, with layers of black fruits and violets that sweep across the tongue. Light tannins and a super-long orange-rind-tinged finish complete this meditative wine. Love the Cognac touch—quite untraditional but unique and very tasty. The port was, without question, the highlight of the portfolio.

NICK'S PICKS

We tasted a great deal of wine on our many excursions throughout California wine country. Because of the nature of this book, we were limited to writing only about wineries that featured "celebrity" vintages. But Nick has been touring California vineyards for many years and he certainly has his favorites. During our research trips, we spent our days at the celebrity wineries but our nights were spent sampling the rest of what the region had to offer. We tried some absolutely awesome wines and wanted to share our favorites.

Our editor limited us to 20 of our top picks but we couldn't whittle it down to less than 22. Some of these wineries have tasting rooms, others only sell through allocation to their wine club members. You can pick a handful of these and go on an amazing winery tour, or you can order wines from these stellar winemakers and be guaranteed a memorable treat. We wholeheartedly recommend these wines to our friends, families, and readers.

Ampelos Cellars

TASTING ROOM:
312 North Ninth Street
Lompoc, CA, 93436
ph: 805.736.9957
www.ampeloscellars.net

Ampelos Cellars produces approximately 5000 cases a year. Owned and operated by Rebecca and Peter Work, this vineyard in the Sta. Rita Hills appellation was one of the first in the U.S. to be certified as sustainable, organic, and biodynamic. The Works combine a respect for tradition with an openness to innovation, always honoring the terroir from which their grapes are produced. Their commitment to eco-friendly, natural farming and winemaking is evident in every bottle.

The tasting room is located in Lompoc's "Wine Ghetto," which is a bit off the beaten Santa Ynez tasting track, but well worth a visit. It is open Thursday to Sunday from 11:00am to 5:00pm and on Monday from 11:00am to 4:00pm. You are invited to bring along a picnic. Please call if your party is larger than eight people.

TASTING NOTE: *Ampelos Pinot Noir, 2005*
This wine was presented to me by the Works to demonstrate how their wines do indeed stand the test of time. The deep ruby color was obviously lighter than the latest released cuvées with muddy-ruddy age replacing the usual bright crimson. The wine has a slightly rustic complexity and secondary aromas of forest-floor decay, dead leaves, black and red forest fruits, and faded oak. All the structural elements of acidity and tannins have melded together and this is now a totally delicious and complex wine to enjoy.

Araujo Estate Wines

2155 Pickett Road
Calistoga, CA 94515
ph: 707.942.6061
wine@araujoestate.com
www.araujoestate.com

Araujo Estate is located in the northeast Napa Valley, just east of Calistoga. The estate was established around the Eisele Vineyard, first planted over 125 years ago and principally dedicated to Cabernet Sauvignon for the past 50 years. Since the inaugural release bearing the Eisele name in 1971, this unique vineyard has been widely recognized as one of the greatest terroirs in the Napa Valley. Over the last 23 years Daphne and Bart Araujo have developed the property's potential, raising it to the status of California "First Growth." In 2013, the historic vineyard was acquired by the Pinault family and Groupe Artemis.

For each vintage, over half of the wine bottled is sent directly to customers on their mailing list. Araujo wines can also be found at fine restaurants and wine shops across the U.S. and internationally in Europe and Asia, which are listed on their website.

Araujo is not open to the public and is unable to offer tours or tastings.

Tasting Note: *Araujo, "Alianza" Meritage, Napa Valley, 2011*

A new cuvée from Araujo, less expensive than the "Estate" wine and more widely available as it's made from sourced fruit. Still, the winemaking team for both cuvées is the same and they utilize the same methods. Think of it as a baby Araujo, with an earlier drinking window and less overt, deep-seated concentration. This cuvée will be discontinued after this vintage, which is a pity but the new owners (Latour) would like to put 100% of their focus on the famous Eisele Cabernet. The 2011 includes some Eisele fruit and is 70% Cabernet Sauvignon, 15% Malbec, and 5% each of Petite Verdot, Malbec, and Cabernet Franc. Only 500 cases were produced of this smooth, elegant, and expressive wine. Displaying a very deep, bloody crimson color with youthful rim, the bouquet is classy and direct, releasing the classic aromas of a Bordeaux wine. Dominated by vibrant scents of super-ripe small-berried cassis fruit, black plums, leather, minerals, earth, light chocolate, tutti-frutti, and sweet vanilla. In the background light floral notes plus a hint of pencil shavings add to its interest.

Restrained (2011 was a cool year) and elegant in the mouth, the wine is medium-bodied (becoming fuller with time in the glass) but contains excellent density and depth of "grapey" fruit. Reveals a wonderful purity of fruit and a precision-like balance of structured yet unobtrusive sweet, tight tannins, and ethereal medium acidity, keeping the wine structured and fresh. Similar to a French Bordeaux but with a splash of Californian sun, it lingers long on the palate, with a supple and graceful ending with a dash of ripe black cherries, blueberries, vanilla spice, and light coffee ground flavors. Made for early consumption, it's a delight to drink.

Clos Pepe Estate Vineyards

4777 East Highway 246
Lompoc, CA 93436
ph: 805.735.2196
www.clospepe.com

The vineyard was purchased by Steve and Cathy Pepe in 1994 as a horse ranch, and established as the ninth vineyard in what would become the Sta. Rita Hills AVA. Specializing in cool-climate, small production, craft-based Pinot Noir and Chardonnay, Clos Pepe is now recognized as a leader in local and national wine culture and wine education, and provides fruit to some of the best winemakers in California.

Clos Pepe Vineyards is a private farm and residence. Vineyard tours and tastings are by appointment only. Email andrew@clospepe.com to schedule an appointment.

TASTING NOTE: *Clos Pepe Chardonnay, Santa Rita Hills, 2012*

The wine presents a waxy golden color with a watery youthful rim. Creamy citrus and buttery nose leads to a quite direct and purposeful mouthful of juice. Much more "old school" than the Liquid Farms Chardonnay, for example, it reveals a classic, sturdy, and foursquare composite. It's leaner and more composed yet less exciting overall. Nonetheless, this is an excellently made wine and would probably go even better with food. It's quietly complex and solid with white pear, citrus, peach, and a good whack of spicy oak.

Minerals abound in the foreground whilst flavors and aromas of honeydew melons, buttercups, citrus, and peaches revolve around a core of minerals and nuts. Big and bold, yet still retains the lushness of the area with good levels of acidity, which buoy the tangy mineral fruits that lead to a long feathered finish.

Dominus Estate

2570 Napanook Road
Yountville, CA 94599
ph: 707.944.8954
info@dominusestate.com

In the late 1960s, while attending UCLA Davis, Christian Moueix fell in love with Napa Valley and its wines. Son of Jean-Pierre Moueix, the famed wine merchant and producer from Linbourne, France, Moueix returned home in 1970 to manage the family vineyards including Chateau Petrus, La Fleur-Petrus, Trotanoy in Pomerol, and Magdelaine in Saint Emilion.

His love of Napa Valley lingered and, in 1981, he discovered the historic Napanook Vineyard, a 124-acre site west of Yountville that had been the source of fruit for some of the finest Napa Valley wines of the 1940s and 1950s. In 1982, Christian Moueix entered into a partnership to develop the vineyard and, in 1995, became the sole owner. He chose the name Dominus—"Lord of the Estate" in Latin—to underscore his longstanding commitment to stewardship of the land.

Due to a restrictive Napa Valley winery use permit, Dominus is not open to the public. For more information on Dominus Estate and its wines, please visit the website of Maisons Marques et Domaines at www.mmdusa.net and the website of Établissements Jean-Pierre Moueix at www.moueix.com

Tasting Note: *Napanook, Meritage, Napa Valley, 2009*

This is the second wine of Dominus, which always proves to be a decently priced cuvée and is exemplary in quality in good vintages. 2009 was a superb vintage and this is a great example of what this second label can achieve. Boasting a very deep ruby color with an opaque core plus a touch of browning age, the bouquet is off the charts. Complex and fascinating aromas bounce around the glass—a mélange of super-ripe black cherries, black currants, saddle leather, graphite, granite, tar, chocolate, mint, vanilla, and camphor.

The palate is equally as busy, exhibiting a plush, full-bodied super-rich character. Decadent and Moorish, it's also streamlined and sleek with obvious use of high quality oak. Chocolaty and densely fruity, this is still a youthful wine that contains medium tannins and expertly judged acidity leading to a long vanilla-spiced finish that lingers—somewhat akin to falling into a plush couch.

Dragonette Cellars

TASTING ROOM:
2445 Alamo Pintado Avenue
Los Olivos, CA 93441
ph: 805.693.0077
www.dragonettecellars.com

WINERY:
55 Los Padres Way #1
Buellton, CA 93427
ph: 805.688.8440

The tasting room is located in picturesque Los Olivos and features regular and reserve tastings for a small fee. It also offers the chance to purchase exclusive, small lot wines not found anywhere else.

Open seven days a week from 11:00am to 5:00pm, private winery tours and tastings are available by appointment only. To schedule a visit, call Jessica Gasca at 805.693.0077.

Tasting Note: *Dragonette Cellars, MJM, Central Coast, 2009*

From one of our favorite new producers, this wine is a blend of 91% Syrah, 5% Grenache, 3% Mourvedre, and 1% of the white grape variety Viognier. Created from ultra low yields and aged for 33 months in new oak, only 225 cases were produced of this immensely concentrated wine. Very purple with an opaque core and a youthful watery pink rim. A dazzling bouquet soars from the glass, releasing initially strong aromas of super-ripe blackberries and black cherries steeped in alcohol combined with more complex notes of blueberries, black sugar-coated plums, meat, tar, and crayons, all swathed in sweet, spicy new oak. There is also a noticeable hint of apricots from the addition of the Viognier in the blend. Slick, round, and smooth in the mouth, almost oily, the wine is full-bodied and very textured with dashing, bold flavors of meaty black fruits, mineral, spices, creamy new oak, and chocolate cake. The medium tannins and good acidity provide a much-needed supporting role. Fragrant, round, and plump in the mouth, this wine lingers endlessly on the palate.

DuMOL

MAILING ADDRESS:
11 El Sereno
Orinda, CA 94563
ph: 925.254.8922
winery@dumol.com
www.dumol.com

Created in the famed Russian River area of Northern California, DuMOL Wines are only available through allocation because they sell out months prior to their individual spring and fall release dates. If you want to ensure a personal allocation/offering for each release, please go to their website and become a DuMOL pre-release member.

Tasting Note: *DuMOL Syrah,*
Russian River Valley, 2012

A great example of Californian Syrah, restrained, complex, and cool climate in style (Northern Rhône). Purple crimson in color with a blue-black opaque core and a broad watery rim, the nose reveals mostly creamy blackberry and blueberry with hints of light raspberry and minerals that mingle with a cornucopia of wild tertiary aromas: tar, tobacco, asphalt, white pepper, coffee grounds, and savory hung meat. Medium-bodied in the mouth with an impressive meaty concentration of spicy ripe blackberries that coat the palate. Lovely textured and smooth palate balanced by quite poky tannins and good levels of acidity that, at present, are hidden beneath the wealth of fruit. Ends with flavors of black olives and black truffles.

HdV Wines
(Hyde de Villaine Wines)

588 Trancas Street
Napa, CA 94558
ph: 707.251.9121
info@hdvwines.com
www.hdvwines.com

HdV is a venture between the Hyde family of Napa Valley and the de Villaine family of Burgundy who, related by marriage, share long histories in French and Californian winemaking.

Tastings are by appointment only. Two tasting flights are offered: The HDV Flight ($45 per person) and the Comandante Flight ($75 per person.) Each tasting lasts between 60 and 90 minutes.

TASTING NOTE: *HdV Chardonnay, Hyde Vineyard, Napa Valley, 2008*

Quite golden in color due to its advanced age. The multi-faceted nose bursts with rich citrus, liquid honey, fresh summer flowers, minerals, and some savory nutty and vanilla notes. It's obviously a warm-climate wine but has elements of fruit that also reveal an earthy red loam note reminiscent of Burgundy. Full bodied, and absolutely packed to the hilt with an abundance of juicy powerful golden fruits such as citrus, golden apple, and ripe pears. The palate is not in the slightest bit heavy but it's nonetheless a very rich wine and perfectly balanced with good acidity. Extremely complex, this is reminiscent of a very good classic Meursault or a Corton Charlemagne but with an extra dollop of warmth. Reflects the deep-seated concentration and ripe fruit of Napa Chardonnays. Drinking well now.

Hirsch Winery

45075 Bohan Dillion Road
Cazadero, CA 95421
ph: 707.847.3600
www.hirschvineyards.com

Perched on a ridge overlooking the Pacific Ocean at Fort Ross, Hirsch Vineyards is the birth ground of great Pinot Noir on the extreme Sonoma Coast. David Hirsch founded the vineyard in 1980 to grow fruit and make site-specific wine. From the start, all efforts have been on the cultivation of grapes that make wines profoundly characteristic of the location, vintage after vintage.

Hirsch Vineyards is closed to the public, but visitors are welcomed by advance appointment for private tours on a very limited basis. Priority for appointments is reserved for active members of the Hirsch mailing list. Hirsch is closed Monday through Thursday each week.

Please note that Hirsch is in a very beautiful but remote location: two to three hours from San Francisco, 90 minutes from Santa Rosa and Healdsburg, and two hours plus from Napa. If you want to visit, go to the website and fill out a visitor request. Hirsch will respond within 48 hours (except during holidays).

TASTING NOTE: *Hirsch Vineyards Chardonnay, Sonoma Coast, 2012*

The style of this Chardonnay deliberately sets off in the opposite direction from any other. This is the new wave of unique winemaking at its best, showcasing and perfectly reflecting the terroir that surrounds Hirsch's coastal vineyards. The cool breezes that sweep in from the sea help highlight the distinctive aromas and flavors that make this wine so beguiling.

Delicacy and natural subtleness are the name of the game here with the wine revealing a very pale gold color with reflective hints. Its nose is discreet yet complex and loaded with aromas of fresh cut lemons and limes, minerals, and stone fruits paired with light unobtrusive oak. Precise and silky on the palate, the wine is restrained but also expressive and flavorsome—it has some serious presence in the mouth. Textured and rich at its core, its balance is precise with an expert use of well-judged light oak and a good extraction of mineral-like fresh stone fruits. This wine seems to float across the palate with adequate texture, all balanced on a spine of fine natural acidity. Long and lingering in the mouth, this is a wine to drink now.

Hudson Vineyards

5398 Carneros Highway
Napa, CA 94559
ph: 707.255.1455
info@hudsonvieyards.com
www.hudsonranch.com

Wines can be purchased by allocation from the website which also lists stores and restaurants that serve and sell the wines.

TASTING NOTE: *Hudson Chardonnay, Carneros, 2012*
This is a big, bold, and broad-shouldered Chardonnay from the cool Carneros region of Sonoma. Shows a very deep gold color that is clean, shiny, and bright. Rich powerful aromas of citrus and grilled nuts with lashings of spicy vanilla oak and hints of jasmine. Full-bodied and rich in the mouth, with decadent levels of concentrated spicy white fruits. Loaded with super-ripe flavors of citrus, pear, peach, golden apples, and creamy vanilla. Good acidity manages to provide

enough structure to shape this mammoth example of Chardonnay. Richly textured with excellent depth of fruit and some bounding minerals. Super ripe and super rich with a high (almost 15%) alcohol content, this is unabashedly Californian in style. Drink now.

Iron Horse Winery

9786 Ross Station Road
Sebastopol, CA 95472
ph: 707.887.1507
info@ironhorsevineyards.com

Founded by Audrey and Barry Sterling in 1979, Iron Horse Winery is an independent, family-owned operation in the Green Valley within the cool Russian River AVA. Today, three generations live on the property, ranging in age from 20 to 86. There are approximately 160 acres planted exclusively to Chardonnay and Pinot Noir with spectacular views from the winery clear across Sonoma County to Mount St. Helena. Not only is it one of the most scenic properties in the area, Iron Horse makes the best uniquely-styled sparkling wines in California. Fittingly, Iron Horse sparkling wines have been served at the White House for the past five consecutive presidential administrations. The winery is famous for keeping its cuvées on their lees for many years prior to disgorgement to increase and add complexity.

The outdoor tasting room is open seven days a week from 10:00am to 4:30pm. Tastings are $20 for a flight of five wines, refunded with purchase, no charge for wine club members with a choice of three flights.

Tours are by appointment only, Monday through Friday at 10:00am and cost $25 per person (including tasting), refunded with purchase. Winemaker David Munksgard offers a truck tour through the vineyards and a private tasting on Mondays at 10:00am, a truly memorable experience. This private tour is limited to four people and costs $50 per person. To make a reservation contact tasting room manager Lisa Macek: lisam@ironhorsevineyards.com.

Tasting Note: *Iron Horse NV Joy! Sparkling Wine*

Simply a mind-blowing sparkling wine that easily competes with the best from Champagne. There's a wonderful balance between richness, delicacy, and complexity in this bottling. Beautiful bronze color with small persistent bubbles, the bouquet positively soars from the glass with powerful aromas of yeasty brioche, citrus, and yellow fruits wrapped in creamy high-quality oak. This multi-vintage bottling is extraordinarily rich and full-bodied for a sparkling wine.

Layered with aromas that mingle with more mineral accents, this wine is fresh and filling in the mouth. It floats over the palate with a soft and silky texture, releasing rich flavors of citrus, poached pears, golden apples, and tangerines buoyed by supportive acidity that slides the wine into an endless finish.

Keenan Winery

3660 Spring Mountain Road
St. Helena, CA 94574
ph: 707.963.9177
info@keenanwinery.com
www.keenanwinery.com

The Robert Keenan winery is located in the Spring Mountain District of the Napa Valley. Tastings may be arranged by prior appointment online. Same-day tasting appointments cannot be scheduled online. Please phone the winery to inquire if there are available appointments on the day you want to visit.

Tasting Note: *Keenan "Reserve Cabernet Sauvignon," 2009*

A mind-boggling, classic, delicious example of Californian Cabernet Sauvignon, one of the very best we've ever tasted. It contained the perfect balance of effortless power and mountainous fruit paired with the elegance provided by good acidity from the elevation of the region. A superb wine made from a great vintage. Inky black purple in color, the whole wine is almost opaque except for some light bricking at the rim. The bouquet is quintessentially Californian, bursting with exciting aromas of fresh ripe liquored black and red cherries bathed in sweet fresh oak. Licorice, damp earth, and a flavor of minerals bring up the rear of the palate. It's an inviting and complex nose that leads on to an even more delicious palate. Due to its age, the palate is textured and ripe and it coats the tongue. There's a great purity of small-berried fruits that saturate the palate yet somehow manage to float across the tongue. Impressively multi-layered with great uplifting acidity, the powerful tannins and depth of pure fruit is stunning. Amazing length to this juice that highlights some of the more mature, savory, aged flavors. Only 650 cases made.

Kongsgaard Winery

MAILING ADDRESS:
4375 Atlas Peak Road
Napa, CA 94558
ph: 707.226.2190
info@kongsgaardwine.com
www.kongsgaardwine.com

The Kongsgaard winery and vineyards are not open to the public. The wines are only available through allocation to members. A list of restaurants offering the wine is available on their website.

Tasting Note: *Kongsgaard Chardonnay, Napa Valley, 2012*
This extraordinarily stunning wine is Kongsgaard's basic cuvée. Without pretending it has any relation to Burgundy, this bold, brazen wine proudly screams California with defiant confidence. A deep golden color leads towards a very expressive and obviously high-quality nose. It boasts lashings of creamy,

smoky oak on the nose with a backdrop of minerals and a depthless core of spicy, ripe, white fruits on the tongue. The theme is definitely one of opulence and extraction yet the winemaker has held back on a typical Californian tropical feel and headed towards developing a more deep-veined "Meursault" feel to the overall taste. Expertly made, long and flavorsome, it's awesomely concentrated yet distinctive and individually fashioned. An utterly fascinating wine.

Liquid Farm

ph: 805.686-7903
liquid@liquidfarm.com

Liquid Farm wines are available direct from the winery through their customizable wine club. For detailed information regarding pricing, wine club benefits, and allocation, log on to Liquidfarm. com. The website includes a list of shops and restaurants that sell LF wines.

Private tastings are by appointment only, as available, and typically require one to two weeks lead time. Email Liquid Farm for more details and to be added to their mailing list to find out about upcoming new releases, special events, and pop-up tastings. For up-to-date news on tastings and events, you can also follow Liquid Farm on Facebook and Twitter.

If you have trouble finding Liquid Farm in your local wine shop, email nikki@liquidfarm.com.

TASTING NOTE: *Liquid Farm Chardonnay, Golden Slope Vineyard, Santa Rita Hills, 2013*

One of the best Chardonnays we tasted; from a superb vintage. Shows a shiny bright golden color reminiscent of ripe golden apples with green reflections of youthfulness. On the nose are pure juicy fruits, fresh powerful aromas of citrus, golden apples, banana, mango, and fresh churned butter. Lush and deep on the palate with expansive and mouth-coating voluptuous fresh fruits. Softly textured but with excellent uplifting acidity. Seems fat but not overdone and becomes ever more complex with air, revealing limes, mangoes, citrus, and a touch of marmalade and minerals.

If anything, the wine reflects the distinctive lush traits of the Santa Rita Hills with an added loamy note that seems unconventional for a Californian wine, and just a smattering of oak and a rich inner core of white fruits swathed in minerals. The palate ends long and tangy with a huge flourish of white pears, marshmallow, and citrus bringing up the rear.

Neyers Vineyard

2153 Sage Canyon Road
St. Helena, CA 94574
ph: 707.963.8840
info@neyersvineyards.com
www.neyersvineyards.com

MAILING ADDRESS:
PO Box 1028
St. Helena, CA 94574

Tastings are by appointment only with a $35 per person tasting fee. Contact the vineyard to arrange a visit; they can accommodate visitors on most days of the week with advance notice.

TASTING NOTE: *Neyers Cabernet Sauvignon "Ame," Napa Valley, 2007*

A beautifully aged, classically styled, quintessential California Cabernet from an up-and-coming producer from the region. Inky purple and brawny color with a malty/brown aged tinge. The fruit is sourced from the highest elevation block of vines on Neyers' Conn Valley ranch and has been certified organic since 2009.

Great nose; mellowed with age and revealing powerful scents of small-berried black and red cassis cherries, licorice, chocolate, earth, and vanilla oak. Medium- to full-bodied, smooth and rich with a deep-veined concentration of ripe black fruits, briar, a touch of oriental spices, and a savory aged malty note. Nicely balanced with small tightly packed yet still powerful tannins and uplifting acidity that balances the richness on the palate. Long, powerful, and age-worthy.

Pahlmeyer

ph: 707.255.2321
info@pahlmeyer.com
www.pahlmeyer.com

TASTINGS:
Ma(i)sonry Napa Valley
6711 Washington St,
Yountville, CA 94599
ph: 707.944.0889

"All I could think about was creating my own Califor-nia Mouton," says winemaker Jayson Pahlmeyer.

A selection of Pahlmeyer wines are available for tasting at Ma(i)sonry Napa Valley in Yount-ville. To request a reservation, please call or email. Preferred members are offered complimentary tastings for themselves and up to three guests, up to two visits each year.

Tasting Note: *Pahlmeyer Merlot, Napa Valley, 2012*

Continually one of our favorite wines produced in the Napa Valley; always drinkable and delicious. Opulent and concentrated yet at the same time beguilingly weightless, its deceptively complex palate always reveals an effortless sweet, ripe, tactile texture. Completely spellbinds the drinker with its drinkability. A mélange of red and black forest fruits are deftly bathed in fresh, creamy yet unobtrusive oak. Nuances of suede and licorice dance with silky elegant flavors of juicy black and red cherries and

currants and earthy notes that glide across the palate. Nicely concentrated yet never over-extracted, this is a wine that displays a phenomenally complex and precise balancing act between its fruit, acid, and tannins. Absurdly long in the mouth, this is a perfect example of what Californian winemaking at its best can produce.

Peter Michael Winery

12400 Ida Clayton Road
Calistoga, CA 94515
ph: 707.942.3200
www.petermichaelwinery.com

County restrictions on their permit require Peter Michael to be closed to the public. Tours and tastings are available on a limited by-appointment basis for active members of the winery's retail mailing list and certain members of the professional wine trade. Due to an overwhelming demand, the winery is not able to accommodate non-members. Appointments are usually booked four to eight weeks in advance. Please contact the retail department at 800.354.4459 or retail@petermichaelwinery.com. Visit the website to join the mailing list.

Tasting Note: *Peter Michael Chardonnay, "Ma Belle-Fille," Sonoma, 2012*

Elegant but rich and complex, this wine is grown high up in the valley thus it's always blessed with fine acidity that matches its concentration; an unfiltered wine, this is medium gold colored and youthful with a slight haze. It's complex, classy nose soars with exotic aromas of ripe peach, poached pears, zesty citrus, smoke, vanilla, cream, kumquats, orange blossoms, honey, almonds, and fresh pastry. The oak is restrained and unobtrusive. In the mouth the wine is equally impressive. Voluminous, rich, and silky on the tongue, this is a very concentrated wine, exquisitely balanced with deft balance of fruit to acid. Though immensely powerful, this wine still floats across the palate. Multi-faceted, revealing layer upon layer of pear-like fruit, the overall balance is very impressive. This concentrated wine is long in the mouth with a spine of fine acidity that holds up the rich ripe fruit; classy and delicious.

PlumpJack Winery

620 Oakville Cross Road
Oakville CA. 94558
ph: 707.945.1220
www.plumpjackwinery.com

PlumpJack Winery sits squarely in the heart of Napa Valley's renowned Oakville region, surrounded by a 42-acre estate vineyard highly regarded for the quality of its Cabernet Sauvignon. Gavin Newsom and Gordon Getty established PlumpJack Winery in 1995, inspired by one of Shakespeare's most memorable characters, Sir John "PlumpJack" Falstaff. PlumpJack's down-to-earth, fun-loving, irreverent nature is rivaled only by his fierce loyalty to Prince Hal (Henry V), with whom he shares more than a few goblets of sack (wine) at the local tavern. "If sack and sugar be a fault," intones PlumpJack, "God help the wicked."

The fanciful tasting room is open to the public daily from 10:00am to 4:00pm, offering a selection of both red and white wines. Fees range from $40 to $65 per person. Parties of seven or more require a reservation.

Tasting Note: *PlumpJack Syrah, Napa Valley, 2012*

A really lovely wine that paired perfectly with our braised beef dish. Here is an age-worthy wine that is complex but also very drinkable, made in a modern style and proudly American. Big and loaded with glycerin, it's a hedonistic wine showing primary spicy fruit with its structure buried beneath a wealth of youthful fruit. Still it displays immense depth of fruit and a long bold spicy finish. The color immediately sets the scene, boasting an opaque dark purple with a wide watery rim. The nose explodes with rich accents of dark sugar-coated plums, ripe black cherries, mocha, dark chocolate, roasted coffee beans, pepper spice, and new French oak. The palate is huge and super dense; full-bodied but not thick.

The alcohol content is high, 15.2%, but the wine is deftly created and hides it well, at least at this point. The acidity and tannins are also high to match and support the wealth of fruit. There is a definite new-world creaminess and opulence to this wine that will age well.

Rochioli Vineyards & Winery

6192 Westside Road
Healdsburg, CA 95448
ph: 707.433.2305
info@rochioliwinery.com
www.rochioliwinery.com

Rochioli Vineyards & Winery is located just south of Healdsburg, in northern Sonoma County. The tasting room overlooks the Russian River Valley floor and offers a range of estate wines available to taste. Visitors are invited to bring a picnic and enjoy lunch on the patio. Tastings are $10 per person refundable with any purchase.

Vineyard hours are Thursday through Monday from 11:00am to 4:00pm, and Tuesday and Wednesday by appointment only. Call or email to make a reservation in advance.

Tasting Note: *Rochioli Estate Chardonnay, Russian River Valley, 2013*

This wine is light in color, almost a very pale gold. With jazzy aromas of poached pear, sweet oak, orange blossom, yellow fruits, citrus, nuts, and hints of black currant spice, it presents a fascinating nose. Medium-bodied and quite structured with natural high acidity. Almost yeasty and quite dry at this stage, this wine seems very youthful at present with high levels of natural acidity that have yet to fully integrate with the fruit. Long in the mouth, it feels almost "autumnal" with some interesting brown leafy notes that really added interest. Definitely a wine to follow, as it will age well in the short term.

Santana Wines

Carlos Santana Series
Mumm Napa
8445 Silverado Trail
Rutherford, CA 94558
ph: 800.686.6272 (Mon-Fri), 707.967.7700 (weekends), 866.783.5826 (private events & group tasting reservations)
www.mummnapa.com

Carlos Santana produces a portfolio of sparkling wines in conjunction with Mumm. All his wines are well-made examples of Napa sparkling wines albeit with slightly higher levels of sweetness, which Carlos prefers. All the whites are wonderful but his Rosé, in particular, happens to be excellent, especially as an aperitif.

A portion of the proceeds from the Mumm Napa Santana collection benefit the Milagro Foundation, a publicly-supported foundation established by Carlos Santana and his family in 1998. The tasting room is open daily from 10:00am to 6:00pm. The last seating is at 5:45pm.

Tasting Note: *Santana Supernatural Rosé, 2007*

The wine reveals a salmon pink color with small tight bubbles and a good persistent mousse. Lively red fruit bouquet packed with bright aromas of red cherries, raspberries, small frambois, exotic spices, vanilla, earth, and minerals are combined with a superb autolytic character; yeasty, bready scents with a piquant note. Initially the wine's bubbles are intensely gripping in the mouth until the rush of sweet, ripe red berries hit the tongue, filling the mouth with spicy red fruits as found on the nose. Surprisingly concentrated for a sparkling wine, it has a good depth of fruit at its core. Made with precision, this is a fun and refreshing wine to drink but also has a serious side and can be enjoyed easily with food, especially Asian flavors. Interestingly, the wine carries a noticeable spicy note that's due to the addition of a splash of Syrah in the blend. All the wines in the portfolio sport awesome psychedelic labels.

Stony Hill Vineyard

PO Box 308
St. Helena, CA 94574
ph: 707.963.2636
fax: 707.963.1831
info@stonyhillvineyard.com

When Fred and Eleanor McCrea bought a 160-acre goat ranch on the northeast slope of Spring Mountain in 1943, little did they envision the sign reading, "Stony Hill Vineyard... visitors by appointment only," at the bend in the road. Yet 60 years later, the sign hangs there as a testament to their passionate dedication to producing quality wines.

In 1952 Fred and Eleanor completed a small winery on the property and produced their first vintage of Chardonnay. After allowing the wine to age for two years, they began marketing Stony Hill Chardonnay through a personal letter to Bay Area friends. Fifty-four years later this annual September mailer is still Stony Hill's primary mode of marketing, albeit less than half now are sent via the postal service as more and more customers opt for email newsletters. Stony Hill wines are also available at select restaurants in the Napa Valley, San Francisco, Los Angeles, and other metropolitan areas across the United States.

Stony Hill is open by appointment Monday through Saturday from 9:00am to 3:30pm. Visits average between 60 and 90 minutes and include a tour of the winery and a wine tasting at the ranch house. The cost is $45 per person. To request an appointment call 707.963.2636 or go to the website and fill out a request. The winery is located three miles north of St. Helena, off Highway 29 in the western hills above the Napa Valley. Directions to the vineyard will be emailed when you make an appointment.

TASTING NOTE: *Stony Hill Vineyard Cabernet Sauvignon, St. Helena Napa, 2010*

There's a new wave of restraint and non-intervention here with the aim of making a much less extracted Napa Valley Cabernet. The wine has noticeably more red fruit and less alcohol (13.5%), and is less overtly rich though no less complex. We were very impressed with this wine and its style. Bright and ruby-colored with vibrant hues and no opaqueness; lively on the palate, showcasing red fruits such as fresh red cher-

ries, raspberries, red currants, and watermelons. A light funky note adds interest and the winemaker's judicial use of oak is welcome and begs for another sip. The oak is discrete and adds to, rather than smothers, this medium-bodied wine. The tannins are sweet and well-integrated, so this wine is already very drinkable. Juicy and dry but with plenty of adequate flesh, this is a lovely little wine with good complexity and a purposeful aim.

Varner Wine

648 Menlo Avenue, Suite 5
Menlo Park, CA 94025
ph: 650.321.4894
jv@varnerwine.com
www.varnerwine.com

In the late 1970s, twins Jim and Bob Varner planted their first vineyard, which now produces some of California's best Chardonnays. Go to the website to join the mailing list which details availability of the wines.

TASTING NOTE: *Varner Chardonnay, "Home Block," Santa Cruz, 2012*
A youthful, pale lemon-colored wine. A touch neutral on the nose at first, but then pure stone citrus aromas emerge, interlocked with minerals and barely-there oak. Medium-bodied, lush, concentrated palate; silky and restrained with lively acidity. Clean, bright, flavors of fresh-cut citrus; guava and minerals coat the

palate. Initially seems very direct and almost simple in the mouth but this wine has hidden dimensions, with notes of merengue, honey, peach, and light vanilla building weight and tension with airing. Long, tangy, and pure on the long finish with a tingle of oak and acidity. Expertly made in a European fashion. Medium alcohol. Drink now.

Walter Hansel Winery

5465 Hall Road
Santa Rosa, CA 95401
ph: 707.525.3614
www.walterhanselwinery.com

MAILING ADDRESS:
PO Box 3437
Santa Rosa, CA 95402

Walter Hansel's informative vineyard tours and tastings are by appointment only. To set up an appointment call or e-mail stacie@hanselwine.com or shansel@hanselwine.com.

TASTING NOTE: *Walter Hansel Pinot Noir, Russian River "North Slope Vineyards," 2012*
Bright and clear, with a lively transparent ruby core and watery rim. Aromas leap from the glass; the nose bursts with raspberries, red and black cherries, and currants swathed in new spicy oak. In the mouth, the wine has a sweet "ripe" feel. Linear but superbly concentrated offering up a lush soft-textured

palate; medium-bodied but with excellent levels of fresh bright acidity that lift up the tangy mélange of black and red cherry fruits. It's a complex wine with nuances of boiled sweets, seaweed, floral notes, and aromas of the forest floor. Delicious, fresh, and complex—it's a perfect example of a youthful New World Pinot Noir, displaying a definite beginning, a succulent mid-palate, and a long, fine, fruity finish.

This is a superb wine displaying excellent balance with good levels of acidity and some serious sweet but buried tannins. It's a classy wine that continually holds its own or triumphs when tasted against high class Premiere Cru Burgundies. It is feminine and silky yet also deceptively seriously concentrated at its core. Will age well in the short term, but since it's so delicious, why wait?

RESOURCE GUIDE

B. R. Cohn Winery

15000 Sonoma Highway
Glen Ellen, CA 95442
ph: 707.938.4064
www.brcohn.com

Tastings are open to the public and offered daily from 10:00am to 5:00pm for a fee of $15 per person. Appointments are not necessary for groups of six or under.

The winery is available for special events; public events (such as concerts) are posted on the website.

Founded by Bruce Cohn, manager of the Doobie Brothers, in 1984, the B. R. Cohn Winery is located in the heart of Sonoma Valley. Now owned by Vintage Wine Estates, the winery is surrounded by the 90-acre Olive Hill Estate Vineyards, where soils warmed by underground natural hot springs and gentle ocean breezes create a unique microclimate resulting in ideal growing conditions for Cabernet Sauvignon.

Chappellet Winery

1581 Sage Canyon Road
St. Helena, CA 94574
ph: 707.963.7136, 800.4.WINERY
fax: 707-963-7445
customerservice@chappellet.com
www.chappellet.com

Tours and tastings are available by advance appointment only and range in price from $35 to $75 per person. (Due to limited seating, please note that the winery charge is based on the number of people participating, not the number of people tasting.) For further details and to book your visit, please call the concierge desk at 707.286.4219 or email toursandtastings@chappellet.com.

The Chappellet family's romance with Pritchard Hill started more than four decades ago when Donn and Molly Chappellet first glimpsed its magnificent vista of forests and wildflower-filled meadows. Inspired by the notion that Bacchus loves the hills, the Chappellets followed the advice of renowned winemaker André Tchelistcheff and settled on Pritchard Hill's rocky slopes, becoming the first winery to plant vineyards exclusively on high-elevation hillsides. From these Pritchard Hill vineyards, the Chappellets have been crafting extraordinary, age-worthy wines since 1967.

Charlie Clay Wines

Mauritson Family Winery
2859 Dry Creek Road
Healdsburg, California 95448
ph: 707.431.0804
www.mauritsonwines.com

Charlie Clay wines are featured in Charlie Palmer's restaurants (listed at www.charliepalmer.com)

and at select wine stores, or can be sampled in the tasting room at Mauritson Family Winery.

Established in 1884 by Clay Mauritson's great-great-great grandfather, the family operation is now vast—spreading across Dry Creek Valley, Alexander Valley, and the Rockpile Appellations. Chef Charlie Palmer is a silent partner in this impressive operation and privately owns a small vineyard dedicated exclusively to his favorite grape, Pinot Noir. His selective plot produces 3 to 3½ tons of fruit per acre.

Chimney Rock

5350 Silverado Trail
Napa, CA 94558
ph: 800.257.2641
fax: 707.257.2036
tourtaste@chimneyrock.com
www.chimneyrock.com

The Chimney Rock tasting room is open to the public seven days a week from 10:00am to 5:00pm. Parties of fewer than six guests may visit without a reservation. Special requests and large parties should make a reservation by visiting the website or calling 707.257.2641 x3218. Please note: reservations are strongly encouraged for weekend visits. Tastings are $20 to $35 for three or four wines; from $30 for private tastings. Special tours are offered by appointment. If you are looking to buy any of the Jack Nicklaus wines,

the best place to order them in California is at the website uncorked.com.

The Chimney Rock estate began to take shape in 1980, when Hack and Stella Wilson purchased a 180-acre parcel—which included a golf course—situated on the east side of the Silverado Trail. In 2000, the Terlato family joined the Wilson family as partners in the winery and assumed sole ownership in 2004. When famed golfer Jack Nicklaus was blending a Sauvignon Blanc in honor of his wife's favorite wine, the grapes were sourced at Chimney Rock. The estate now comprises 119 acres of vineyards divided into 28 distinct blocks, allowing for highly specialized viticulture suited to each specific site.

Fess Parker Winery

6200 Foxen Canyon Road
Los Olivos, CA 93441
ph: 805.688.1545
www.fessparkerwines.com

The tasting room at the Fess Parker Winery is open to the public seven days a week from 10:00am to 5:00pm. No reservations are required for tastings. Check the website for additional events such as the Private Food & Wine Exploration and the Fess Parker Group Tasting Experience. These events do require a reservation. Fess Parker Wines are available in many wine stores and on their website.

Founded in 1987, Fess Parker's 1,500-acre vineyard has won over 30 medals for its wines. In the entrepreneurial spirit that created the winery, Fess Parker's Wine Country Inn and Vintage Room Restaurant was opened in 1990 in Los Olivos and has become a hugely popular dining destination.

GoGi Wines
www.gogiwines.com
info@gogiwines.com

GoGi Wines are produced in very limited quantities, so the best way to insure delivery is to join the wine club on their website. Membership is limited and includes a personal invitation for the member and one guest to an annual private members' party with Kurt Russell, which is held at the Wine Saloon in the 1880 Union Hotel in Los Alamos, California (members receive a 20% discount on hotel rooms for the event). Membership includes a minimum purchase of one case of GoGi Pinot Noir (membership rate: $720; retail price: $900). Shipments are made in November. Members also receive discounts on small lots of "Goldie" Chardonnay. Membership is currently limited to those whose wine can be shipped to California, Florida, Minnesota, and Washington, DC. Further details about membership can be found on their website.

In California and Colorado, GoGi Wines are available in the restaurants listed on their website

and in a few select wine shops. Wine can be purchased on the website but can only be delivered to CA, FL, MN and DC.

The actor Kurt Russell fulfilled a heartfelt passion by creating GoGi Wines with Peter and Rebecca Work of Ampelos Cellars. Russell experiences winemaking as a personal and intimate endeavor and his favorite part of the process is "blending day." "To make it truly my wine, I am entrusted to rely on my nose and palate to blend what I believe makes the best combination of Pinot Noir clones that will result in that year's vintage of GoGi," Russell writes on his website. "And there it is—a bottle of GoGi to be enjoyed some time, some place by someone I'll probably never know. But I will most definitely be there sharing the experience. I am there because all of my senses are there pouring out of the bottle and into the glass."

Inglenook
1991 Saint Helena Highway
Rutherford, CA 94573
ph: 707.968.1100
www.rubiconestate.com

Francis Ford Coppola Winery
300 Via Archimedes
Geyserville, CA 95441
ph: 707.857.1400
www.francisfordcoppolawinery.com

Tasting rooms in both wineries are open to the public daily from 11:00am to 6:00pm. The Francis Ford Coppola Winery in Sonoma also offers guest accommodations, winery events, and family entertainment.

In 1975, Francis Ford Coppola and his wife Eleanor bought 1,560 acres of the Inglenook Estate and created the Niebaum-Coppola Estate Winery. Twenty years later, Coppola purchased the remainder of the original Inglenook vineyards and, in 1997, opened the newly restored Chateau. In 2002, Coppola opened the Rubicon Winery and in 2006, Rubicon Estate retired the name Niebaum-Coppola Estate Winery. The Inglenook trademark was purchased in 2011 and the property was once again and forever "Inglenook." In 2011, Coppola purchased a property in the Alexander Valley and named it the Francis Ford Coppola Winery.

Kamen Estates

111B East Napa Street
Sonoma, CA 95476
ph: 707.938.7292
fax: 707.938.7695
info@kamenwines.com
www.kamenwines.com

Kamen's sleek new tasting room is located in the historic downtown square of Sonoma and is open to the public daily—noon to 6:00pm from Monday to Thursday, and 11:00am to 6:00pm

from Friday to Sunday. A signature flight is $20 per person, waived with a two-bottle purchase. The premiere flight is $35 per person, waived with a three-bottle purchase. A vineyard tour is $80 per person and takes between 1½ and 2 hours. Guests taste four wines complemented by artisanal cheeses, while enjoying sweeping views of the Mayacamas Mountains and San Francisco Bay. Offered daily by advance appointment only.

Kamen Estates was established in 1980, by renowned screenwriter Robert Kamen. The vineyard's mountainous terrain was formed by ancient volcanic activity. Volcanic lava flows created soil variations so extreme, that one end of a vine row can be markedly different from the other. The vines here fight for survival among shallow soil and rocks, creating intense, flavorful fruit and wines.

Lewis Cellars

4101 Big Ranch Road
Napa, CA 94558
ph: 707.255.3400
www.lewiscellars.com

Daily winery tastings are available by appointment only at 10:30am and 1:30pm, Monday through Friday, and include a one-hour seated tasting of four wines. Sunday visits are available during September and October only. There is a maximum of six people per seating. Cost is $40 per person.

Mailing list customers who've purchased one case directly in the past twelve months receive a complimentary tasting for themselves and one guest. A credit card will be charged at time of booking with a 48-hour cancellation policy. To book a tasting, contact David at 707.255.3400 x108 or email him through the website.

In 1992 Debbie and Randy Lewis established a small family winery in Napa Valley. The estate has remained small and intimate. Total production is less than 10,000 cases of wine per year from thirteen different wines. The estate offers four Chardonnays, two Sauvignon Blancs, a Merlot, a Syrah, Alec's Blend, and four different Cabernets.

Mario Andretti Vineyards

4162 Big Ranch Road
Napa, CA 94558
ph: 707.259.6777
www.andrettiwinery.com

The tasting room is open to the public seven days a week from 10:30am to 5:00pm.

Founded in 1996, Andretti makes European wines with a splash of Californian sunshine. Differing from many heavy, fruitful, Napa wines, Andretti's wines are crafted with food in mind. Using moderate but ripe fruit and low levels of tannins retains a decent acidic balance that keeps the wines focused and fresh.

Raymond Burr Vineyards

8339 West Dry Creek Road
Healdsburg, CA 95448
ph: 707.433.4365
www.raymondburrvineyards.com

The tasting room is open to the public on Monday, Saturday, and Sunday, from 10:00am to 4:00pm.

In 1986, 30 years after creating his brilliant television hero, Perry Mason, Raymond Burr planted his Dry Creek Valley Estate with his favorite Cabernet Sauvignon grapes and began to cultivate orchids on the property. On a steeply terraced hillside, the well-drained soil and a healthy mix of sun, shade, and ocean breezes keep the growth and maturation of these grapes steady. After Burr died in 1992, his partner Robert Benevides christened the wine after the actor and has been running the winery (and growing the orchids) ever since.

Rutherford Hill

200 Rutherford Hill Road
Rutherford, CA 94573
ph: 707.963.1871
info@rutherfordhill.com
www.rutherfordhill.com

The winery is open daily from 10:00am to 4:00pm. Tasting flights are from $20 to $30. The tasting room off the Silverado Trail offers one of the best views in the Napa Valley and a lovely place to picnic. Tours of their nearly mile-long caves are offered daily at 11:30am, 1:30pm, and 3:30pm; the cost is $35 per person and tours are limited to fourteen guests (reservations are recommended).

For a very special treat, sign up for a Blend Your Own Merlot seminar and learn how to blend, label, and cork your unique bottle. These seminars are on Friday, from 11:00am to 1:00pm, and cost $105 ($85 for club members). If you are looking for the Luke Donald Collection, Jack Nicklaus Wines, or Mike Ditka Wines, the best place to order them in California is at the website uncorked.com.

Founded in 1972, Rutherford Hill Winery is a pioneer in the development of California Merlot. When the Terlato family of the Terlato Wine Group (TWG), Lake Bluff, Illinois, purchased Rutherford Hill in 1996, they immediately began to apply their guiding principle: Quality is a way of life. The philosophy that Anthony, Bill, and John Terlato bring to all their ventures was evident at Rutherford Hill from the start. Their first step was to reduce production by 14,000 cases. This eliminated inferior lots from the final blend and met the demanding, new, high-quality standard they had set. When legendary football coach Mike Ditka wanted to improve the signature wine he was selling in his numerous restaurants, he came to Bill Terlato and together they created the perfect wines to complement the red meat served at Ditka's. Golfer Luke Donald also blends his Bordeaux-style wines at Rutherford Hill.

Sanford Winery

www.sanfordwinery.com

SANTA BARBARA TASTING ROOM:
114 State Street, Suite #26
Santa Barbara, CA 93101
ph: 805.770.7873
SBtastingroom@sanfordwinery.com

STA. RITA HILLS TASTING ROOM:
5010 Santa Rosa Road
Lompoc, CA 93436
ph: 805.735.5900 ext. 2
info@sanfordwinery.com

The tasting room in Santa Barbara is open Friday and Saturday from 12:00pm to 7:00pm and Sunday through Thursday from 12:00pm to 6:00pm. A variety of wine-tasting options and wines by the glass are on offer. Also available are private tastings, vertical tastings, clonal tastings, chocolate and wine pairings, and a wine education series.

Open seven days a week from 11:00am to 4:00pm, the tasting room in Lompoc is located in the heart of the Sta. Rita Hills and offers a 360-degree view of the winery and vineyards. A private room is available for small groups or educational tastings by appointment.
If you want a tour, a private tasting, or a special vertical tasting, call to make an appointment at least 24 hours in advance. Tours last for one hour and range from $35 per person to $75.

Discounted prices are offered to wine club members. Please note that for both tasting rooms, groups of eight or more people must make a prior appointment. Contact tasting room manager, Lesley Ann Becker, at Lesley@sanfordwinery.com or call 805.735.5900 ext. 8 to book a group reservation. If you're looking for the Luke Donald Collection, wines can be ordered for delivery in California at the website uncorked.com.

In 1971, Sanford planted the area's first Pinot Noir in its Sanford & Benedict vineyard and Pinot Noir has thrived in the Santa Rita Hills ever since. Certified as an American Viticultural Area (AVA) in 2001, today the area is also renowned for its Chardonnay. Sanford's estate vineyards—Rancho La Rinconada and Sanford & Benedict—lie within the 100 square miles of the Santa Rita Hills AVA. Majority ownership of Sanford belongs to the Terlato family.

Silverado Vineyards

6121 Silverado Trail
Napa, CA 94558
ph: 707.257.1770
www.silveradovineyards.com

The gorgeous tasting room at Silverado is open to the public seven days a week from 10:00am to 5:00pm with no reservation required. In addition, several specialty tours and private

tastings are available by appointment only and are highly recommended. Check the website for a detailed listing.

Named after an abandoned mining town in Napa Valley, the Silverado Vineyards have been producing quality wines at fair prices for over 100 years. Bought in 1970 by Walt Disney's daughter Diane and her husband, Ron Miller, it has expanded through three generations. The vineyard produces a range of wines from critically acclaimed Chardonnays and Merlots to unique, inspired, and experimental bottlings.

Vermeil Wines

CALISTOGA TASTING ROOM:
1255 Lincoln Avenue
Calistoga, CA 94515
ph: 707.341.3054

NAPA TASTING ROOM:
1018 First Street
Napa, CA 94559
ph: 707.254-9881
www.vermeilwines.com

Both tasting rooms are open to the public. The Calistoga tasting room is open from 10:00am to 5:30pm, Sunday through Thursday, and from 10:00am to 8:00pm, Friday and Saturday. The Napa tasting room is open from 10:00am to 10:00pm, Sunday to Wednesday, and from

10:00am to 11:00pm, Thursday to Saturday. Private parties and tastings can be arranged by contacting the winery.

Born and raised in Napa Valley, football coach Dick Vermeil created his Cabernet Sauvignon in honor of his great-grandparents who brought the Vermeils to Calistoga and the Napa Valley.

Yao Family Wines

ph: 707.968.7470
www.yaofamilywines.com

Yao Family Wines do not have a tasting room but private tastings can be arranged by calling the above number or contacting the winery through their website. Yao Family Wines consists of three artfully crafted wines: The Napa Valley Cabernet Sauvignon, the Family Reserve, and Napa Crest. The first two wines are only available by joining the Yao Family Wine mailing list. Napa Crest is available on the website and in fine retail stores and restaurants.

In November 2011, global humanitarian and recently retired NBA star Yao Ming announced the establishment of his new Napa Valley wine company: Yao Family Wines. Yao Family Wines sources the grapes for its YAO MING® Napa Valley Cabernet Sauvignon from prestigious valley vineyards and selects individual blocks to blend for flavor and

texture. The vineyards are located from north to south along the Napa Valley, where the variation in climates and soils provides the grapes with distinct characteristics that add complexity to the final blend. The distinctive label was designed by Chuck House and features a hand-drawn image of the Napa Valley with the ancient Chinese character for "Yao," elegantly representing both cultures in which Yao Ming has made his home. One of his goals in creating the winery is to introduce the stupendous wines of California to his native home of China.

GLOSSARY OF TERMS

A

AVA

The initials AVA stand for American Viticultural Area. An AVA defines a designated wine grape-growing region within the United States and is validated by the Alcohol and Tobacco Tax and Trade Bureau (TTB) of the U.S. Department of the Treasury. Wineries and other petitioners request a defined AVA to establish their place in the wine world. In early 2015, there were 230 designated AVAs in the U.S. Once an AVA is established, at least 85% of the grapes used to make a wine must be grown within that specified area for the bottle to be labeled as part of that AVA.

Acid

Acids are extracted from the fresh grapes and are intensified in the winery by the fermentation process. These acids are essential in the creation and makeup of balanced wines. Acidity enlivens the taste and bouquet and provides stuffing for further development, similar to the way that tannin creates structure. Without these two essential elements a wine becomes "flabby."

Aftertaste or Finish

The flavor that persists in the mouth after swallowing is an important factor in determining the quality of a wine, as the flavor of most well-made wines will linger in the mouth. The longer the aftertaste, the more indicative of a superbly made wine.

Alcoholic Fermentation

A biological process where yeast consumes the inherent sugars in the grape juice and converts those sugars into alcohol and carbon dioxide.

Astringency

A rough, coarse, unpleasant sensation in the mouth caused by excessive tannins and acidity, especially when a wine is young or at the end of its life. Extended bottle age will undoubtedly "smooth" out tannins, but a wine's acidity will never recede once bottled, thus old wines with faded tannins still can easily exude an astringent quality.

Austere

Severe tasting; typically a young wine, tight with youthful tannins cloaking the submerged fruit. Age is the remedy, usually softening and opening up this angular description. Austerity with age is most commonly indicative of a loss of the wine's fruit while still retaining an overly tannic frame. However, on a bright note, it can also describe a desired "lean" style of winemaking that purposely showcases its delicate mineral and terroir attributes rather than a simple swath of monolithic fruits.

B

Balance

This term is used when all the components in winemaking supposedly merge—acidity, tannins, fruit, and alcohol—either harmonizing or, in some cases, not.

Barrel Aging

Once the fermentation of the juice is completed, the finished wine can mature and soften its overt tannins in a variety of different barrels, depending on the producer's desired style. New Oak imparts a powerful, creamy taste; second-year barrels have a soft, vanilla edge, while inert barrels and stainless steel impart no influence at all. Where the barrels are made is also a factor: New American Oak creates strong-tasting and direct flavors of vanilla, as the wood grain is small. French Oak is also powerful, but more creamy and complex in final taste due to its larger grain. Elapsed time in barrel is also an important consideration in terms of taste; the more time spent in barrel, the more the wine will taste of oak.

Barrel Fermentation

A relatively new method where fermentation takes place in small oak barrels instead of the usual stainless steel. This gives the resultant wines a very dense, oaky taste.

Biodynamic Viticulture

An ancient yet recently revived method of grape growing that revolves around the awareness of planetary movements and its calculated effect on what we grow on our own planet. The aim is to create harmony in growth between all the natural elements the land offers, thus ensuring a better balance between its components. "Magnetic" forces between the moon, planets, and stars are carefully calculated and a mystical timetable of when to plant, pick, etc., is strictly adhered to. Bizarre pagan rituals, such as burying goat horns, are taken very seriously by some of the best wine producers all over the world. Chemicals in the vineyards are kept at a bare minimum with winemakers choosing and promoting alternative natural defenses such as carefully introduced insects and other wildlife to keep natural pests at bay.

Body

This is the physical weight of the wine in the mouth and can range from delicately light as in the wines of the Mosel Valley in Germany, to rich and thick as in those found in the southern Rhône. Neither, of course, is "wrong," it is just a matter of preference.

Botrytis Cinerea

There are two main types of rot that affect grapes, both are caused by excess moisture. One, the dreaded Gray Rot, is extremely bad and can decimate a vineyard overnight, turning grapes to mush. The second kind of rot, known as "Noble" is good for the grape and extremely valued to a select few. Both kinds of rot, Gray and Noble, attack the grape in the same way, shriveling the fruit by sucking out all the water, which causes the sugar content to become super-concentrated. The end result is that Gray Rot causes a foul and dirty taste, while Noble Rot produces an intense honey-flavored wine.

Bouquet

The smell of the wine.

 C

Carbonic Maceration

A type of fermentation where whole clusters of uncrushed grapes are placed inside a closed tank. The weight of the clusters on the top crushes those on the bottom and they ferment quickly and at a higher temperature. For the bunches on top, fermentation takes place inside each grape. This method quickly extracts pigmentation (color) and flavor, yet little tannin, and produces a bouncy, juicy, and immediately approachable wine. This style of fermentation is used in Beaujolais.

Chaptalization

This is the legal addition of cane or beet sugar during fermentation, which increases the alcoholic strength of the wine. The process is used particularly in areas that struggle with grape ripeness on the vine. It is not permitted in warm climates such as California, where it is not necessary but can cheaply produce a flavorless wine that is extremely high in alcohol.

Clone

A clone is a recognized strain of an individual grape that has been endowed or enhanced with certain attributes in a laboratory, usually for the purpose of being resistant to certain diseases.

Cold Fermentation

A method that utilizes slow, long fermentation temperatures in a closed tank to gently coax maximum freshness out of the grapes.

Cuvée

A bottle from a particular vat or selected barrel, derived from the French word cuve, meaning vat. It could also be a wine made from a certain combination of grapes, such as champagne cuvées. When used with champagne, it also means the house's most prestigious wine.

D

Diurnal Temperatures

This is a meteorological term that relates to the variation of temperatures from the high of the days to the cool of the nights. These shifts are particular in terms of viticulture, with the variation ensuring good levels of acid and sugar and increasing the ripeness during the day while the sudden drop at night preserves natural acids.

F

Filter

The separation of solids and liquids by filtration of the juice through a semipermeable membrane, leaving a fine liquid. In winemaking, filters can remove bacteria and yeast cells. Some winemakers use extensive filtration, some filter in moderation, and others don't use any.

Fining

This is a method of wine clarification that adds certain coagulants, the best known being egg whites, to the wine while in the barrel to remove the proteins that give the wine an unsightly haze in the bottle.

I

Ice Wine

An intense, rare wine that's produced by letting the grapes freeze on the vines before and during the very late harvest. Upon reaching the winery the frozen grapes are pressed and the water, as ice, is easily separated from the intensely sweet fruit juice and discarded.

L

Lees

The sediment or junk that settles on the bottom of the tank after fermentation. It is a mixture of dead cells, tartrates, and organic matter. In some cases lees are desired and wines (mostly white) can often be left "on the lees" for extended periods, as they can add extra richness and flavor.

M

Malolactic Fermentation

This is a second fermentation where the sharp malic acid (think apples) is converted into soft lactics (milk) and carbon dioxide. Most common in the production of red wines, it is often not used by white-wine makers who want to keep the malic acid to add zip and freshness to their wines.

Must

The mixture of solids and juice produced after crushing the unfermented grapes in the winery.

N

Noble Rot (Botrytis cinerea)

A fungal disease that attacks white grapes, causing them to shrivel and lose their water content. However, it is necessary to the production of the world's great sweet wines. The mold concentrates the sugar, flavor, and acid, giving white wine a pleasant white truffle flavor.

Oaky

Term used to describe the woody or vanilla smells and flavors contributed to wine that is stored in oak barrels. Newer barrels provide a stronger impact. The longer the wine is left in the oak barrel, the more the flavor will be influenced. If the oak flavor dominates, the wine is termed over-oaked, meaning it is flawed.

Old World

In wine, this refers to the places where wine was first celebrated, particularly in the Mediterranean region. Old World techniques refer to the ancient methods of winemaking, relying more on tradition and less on science. Wine producers are fond of saying they employ Old World techniques to indicate that their wines are at least partly made in traditional ways.

Oxidation

This occurs when the grapes, juice, or wine have been exposed to air, which alters the wine. A small amount of oxidation can open up a wine and be beneficial to the taste. Too much can ruin it, turning the wine brown and giving it the taste of cheap port.

Phylloxera

An aggressive louse that attacks the roots of the vine and destroys the plant. In the late 1880s, Phylloxera devastated the vineyards of Europe and eventually large parts of the world. Winemakers have successfully curbed its influence by grafting American rootstocks, resistant to the bugs, onto the initial vine. It still remains a problem as the insects evolve and become resistant even to the grafted stock.

Racking

A method of clarifying wine by siphoning off the sediment from a barrel of wine and pouring it into a clean barrel, thus leaving behind the murky lees.

Table Wine

Winemakers around the world use the term to describe wine that is moderate in alcohol. Most commonly, table wines refer to dry, still wines used for meals, as opposed to sweet wines or sparkling wines intended for dessert.

Tannin

These mouth roughers are born out of the initial crush of the grape skins. They give a necessary structured feel or framework to a wine while providing extended longevity in the bottle. The harshest of tannins are usually softened by initial oak aging in the winery, but some powerful extracted wines need even more softening and this comes in the form of bottle maturation.

Terroir

From the French *goût de terroir* or taste of the earth, a combination of aspects that go into the entirety of the vineyard's climate, soil, and exposure to sun—and everything else that affects the grapes. Every vineyard is believed to have its own unique terroir, and so every wine reflects where it was planted. Many wines of today have become ubiquitous, and with the addition of new oak, have taken on a universal feel that makes it difficult to place their origin.

Ullage

The space at the top of the bottle when wine is lost by leakage or evaporation. If the space is significant, the wine can be spoiled due to the presence of too much oxygen in the bottle.

Unfiltered

Wine that has not been filtered for clarification. Some winemakers believe that filtering can strip the wine of flavor. Unfiltered wine can be less clear than its filtered counterparts.

Vinification

Turning grapes into wine.

Vintage

The year the grapes were grown and harvested. The vintage year usually appears on the wine label, though some famous wines carry no vintage year because they are a combination of wine blends from various years. In the United States, law dictates that the vintage year on the bottle indicates that 95% of the grapes were harvested that year.

Vintner

The person who makes, or sells, the wine.

Viticulture

The science, management, and growing of the vines and grapes in the vineyard.

Yield

How much fruit a vineyard will produce over a given year. Yields are dependent on the weather conditions, the age of vines, their exposure to the sun, the planting density, and the grape variety utilized. In general, high yields are associated with lower quality wines while smaller yields denote higher quality wine. However, the ratio of yield to quality is highly complex.